European Economic Integration

To Beryl

European Economic Integration

The Common Market, European Union and Beyond

Dennis Swann

Professor of Economics, Loughborough University, UK

Edward Elgar
Cheltenham, UK • Brookfield, US

Published by
Edward Elgar Publishing Limited
8 Lansdown Place
Cheltenham
Glos
GL50 2HU
UK

Edward Elgar Publishing Company
Old Post Road
Brookfield
Vermont 05036
US

British Library Cataloguing in Publication Data
Swann, Dennis
European Economic Integration:Common
Market, European Union and Beyond
I. Title
337.142

Library of Congress Cataloguing in Publication Data
Swann, Dennis.
European economic integration : the Common Market, European Union,
and beyond / Dennis Swann.
p.   cm.
Includes index.
1. Europe—Economic integration.   2. European Union countries—
Economic policy.   I. Title.
HC241.S93   1996
337.1'4—dc20   95–11008
                                                                   CIP

ISBN 1 85278 734 1 (hardback)
     1 85278 773 2 (paperback)
Printed and bound in Great Britain by
Hartnolls Limited, Bodmin, Cornwall

Contents

Figures

Tables

Preface

Writing about the European Community has always been a hazardous business. When I first began to study it, which was in 1961, the main problem was that the object under investigation might indeed disappear, as when the French boycotted the Community in 1965 and when they from time to time issued dire threats about what they might do if a Common Agricultural Policy to their liking was not forthcoming. In due course this problem disappeared, only to be replaced by another one: would the UK ever be admitted? When the negotiations were proceeding in 1961–3 and 1967, UK scholastic interest perked up, but then flagged when General de Gaulle said 'no'. Only a few of us stuck with it through thick and thin. There has of course been the perennial problem that whatever one wrote could confidently be expected to be out of date by the time it was published. More recently, uncertainty about the nature of the beast has been extreme, as when the Danes rejected Maastricht in the first referendum and the EMS tottered. Fortunately, and let us hope this is not tempting fate, matters now seem to have settled down and a degree of stability is in prospect. The single market is substantially, but not wholly, in the bag. The CAP has been reformed – yet again. EMU seems some way off – perhaps it will be a reality by the end of the decade. The broad lines of the Community budget have been agreed until 1999. The immediate and major new member issues have been dealt with. Some change may occur as a result of the 1996 Maastricht review, but 1995 seems a propitious time to launch yet another book on Europe. In doing so I have been greatly assisted by David Allen, who has read and commented on the manuscript. I am greatly indebted to him, but he is not responsible for any errors or omissions. I am also grateful to Beryl, my wife, who has been a tower of strength in manuscript and proof reading. I am also extremely grateful to Lorraine Whittington, who has typed the whole manuscript, dealt with all the tables and figures and done all of this with great skill, good humour and patience.

Dennis Swann

Abbreviations

CAP	Common Agricultural Policy
CEEC	Committee for European Economic Cooperation
CEECs	Central and East European Countries
CEP	Common Energy Policy
CFSP	Common Foreign and Security Policy
CMEA	Council for Mutual Economic Assistance
Coreper	Committee of Permanent Representatives
COREU	Correspondance Européenne
CTP	Common Transport Policy
EAGGF	European Agricultural Guidance and Guarantee Fund
EBRD	European Bank for Reconstruction and Development
EC	European Community(ies)
ECB	European central bank
Ecosoc	Economic and Social Committee
ECSC	European Coal and Steel Community
ECU	European Currency Unit
EDF	European Development Fund
EEA	European Economic Area
EEC	European Economic Community
EES	European Economic Space
EFTA	European Free Trade Association
EIB	European Investment Bank
EMCF	European Monetary Cooperation Fund
EMI	European Monetary Institute
EMS	European Monetary System
EMU	economic and monetary union
EPC	European Political Cooperation
ERDF	European Regional Development Fund
ERM	exchange rate mechanism
ESA	EFTA Surveillance Authority
ESCB	European System of Central Banks
ESF	European Social Fund

Euratom	European Atomic Energy Community
Europol	European Police Office
G24	Group of Twenty-Four Countries
GATT	General Agreement on Tariffs and Trade
GDP	gross domestic product
GNP	gross national product
IGC	Inter-Governmental Conference
IMF	International Monetary Fund
MEP	member of the European Parliament
NATO	North Atlantic Treaty Organization
NCB	national central bank
NTB	non-tariff barrier
OECD	Organization for European Cooperation and Development
R&D	research and development
R&TD	research and technological development
SEA	Single European Act
VAT	value added tax
VER	voluntary export restraint
WEU	Western European Union

1.   The original Community blueprint: the form and process of integration

THE THREE COMMUNITIES

The main focus of this book is on the process by which the European Community (EC) chose first to establish a true Common Market and then to transform that Common Market into a European Union. Central therefore to the discussion are the Single European Act (SEA) of 1986 and the Maastricht Treaty on European Union of 1992. Their aims and achievements, and the prospects they have held out, constitute the main burden of this book. However before we proceed to discuss the shape of the transformed EC we need to delineate the nature, aims and aspirations of the original Community.

In the first place we have to take account of the fact that there were not one but three Communities. The European Coal and Steel Community (ECSC) was founded by the Paris Treaty of 1951. This was an exercise in limited economic integration since it covered only two sectors. Within the overall European Community economy they have over time become proportionately less significant. Nevertheless the ECSC was important for three reasons. First, it was the first successful exercise in economic integration as part of the postwar drive for closer unity in Europe. Second, it set up a series of institutions which, in modified form, continued to exist. These included the High Authority – predecessor of the European Communities Commission – a Council of Ministers, a Court of Justice, a Common Assembly (later transformed into the present-day European Parliament) and a Consultative Committee foreshadowing the Economic and Social Committee (Ecosoc) of the European Economic Community (EEC).[1]

It is, however, the third reason which must detain us since its vital message is that underlying the drive for closer economic ties has been the parallel desire for political union. In short, in the minds of the integrationists, economic and political motivations have been inextricably intertwined. An appreciation of this point is absolutely essential if we are to make sense of what has happened in Western Europe since the early 1950s. The ECSC was indeed an economic response to what was ultimately a political problem. The problem was whether the West German economy should be allowed to revive in the key sectors of steel and coal, basic materials of a war effort. The answer – at that time a visionary one – was contained in the Schuman Plan (Diebold, 1959). The latter was named after Robert Schuman, the then French foreign minister who was ably assisted by a key European, Jean Monnet. The solution lay in the creation of the ECSC. The partners (the original Six – France, West Germany, Italy, Belgium, the Netherlands and Luxembourg) agreed to form what was essentially a free trade area in coal and steel. Trade flows between the Six had to be free and tariff (customs duty) and quota protection had therefore to be dismantled. No country could arrogate to itself these vital materials of a war effort, which had to be made available to all buyers whatever their nationality: that is, on non-discriminatory terms. This, it was declared, would render war not only unthinkable but also materially impossible. For West Germany this was a key development since, apart from removing dampers on economic expansion and opening up trading opportunities, it was a milestone in its return to the comity of nations.

Attempts were subsequently made to develop a European Defence Community and a European Political Community but they failed (Swann, 1995). Subsequently the Benelux states in particular appear to have correctly judged that the supporters of European integration had been overambitious: it would make more sense to proceed on the path of further economic integration in the hope that in turn this would pave the way for developments on the political front. Perhaps at this point it is worth observing that this distinction is capable of producing some confusion. Since politics is about the use of power, it is reasonable to argue that economic integration is political since it too gives rise to the surrender of previously sovereign powers. Nevertheless a distinction can be made between developments which touch upon economic sovereignty and those which have implications for areas such as foreign policy, security and defence. The idea that one thing might lead to another emphasized the expectation that economic integration might spill over into other areas of policy concerned with home affairs, foreign relations, security and defence.

The ultimate result was the signing by the Six of two more treaties in 1957. The first created the European Atomic Energy Community (Euratom). This was to be a vehicle for the collaborative development of the peaceful uses of atomic energy. In practice members tended to go their separate ways and Euratom must be judged to have been largely a failure. Matters were otherwise with the EEC. It covered potentially every other sector apart from the coal and steel and atomic energy matters. Its relative success and the further development of it constitute the second main burden of this book.

THE CONCEPT OF ECONOMIC INTEGRATION

Economic integration denotes a state of affairs, or a process, involving the combination of previously separate economies into larger arrangements. A distinction should be made between *overall* economic integration, via institutions such as the General Agreement on Tariffs and Trade (GATT), and *regional* integration. In this study it is the regional variety, with its attendant element of discrimination against the rest of the world, which we are interested in. One way of achieving integration is to eliminate the barriers to the free flow of goods, services, factors of production and money and to leave matters to free market forces and competition. However this essentially negative process may be accompanied by a positive process of common policy development. We will discuss this later in the context of the distinction between negative and positive integration.

FORMS OF INTEGRATION

The simplest form of economic integration arises in the case of a preferential tariff agreement. This assumes that the tariffs on trade among the signatory countries are lower than those on trade with third countries (Jovanovic, 1992, p. 9).

In a free trade area the parties to the arrangement agree to remove *totally* the protection on the trade in goods flowing between them but are left free to determine the level of protection to be applied to goods coming from without.[2] The European Free Trade Association (EFTA) was an excellent example. Free trade areas may be *partial* in the sense that only certain economic sectors may be covered. The ECSC was a case in point, since it covered only two industries and fell into the free trade area category by virtue of having, at least initially, no common level of protection against imports from third countries. Likewise EFTA was partial since agricultural trade was largely excluded. It should be emphasized that the freeing of internal trade also requires that quota restrictions should be abolished as well as a host of other forms of protection which generally go under the title of 'non-tariff barriers' (NTBs) – see below.

In a customs union the parties agree to remove tariff and quota protection on the trade in goods flowing between them. The vital distinction between a free trade area and a customs union is that in a customs union the contracting parties also agree to apply a *common* level of protection against goods coming from third countries. This is generally referred to as the 'common external tariff' although the Rome Treaty refers to it as the 'common customs tariff'. In a common market, a customs union is complemented by free movement of factors of production such as labour, the professions, capital and business enterprise. In the context of the EEC, the latter freedom was referred to as the 'right of establishment'.

The process of dismantling internal protection, which is common to all these arrangements, is a complex matter. There are two reasons for this. First, as we have already observed, the internal free movement of goods requires not just the removal of tariffs and quotas but also the elimination of NTBs. In other words trade between the partners must not be prevented or distorted by state subsidies, anti-competitive business practices, domestic fiscal arrangements, discriminatory public purchasing, the imposition by the state or other bodies of standards which effectively exclude imports, border controls and administrative processes, and so forth. The removal of such barriers poses major problems. Second, the process of integration also requires that there should be a parallel freedom to supply *services*. Here, typically, the problem is not one of tariffs and quotas so much as of government regulation. For example, in the past international air passenger transport was governed by bilateral air services agreements by means of which the two countries involved tended to reserve the traffic on inter-country routes for their own national flag-flying carriers and in addition gave their joint blessing to the products of air fare-fixing cartels. The former aspect had the effect of excluding third country airlines. It should also be added that in a common market the free movement of factors requirement throws up the same kind of problem. Again it is not tariffs and quotas which pose the problem but the regulatory activities of the state and these again impose major problems for those who seek to liberalize factor flows. Two examples will suffice. Professionals may not be able to practise in another member state because they do not satisfy the latter's training and practical experience requirements. In financial services, such as banking, firms may encounter restrictions which prevent them establishing a branch or subsidiary in another member state. This may arise because governments operate systems of prudential regulation which are designed to guarantee the stability of their banks and to protect the interests of depositors. If a branch or subsidiary is to be set up in member state B it will nevertheless be underpinned by the financial strength of the parent whose head office may be in country A. But the regulatory authority in country B may deem the prudential standards adopted by the regulators in country A to be inadequate. Country B regulators will therefore refuse to license the branch or subsidiary.

We now come to the concept of economic union. The European Community prefers to refer to this state as one of economic and monetary union (EMU) since it envisages a situation where a common market (which is the 'economic' aspect) takes the further step of monetary union (the 'monetary' aspect) – see Figure 1.1. In an economic union or EMU the member states become mere regions within the enlarged grouping, although the degree to which this happens does depend on the particular model which is adopted (see below).

What then does an EMU involve? As Figure 1.1 indicates, there is a choice in respect of the monetary aspect and it should be emphasized that we are at this point defining the word 'monetary' in a rather narrow

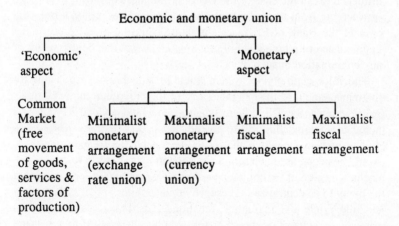

Figure 1.1   The ingredients of economic and monetary union

sense. The parties to the union could agree to fix their exchange rates irrevocably and combine that with full convertibility of their currencies. The latter refers to a situation where individuals, companies, and so on can change one member state currency into another in whatever quantity they wish whenever they wish. In other words, exchange controls are eliminated. The continued existence of fixed exchange rates would also require a coordination of national monetary policies. This is a *minimalist* approach to the monetary aspect. The *maximalist* approach can be viewed as a logical progression from the minimalist. If a fixed quantity of one currency can always be exchanged for a fixed quantity of another then one is to all intents and purposes a substitute for the other and it could then be argued that for convenience and economy it would be logical to take the further *but considerable* step of replacing the separate currencies with a *common* currency.[3]

If the latter path was followed then there would be a need to create a central organ (a union central bank system) to control the supply of the common currency and to determine the union interest rate (more precisely the union interest rate *structure* of long, medium- and short-term rates). An identification of the ingredients of monetary union does not suggest that there is any unique formula governing the organization, political relationship or objectives of a union central bank system. It could be monolithic or it could be based on a federal arrangement in which the union central bank was linked to the old national central banks. The union central bank system could be independent of political influence (as in the case of the Deutsche Bundesbank) or it could take instructions from the political authorities (as in the past has been the case of the Bank of England).[4] Its aims could be price stability, the maintenance of a high level of employment, economic development or any combination of such objectives.

The union central bank system would presumably be responsible for the management of the external value of the union currency, that is its value against the US dollar, Japanese yen and so on. To this end member states would have to agree to pool their reserves of gold, US dollars and so on within the union central bank system, since these would be necessary to underpin any support operations in respect of the exchange value of the common currency. Certain other functions would be likely to be centralized. These would include the lender of last resort and the prudential regulation functions. The former is designed to provide a mechanism whereby banks can be supported if they get into liquidity difficulties. For example, a lack of depositor confidence (for whatever reason) in a bank could lead to a drastic withdrawal of cash which individual banks, working as they do on a fractional reserve basis, cannot cope with. The resulting individual bank failure could be contagious, leading to a widespread banking collapse. A central bank therefore has to support the commercial banks in such circumstances. The second function relates to the setting down and enforcement of rules which are designed to prevent imprudence in the day-to-day conduct of banking operations. This helps to prevent systemic failure and also protects the interests of depositors.

All this is concerned with monetary matters, that is the supply of the common currency, its rate of interest and its exchange rate. However monetary union would also impinge on national *fiscal* policies. Indeed here, too, it is possible to identify minimalist and maximalist models. However, before we discuss that, we need to establish the point that member states would no longer be able to run budget deficits of any magnitude they chose since the larger the deficits (assuming these to be financed by borrowing) the more they would be likely to drive up interest rates. Moreover, since there would no longer be separate national monetary systems, the effect of driving up interest rates would be felt by *the union as a whole*. Indeed the effect upon interest rates would probably be contrary to that desired by the union central bank system *in the interests of the whole of the union*. A control over the level of national budget deficits would therefore be a feature of a monetary union.

What we are specifying here is a minimalist fiscal condition in which taxing and public spending formally remain in the hands of the member states of the union but taxes are harmonized to avoid competitive distortions in the Common Market (see discussion of EEC policy aims in the next chapter) and the size of national budget deficits is controlled. However it is also possible to envisage a maximalist model where the levying of taxes and public spending, together with the consequent level of what would be a *union* budget deficit or surplus, were all *centralized* in some union body. As a modification of such a centralizing arrangement, it is possible to envisage the injection of a federal element by means of which some of the centralized budget income would be transferred back to the constituent states for locally determined allocation. The reader will readily discern that we are outlining a system of the kind which exists in the USA. However it is important to note that some limited fiscal autonomy is enjoyed by the individual states of the American union.

Even on a minimalist view of the kind discussed above it is generally argued that EMU would require the existence of a union budgetary system which would be capable of giving rise to a substantial transfer of resources to the less successful states (regions) with below-average per capita income levels and above-average unemployment levels. It could be argued that states would be reluctant to give up their economic sovereignty (such as the power to devalue the currency) unless they could be assured of some resource transfer if their economies were to underperform. This would be all the more necessary if individual member states, whose economies were uncompetitive, did not believe that automatic correction mechanisms such as wage/price flexibility or emigration would come to their rescue.[5]

It can be argued that EMU would require a degree of political unification. Even on a minimalist view of the budgetary process, the scale of the redistribution of income would require a strong central decision-making system. *A fortiori* a high degree of political centralization seems to be an indispensable accompaniment of a maximalist system since the wholesale centralization of the budgetary process would not make sense unless there had already been a parallel agreement to shift major activities such as defence to the centre. Moreover such a wholesale shifting of the budgetary process would require a parallel centralization of the system of political and democratic oversight – no taxation without representation! In such circumstances the member states do indeed become mere regions of the union.

THE PROCESS OF ECONOMIC INTEGRATION

The above discussion still leaves open the question of how economic integration, at least up to the stage of a Common Market, is to be achieved. There are two broad possibilities. A Common Market involves a situation in which national economies are interconnected and enmeshed. Such a state of integration could be achieved by a planning mechanism. Let us think purely of the trade in goods. Country 1 could be instructed to produce good A and country 2 could be commanded to produce good B, and so forth. They could also be commanded to exchange their surpluses of A and B and a price could be prescribed – so much A for so much B. Alternatively the integration of economies can arise through competitive trade interpenetration. In simplistic terms, if country 1 was indeed more efficient at producing good A, then the removal of trade barriers would enable it to expand its sales of A to country 2 whose industry would contract. If country 2 was more efficient at producing good B, its B industry would expand if the barriers to trade were removed. It would sell B to country 1 whose industry would consequently contract. The countries would become enmeshed in beneficial trade exchanges (we are assuming that in each country unemployed factors could shift from declining to expanding industries). In the case of the EEC, the matter was really a *fait accompli* since the predominant mode of economic operation was and has increasingly become the free market system and the planning approach was unthinkable.

Two other features of the integration process are worth highlighting at this stage. The first is the distinction, mentioned earlier, between negative and positive integration. A good deal of the process of economic integration, certainly in a free enterprise economy context, is indeed negative. It consists of removing barriers to the free and undistorted flow of goods, services, factors and so on. But integration activity can also be positive: it can take the form of the development of common policies. An example of the latter would be cooperative arrangements to develop particular areas of high technology. An illustration would be the European Community's joint European Torus project which seeks to produce energy from nuclear fusion rather than fission. Another example would be the joint financing of productive investments whose outputs would serve the whole union. Even the famous (or infamous) Common Agricultural Policy (CAP) has had its positive aspect since, alongside the dismantling of barriers to internal trade in agricultural produce, and the elimination of different national systems of agricultural price support, there has been the positive aim of trying to raise the level of farmers' incomes nearer to those of their industrial counterparts. More recently environmental protection has become a major feature of the policy.

The second relates to the concept of spillover, which was briefly referred to earlier. Theorists of the economic integration process – referred to as neofunctionalists – have pointed to what has been called the 'expansive logic of integration' (George, 1985, p. 21). Functional spillover emphasizes the idea that, when a group of countries embark on a scheme of limited economic integration, spillover effects arise which drive them on to higher levels of integration. The following is an example of spillover effects. Assume that a group of countries have indeed embarked on a limited economic integration exercise which involves the free movement of goods, services and factors, but excludes monetary matters. Because of the latter exclusion, exchange rates are free to rise and fall as market forces dictate. Subsequent experience may suggest that flexible exchange rates inhibit the flow of goods, services and factors. This arises from the uncertainties which are associated with exchange rate volatility. It may therefore be argued that flexible exchange rates should be replaced by fixed rates. But exchange rates cannot remain fixed unless the monetary conditions in the member states are harmonized so as to give rise to uniform rates of inflation (or deflation). Such harmonization would require that national sovereignty over monetary matters be given up in favour of Community monetary coordination. It might indeed be concluded that stability would be better achieved by having a common currency. In short, although the member states may embark on a limited integration exercise they may be remorselessly driven down the path to greater and greater economic integration. That at least was the expectation entertained by these theorists. Subsequent chapters will reveal to what extent that expectation has been fulfilled.

The neofunctionalists also expected that economic integration would give rise to a political spillover. Their theorizing was somewhat obscure but the general proposition was very credible. In the first place it was not unreasonable to expect that the process of economic integration could have a confidence-building effect. Successful efforts in the economic sphere could suggest the possibility of successful outcomes in policy areas which were not economic in character. Not only that, but pooled efforts could be expected to carry more weight than individual ones. Equally important was the point that a distinction between the economic and non-economic is often difficult to draw. Economic sanctions are both economic and political. A policy regarding free movement of persons also has implications for home affairs policy, that is the apprehending of criminals and dealing with terrorists and drug traffickers. Equally important is the point that control of immigration is undermined if other countries have a lax policy and immigrant workers can move anywhere within the union.

THE STATUS OF THE ORIGINAL EEC

In the review of the institutional arrangements and policy aims and achievements in Chapter 2 we will focus primarily on the EEC. We will also concentrate on the period from the inception of the EEC on 1 January 1958 until the formal adoption of the Single European Act in 1986. Central to the aspirations of the EEC was the creation of a Common Market. The Rome Treaty did not provide for establishment of a full-blown EMU of the kind discussed earlier. Attempts were subsequently made in the early 1970s to move in that direction but they failed. It is true that a much less ambitious arrangement in the form of the European Monetary System (EMS) with its equally famous exchange rate mechanism (ERM) did come into being in 1979. We will discuss these later.

THE ADVANTAGES OF ECONOMIC INTEGRATION

The advantages are most conveniently discussed by focusing on the stage of integration up to a customs union. The advantages of liberalizing factor movements will be considered thereafter and this will be followed by a consideration of EMU. Although a customs union is an exercise in free trade, it is not a substitute for universal free trade which economists have always regarded as beneficial. A customs union represents free trade within a bloc, but discrimination against the rest of the world. Because of this its effects may be beneficial or disbeneficial. In other words, it may give rise to trade creation or trade diversion and is therefore not unambiguously beneficial. In Table 1.1, in the case of good A, country I initially applies a non-discriminatory 50 per cent tariff in respect of imports from country II and country III. The most efficient source is country II but it is excluded by the tariff. If country I and country II form a customs union, but leave country III facing the tariff, then there will be a *beneficial* switch of production from less efficient country I to more efficient country II. This is *trade creation*. But in the case of good B, the most efficient supplier is country III and prior to the union it supplies the good to country I. After the union, country II can undercut country III. There will be a *disbeneficial* switch of production from more efficient country III to less efficient country II. This is *trade diversion*.

Whether a customs union is, on balance, beneficial partly depends on the relative magnitude of these types of conflicting effects. However this static analysis does not take account of two further benefits, namely the possibility that the enlarged market will give greater scope for economies of scale and that it is likely to give rise to a more intensely

Table 1.1   Trade creation and trade diversion (£)

Good	Cost or cost plus duty per unit	Country III exporting to country I	Flow of trade	Goods produced by country I	Flow of trade	Country II exporting to country 1	Results
A	Cost	14		17		12	Trade creation
	Cost plus duty prior to customs union	21	No trade: country I produces A	17	No trade: country I produces A	18	
	Cost plus duty after customs union	21	No trade	17	←	12	
B	Cost	12		20		14	Trade diversion
	Cost plus duty prior to customs union	18	→	20	No trade	21	
	Cost plus duty after customs union	18	No trade	20	←	14	

competitive environment. The latter could lead to a lowering of costs and increased levels of investment and research and development (R&D) spending. The customs union is also likely to confer greater bargaining power in international trade negotiations than would be enjoyed if the union states acted independently. A common market also involves the free movement of factors. Here the major benefit is that factors are free to flow to the locations where they earn the highest return and produce the greatest economic welfare.

A minimalist monetary arrangement, particularly with irrevocably fixed exchange rates, removes the uncertainty which floating exchange rates give rise to. This facilitates intra-union trade exchanges of both goods and services and thus enables the integrating states to enjoy more fully the advantages of specialization according to comparative advantage, economies of scale, greater competition and wider choice. The removal of exchange rate uncertainty also facilitates the intra-union flow of factors of production. Thus, for example, it enables further advantage to be taken of their ability to flow to those locations where they will earn the highest return. If a maximalist arrangement is introduced in which a common currency emerges, two further advantages arise, namely the elimination of the transactions cost which arises when differing currencies have to be exchanged, together with the greater transparency which arises when economic transactions can be evaluated in terms of one currency.

The pool of reserves needing to be held when a common currency emerges will be less than the sum of the national reserves held prior to union. The member states will therefore enjoy a temporary gain in that an external trade deficit can be financed by allowing reserves to fall to the lower required level. If the common currency becomes an international currency an element of seigniorage will arise. That is to say, countries outside the union will be willing to hold the union currency as an asset and therefore imports of goods and services into the union can be financed by increased outside holdings of the union currency rather than exports. This seigniorage advantage can be exaggerated, since there will also be an outflow of interest payments. Finally a common currency greatly increases the bargaining power of the participating states when engaging in international monetary negotiations. Individually the members may carry little or no weight but collectively they can exert an influence which reflects their regional interests.

NOTES

1. As a result of the Maastricht Treaty the EEC has been retitled the European Community (EC). However at this point we shall refer to it as the EEC.
2. In a Free Trade Area rules of origin have to be devised. These prevent what is called 'trade deflection', which can be defined as the import of goods from third countries into the Free Trade Area by member state A, which has a lower external tariff than member state B, in order to re-export them to member state B.
3. It has also been proposed that there is another form of monetary union in which a *single* currency is introduced which does not immediately replace the national currencies but exists alongside them and in competition with them. If successful, it might replace them and thus become a *common* currency.
4. From a practical standpoint it seems likely that a union central bank would have to be politically independent. Otherwise it would be in constant danger of being pulled violently in a variety of different directions as a result of differences of national interest as between the member states.
5. Automatic correction mechanisms imply that workers would price themselves back into jobs or would emigrate and find jobs elsewhere.

REFERENCES

Diebold, W. (1959), *The Schuman Plan* (New York: Praeger).

George, S. (1985), *Politics and Policy in the European Community* (Oxford: Clarendon).

Jovanovic, M.N. (1992), *International Economic Integration* (London: Routledge).

Swann, D. (1995), *The Economics of the Common Market* (Harmondsworth: Penguin).

2. The original Community blueprint: institutions and integration policies

Before we discuss the policy aims of the Rome Treaty, and the actual policies adopted, we need to outline the EEC's institutional structure. This can be viewed under two headings: (1) the institutions concerned with economic policy making, (2) the institutional arrangements concerned with financing those policies.

THE EEC INSTITUTIONAL STRUCTURE

The Decision-making Institutions

These institutions are outlined in Figure 2.1 where we find it convenient to assume initially that the authority upon which policy was founded was the original Rome (EEC) Treaty. The task of the European Communities Commission was to make policy proposals which were designed to achieve the stated aims of the EEC which were contained in Article 3. At the head of the administration was a group of commissioners, each with a particular policy portfolio, together possibly with an administrative function. The president of the commission, together with his/her fellow commissioners, enjoyed a sole right of initiative (and the Council of Ministers (see below) could only amend such proposals by unanimous vote). Hence when reading the Rome Treaty we repeatedly come across the phrase, 'on a proposal of the Commission'. Thereafter other bodies had a role to play. This proposal role is indicated by track 6 of Figure 2.1. It is perhaps worth mentioning at this point that in earlier days each of the three communities had its own commission-type body (a High Authority in the case of the ECSC) but from 1967 these were merged. Thus the European Communities Commission came to be responsible for all three communities and operated the provisions of three different founding treaties.

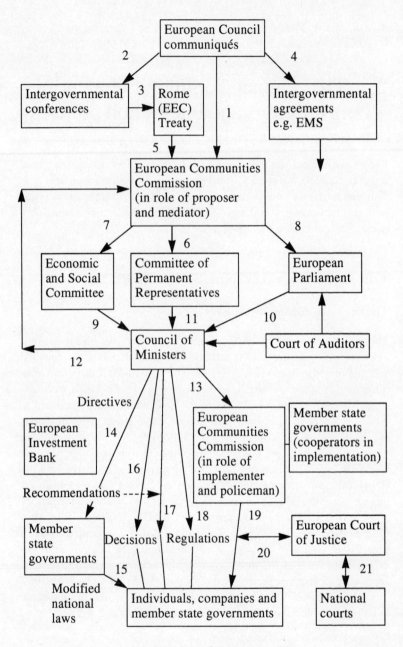

Figure 2.1   Decision-making institutions of the EEC

Tracks 7 and 8 indicate that two other actors also had to be involved in the decision-making process: Ecosoc (a broadly based representative body drawn from the member states) and the more important Common Assembly or European Parliament. Originally the European Parliament was drawn from the national parliaments but the Rome Treaty envisaged that eventually it would be directly elected by the people and this occurred for the first time in 1979. As we shall see in Chapter 3, this was a significant event. The treaty indicated that on various issues the Community's law maker, the Council of Ministers, had to consult these two before it enacted legislation. Moreover to act without first carrying out the stipulated consultation would render the act invalid. Of the two, the parliament was originally, and was increasingly to become, the more important. However the parliament was not in any significant sense a legislature. It was essentially a debating chamber, with a related committee structure, where *consultation* took place. This observation needs to be complemented in two respects. The parliament had the power to dismiss the commission on a vote of no confidence. Later it acquired limited law-making and approval powers in relation to the Community budget (see Chapter 8).

Tracks 9 and 10 show the results of these consultations flowing into the decision-making system. It will also be noted that commission proposals did not go directly to the Council of Ministers. Rather they went via the Committee of Permanent Representatives (Coreper for short). Each member state had a permanent delegation in Brussels and its task in Coreper was to consider proposals prior to their arrival on the council table. Thus areas of agreement could be quickly identified, areas of disagreement resolved and areas of continuing disagreement highlighted and left for the council to settle. The council was not a fixed body: its ministerial membership would vary according to the policy area under discussion. Council meetings were presided over by one member state and this presidency role rotated among the member states on a six-monthly basis. As we have indicated, the council was the body which finally made the laws. To this end the Rome Treaty prescribed a system of voting. Whilst the treaty contained a general presumption in favour of majority voting (for a definition see below), in the early days unanimity was generally the rule and it was only in the later stages of the 12-year transition period that on a wide range of issues decisions could be taken by qualified majority voting.[1] Under the original arrangements France, West Germany and Italy had four votes each, Belgium and the Netherlands had two each and Luxembourg had one vote. Twelve votes constituted the necessary *qualified* majority. (There was also a provision designed to protect the interests of the smaller countries.) This qualified majority arrangement represented the main supranational element which advocates of closer European unity placed great store by. Subsequently it was to be challenged by France and fell into abeyance (see Chapter 3). It was not greatly appreciated by the British but was later revived, partly by virtue of the SEA (see Chapter 4).

Track 12 indicates that initially the commission might not secure agreement for a policy proposal, in which case it would have to be taken back for further consideration. Here we are emphasizing the role of the commission as mediator – seeking an alternative formulation which it hoped would secure acceptance in the council.

From the council there emerged a variety of instruments, namely regulations (track 18), directives (track 14), decisions (track 16) and recommendations (track 17). The last had no binding force, the others did. Regulations were in effect laws which applied directly but without naming specific individuals, enterprises or states. Decisions were laws which also applied directly but in this case to those named in them. Directives did not apply directly.[2] Rather they were addressed to member states and required them to modify their laws in some particular way. Citizens and companies would then have to obey the modified national law. A good example would be a directive harmonizing standards in the composition of a foodstuff. Food manufacturing companies would not be directly affected; rather it was for the member state governments to modify their national food laws in line with the directive and food manufacturers throughout the Community would obey their harmonized national laws.

Tracks 13 and 19 indicate that the commission also played two other key roles. One was that of implementer. For example, the CAP, which we discuss later in Chapter 8, required active intervention in the market in order to manipulate prices. This was done by imposing levies on cheap imported food and taking excess supplies off the market. Here the commission had an implementing role to play but, given its relatively small size, it was one which it discharged in collaboration with national governments, as Figure 2.1 indicates. Second, there was the task of policeman or enforcer. Here the commission needed to know what states, companies or individuals were doing: whether, for example, by cartel or state subsidy cross-frontier competition was being distorted. It needed to be able to take action against such breaches of

Community law. Later we shall see how the council delegated appropriate enforcement powers to the commission.

We now come to an important Community institution which, as we shall emphasize later, must not be underestimated. Indeed its role in the development of Community policy has on occasions been crucial. We are referring to the European Court of Justice which served three principal functions. First of all it was a body to which individuals, companies and governments could appeal against the actions of Community organs. Thus, if a group of companies was attacked by the commission for an alleged breach of the competition rules, they could ask the court to review the commission's decision. This might relate to the reasoning which lay behind it, to the size of any penalty imposed, or both. This is represented by track 20. Second, it was possible for any Community organ to appeal to the court on the grounds that another Community organ had acted in ways contrary to the treaty. For example, on one occasion parliament challenged council before the court on the grounds that council had acted before going through the proper consultation process. In another case the parliament attacked the council because the latter had failed to implement the Common Transport Policy (CTP) – notably those features specifically called for in the Treaty. Unfortunately we cannot easily portray this function in Figure 2.1. Third, it is essential to recognize that Community law is supreme and that, if there is a conflict between Community and national law, then national law must give way to Community law. Inevitably cases arise in which the possible implications of Community law are at issue. However a national court may not feel able without guidance to pronounce on the implications of the Rome Treaty in a particular case. It can therefore approach the court for help – for a preliminary ruling. This is represented by track 21.

Initially we chose to regard the original Rome Treaty as the unique basis upon which policy is based. However the picture is somewhat more complicated than that. First, we need to note the existence of another body which did not feature in the treaty. This is the European Council. Over many years the heads of state and government had been in the habit of holding summit meetings from time to time. In 1974, at the suggestion of the then French president, it was decided that these summits should be given the title, European Council. The council came to play several roles. It was a forum where new initiatives were identified. Here we are thinking of developments which were consistent with the stated objectives of the existing Rome Treaty. This is represented by track 1. It is essential to recognize that the council would not normally be involved in the finer detail of Community law making – that task would be remitted to the decision making system which we have just discussed, track 6 onwards. Second, it was essential that the Rome Treaty should not be a static document since otherwise, as time passed, new problems and opportunities would emerge but the Community would be saddled with treaty objectives and associated powers which were only relevant to the mid-1950s. Hence the importance of Article 236, which enabled the treaty to be modified, but this required the calling of an intergovernmental conference. The convening of such conferences (track 2) was the task of the European Council, as was the wrapping up of the details at a final conference. These final results, when ratified by national parliaments, would take the form of modifications to the original treaty – track 3. The emergence of both the Single Act and the Maastricht Treaty on European Union were instances of this process at work. Third, the Council was a forum to which the Council of Ministers and the commission could resort if the Community decision-making system was locked in disagreement. The resolving of such wrangles is represented by track 1. It is necessary to observe that, whilst the council would not normally be involved in the finer details of Community decision making, there were occasions when it did get quite deeply involved. Here we are thinking of its work in connection with the pattern of future Community budget spending, the so-called 'financial perspective' (see Chapter 8).

It does need to be emphasized that not all the activities which we tend to regard as Community policies have been based on the Rome Treaty. Some have been the products of separate intergovernmental agreements outside the scope of the Rome Treaty. A good example is the EMS – see track 4.

Financing the Community

The main institutions concerned with Community financing were the following: the Community budget, various international loan-raising facilities, the European Investment Bank (EIB) and the European Development Fund (EDF). Had the Rome Treaty given rise to nothing more than a Common Market, plain and simple, then the financial requirements of the Community would have been modest and would have consisted of the funds necessary to pay the salaries, expenses, pensions and general administrative running costs of the institutions outlined above. However, as will become plain later in this chapter, the Community chose to develop policies which in fact cost very much more than mere administration. We will not go into much detail at this point since the role and structure of the Community budget will be extensively discussed in Chapter 8. Suffice it to say that the EEC was originally financed by national contributions. However the Rome Treaty envisaged that in due course the Community budget would be able to draw on what were called the Community's 'own resources'. Subsequently these were identified as the proceeds of the common external tariff (less 10 per cent which the states could keep to cover collection costs), the proceeds of the levies imposed on imports of agricultural products from third countries (again less the 10 per cent) and finally a value added tax (VAT) component. Briefly this latter element consisted of the proceeds of a *uniform* rate of VAT, on an agreed collection of goods and services, which each member state would pay into the budget.

We turn now to non-budgetary instruments. The commission came to dispose of various loan facilities by means of which it could raise funds on the international capital market. Some of these were inherited from Euratom and the ECSC. The old High Authority of the ECSC had been able to borrow for the development of the coal and steel industries, to provide alternative employment in areas dominated by these industries and to modernize housing in these areas. The EEC itself set up a series of loan facilities. In 1975, it established a mechanism for assisting member states in balance of payments difficulties. Then, in 1978, it introduced the Ortoli facility (named after the then president of the commission). Formally it was called the 'new Community instrument' and the loan proceeds could be used to finance projects which fitted in with Community priority objectives (such as the stimulation of small and medium-sized enterprises). The funds were handled by the EIB, to which we now turn.

The bank has a separate legal personality, independent of the commission and the Community budget. It was expressly called for in Article 3(j) of the Rome Treaty and its operations were governed by Articles 129 and 130 whilst its statute was the subject of a protocol annexed to the Treaty. The subscribers to the bank were the member states. However only a limited amount was actually paid up and so the unpaid balance acted as a guarantee. In practice therefore, whilst some of its lending was financed from the paid-up contributions, most came from international borrowings. These were used mainly to finance internal operations, notably the development of backward regions, industrial restructuring, environmental protection and projects of common interest. Later the bank's objectives were widened to include countries which had association or other agreements with the Community (see below).

Mention should also be made of the EDF, which was established to aid the colonial and ex-colonial dependencies of the member states. These territories enjoyed a special trade and aid relationship with the EEC. The fund, although in the business of giving grants, was not financed through the Community budget but by separate member state contributions.

THE POLICY AIMS AND ACHIEVEMENTS OF THE ORIGINAL EEC

As with the institutions, we will concern ourselves with the EEC in the period up to the signature of the Single Act. The development of EEC policy can be viewed under four heads: (1) the establishment of a Common Market; (2) the introduction of common policies in *specific sectors*, such as agriculture; (3) the development of common policies on *particular issues*, such as R&D, the environment and regional policy; and (4) the evolution of trade relationships with the colonial and increasingly ex-colonial dependencies and other third countries. This can be broadened to include the admission of new members.

The Common Market

It has already been made plain that the Rome Treaty envisaged a process of economic integration based on competition; indeed we described this as a process of competitive trade interpenetration. The key role that competition had to play was highlighted by Article 3(f) which declared that the Community should seek to establish a system which ensured that competition in the Common Market was not distorted. Competition was to be the guiding factor and, moreover, it should be undistorted.

Central to the creation of a Common Market was the setting up of a customs union. This in turn required the erection of a common external tariff (Articles 3(b) and 18 to 29). This seemed to raise the possibility of a conflict with GATT principles, since the latter emphasized the importance of non-discrimination in postwar tariff arrangements. However, while a common external tariff is undoubtedly discriminatory, since the rest of the world pays the tariff but the partners do not, the GATT provided a convenient escape clause. A common tariff was acceptable if it was no higher than the average of the national tariffs which preceded it. The Community was able to complete the common tariff by the middle of 1968, somewhat ahead of the end of 12-year transition period. Subsequently the level of the tariff was reduced in a series of GATT negotiating rounds, the most recent being the long drawn-out Uruguay Round. Alongside this, Article 3(b) envisaged the establishment of a common commercial policy, the detailed aims of which were to be found in Articles 110–16. This gave rise to common action not only in reducing the common external tariff but in the conclusion of trade agreements with individual countries or groups of countries (sometimes these were restrictive, as in the case of the quotas contained in the multi-fibre arrangements). The EEC also elaborated various protective instruments. These included a mechanism to combat foreign dumping in the Community market. In 1984, the EEC followed this up by introducing the new commercial policy instrument, which enabled the EEC to retaliate (by quota or import duty) against illicit trade practices affecting Community exports as well as imports.

The customs union also required the elimination of *internal* protection. As far as goods were concerned, this had five main elements: the member states had to remove (a) tariffs and (b) charges equivalent to tariffs (Articles 3(a) and 12–17); to abolish (c) quotas and (d) measures equivalent thereto (Articles 3(a) and 30-35); and (e) to tackle the thorny problem of NTBs.

Internal tariffs were removed by mid-1968. Charges equivalent to tariffs were also rooted out. The Italian government, for example, was in the habit of applying what it called a 'statistical levy' to imports and exports. The commission pointed out that this was equivalent to a tariff and should be eliminated. When the Italian government refused to comply, the matter was referred to the Court of Justice, which upheld the commission's action. The removal of quotas posed no great problem since many had already been eliminated thanks to bodies such as the GATT, the International Monetary Fund (IMF) and the Organization for European Cooperation and Development (OECD). A particularly good indication of the kind of problem posed by measures equivalent to quotas was provided by the *Cassis de Dijon* case (CMLR, 1979) which we will discuss further in Chapter 4. Cassis de Dijon is a French liqueur manufactured from blackcurrants. The German company Rewe-

Zentrale A.G. sought to import the French liqueur and requested an authorization from the West German Federal Monopoly Administration for Spirits. The latter informed Rewe that West German law forbade the sale of liqueurs with less than 32 per cent alcohol content, although for liqueurs of the Cassis type a minimum of 25 per cent was allowed. This was no help to the Cassis importer since Cassis had an alcoholic content of only 15–20 per cent and thus it was illegal to import it. Rewe contested the ban in a German court and the matter was referred to the Court of Justice for a preliminary ruling. The Court declared that the German law in question was in these specific circumstances an equivalent measure of the kind prohibited under Article 30 of the Rome Treaty. The minimum alcoholic content rule had in this particular case the effect of a zero import quota. In the process of delivering its judgement the Court of Justice also made the point that any product legally made and sold in one member state had in principle to be admitted to the markets of the others. National rules and standards could only create barriers where they were necessary to satisfy 'mandatory' requirements such as public health, consumer protection and so on. Moreover, and this was the key point, any rule had to be the 'essential guarantee' of the interest, the protection of which was regarded as being justified. It will be remembered that in the *Cassis* case the German government defended its minimum alcoholic content rule on grounds of consumer protection. But the court implied that the objective could have been achieved by merely requiring the label to show the actual alcoholic content. The rule was not essential to guarantee the protection of the consumer.

In practice, and for the most part, the tariff and quota aspect posed no major problem. NTBs, however, were much more difficult to deal with and it must be admitted that, whilst significant progress was made in the transition period and after, by 1986 much still remained to be done. This indeed is a major reason why the Community was finally impelled to sign the Single Act in 1986. Its major task was to provide the impetus necessary to complete the creation of the single internal market, the target date being the end of 1992. We will discuss this later in Chapter 4.

The Community made good progress in the field of anti-competitive practices. Article 85 pronounces a prohibition on cartels which restrict competition and affect inter-state trade. However it holds out the possibility of exemption where benefits can be shown to arise. Article 86 deals with dominant firms and prohibits the abuse of a dominant position, provided again that it affects inter-state trade. In order to give effect to these principles the Council of Ministers in 1961 delegated the enforcement task to the commission and provided it with significant enforcement powers. As a result a stream of cases emerged so that, by 1986, two things could reasonably be said. First, the significance of Articles 85 and 86 in different case situations was apparent to market operators. Second, the commission and the court were disposed to take a firm line in respect of practices which merely compartmentalized the customs union. The major gap was the lack of a specific merger-controlling power. Although the celebrated *Continental Can* case (CMLR, 1973) had indicated that Article 86 could be invoked against mergers, its practical impact was limited.

A major issue in the creation of a customs union is the need to deal with state subsidies (that is, state aids) which if not addressed are likely to lead to major distortions of competition and unfair trade. The Rome Treaty faced this problem in Articles 92 to 94. Basically they pronounce a ban on state aids which affect inter-state trade, but allow exceptions to be made, notably for regional development and assistance to individual industrial sectors. Here again the enforcement task fell to the commission, which established a system of prior notification and a vetting procedure. General principles were laid down on the acceptability of regional aids (the intensity of aid given and the aid instrument employed) and sectoral aids, while pure export aids were always condemned. The commission also sought to deal with two major problems in connection with sectoral aids. One arose from the financial links (which often involved elements of subsidy) between member state governments and their *public* enterprises, together with the possibility that governments could take financial stakes in *private* as well as public enterprises in which the capital was advanced at less than commercial rates. The other was that, as time passed, the nature of state assistance to industry changed and new aid phenomena had to be addressed. One was aid for R&D which could be justified by the need to compete with the USA and Japan but had to be kept in bounds. An additional complication was that in times of recession, as after the oil price increase of 1973, some temporary aid to industries in difficulties had to be countenanced if severe social shocks were to be avoided.

Public procurement poses a major problem in a customs union context since it constitutes a sizeable proportion of total spending (about 15 per cent in the case of the EC during the early 1980s) and typically it has been conducted on a 'buy home produced goods' basis. The Rome

Treaty did not specifically address the issue but clearly such behaviour offended the non-discrimination provisions of Article 7 and could be classed as a measure equivalent to a quota and was thus caught by Articles 30–33, 52 and 59. Articles 30–33 relate to quantitative restrictions whilst the latter two are respectively concerned with the right of establishment and freedom to supply services. The Community sought to address the problem by elaborating rules governing the award of public contracts; specifically they covered public works contracting and public supply contracts. Unfortunately they contained loopholes which were efficiently exploited by the member states and in addition important areas of the economy were excluded from their coverage.

Standards relating to the design, composition, packaging, labelling and so on of goods such as cars, food, pharmaceuticals and electrical equipment give rise to major problems in a supposedly unified market. These are often introduced to protect consumers and assist industrial users and are frequently a product of state regulation or of bodies which enjoy some official status. To the extent that standards differ (and there is scope here for deliberate manipulation) they either totally inhibit trade and choice or require that goods be adapted to the needs of each market with a consequent loss of the economies of large volume production. This kind of problem is compounded by Article 36, which empowers states to refuse the importation of goods which threaten the health and life of humans, animals and plants (there are also other grounds for refusals). Whilst some national differences in standards may be regarded as not sufficiently serious to justify a refusal to import, there may be other situations where real threats to life, health and so on could legitimately be claimed. That being so, the powers contained in Article 36 threaten the unity of the internal market. The obvious way around the problem is to devise common standards, which by definition would preclude the blocking of imports. It was here that Articles 100–102 of the Rome Treaty came to the rescue since they provided for the harmonization of national laws and practices – the actual word used is 'approximation'. The Community proceeded along these lines but the technical complexity of the process, the unanimity requirement of Article 100 and the fact that technological progress renders standards out of date all tended to inhibit progress.

Fiscal factors were explicitly identified in the treaty as a possible problem area. Since we are discussing goods at this point, only indirect taxes (which in the customs union context meant turnover taxes and excise duties) are relevant matters. Broadly, Articles 95 to 99 provided for two kinds of action. First, they enabled the Community to put a stop to fiscal manipulations as, for example, when a beer-producing but wine-importing country loaded the excise duty on wine as compared with the tax burden imposed on beer. Second, Article 99 invited the Community to consider whether, in the interests of the customs union, there was a case for harmonizing indirect taxes. The conclusion reached was that there were grounds. Ideally both their structures and their rates should be harmonized. The Community began by addressing the turnover tax issue and decided to adopt the VAT model. In so doing it sought to achieve two aims. One was to remove any biasing effect on industrial structures. Other forms of tax did have this effect, but VAT was neutral. The other was a product of member state reluctance to harmonize VAT *rates*. In the absence of rate harmonization, competitive distortions were likely since the exports of high VAT rate countries would suffer in competition with low VAT rate countries. The less than ideal response was therefore to zero rate exports and for the country importing those goods to apply its domestic rate of VAT, thus providing a 'level playing field'. This was the so-called 'destination principle'. The VAT had the additional advantage that, as compared with other tax systems, it was relatively easy to assess whether the tax remission on exports was accurate or whether it was excessive and constituted a hidden export subsidy. Even so the system did not prevent the distorting phenomenon of cross-border shopping which arose when one country imposed a lower VAT rate than a neighbour and in addition zero rating provided scope for fraud, as when goods which were officially for export crept back into the home market to be sold at a tax-inclusive price. Ideally VAT rates needed to be harmonized and then goods could be exported inclusive of VAT – the so-called 'origin principle'. Apart from adopting the VAT system, little else happened and in respect of excise duties the harmonization cupboard was still virtually bare when the Single Act came under consideration.

The Rome Treaty also declared that restrictions on the freedom to supply services should be progressively removed (Articles 59–66). Some progress was achieved (sometimes in parallel with the right of establishment – see below) but in areas such as international air passenger transport and financial services (notably non-life insurance) national regulatory obstacles contained to frustrate the Commission in its search for a single market.

We noted earlier that the treaty envisaged the process of economic integration being pressed to the stage of a Common Market. That being so, it was equally essential that factors of production should be free to flow across frontiers. Articles 67 to 73 related to the free movement of capital and Article 67 stipulated that, to the extent necessary to ensure the proper functioning of the Common Market, member states should abolish restrictions on capital movements. This posed two main problems, the existence of exchange controls and of national corporation taxes whose varying structures and different rates were capable of distorting capital investment. Some early moves were made to dismantle exchange controls since the treaty required member states to supply foreign currency for current transactions, that is the purchase of goods. In other words, a French importer needed to be able to obtain Deutsche Marks if he was going to pay for goods supplied by a German manufacturer. A refusal of currency by the French authorities would have had the same effect as a zero import quota. But in respect of *capital* transactions, only limited liberalization was achieved by the directives of 1960 and 1962.

As early as 1975, the commission sought to persuade the member states to harmonize the rate and structure of corporation taxes since unharmonized rates were likely to induce investors to favour low-tax countries and the associated system of tax credits tended to favour domestic investment as opposed to investment in other member states. Again the problem was one of avoiding distortions by establishing a 'level playing field'. However no progress was made on this front.

Free movement of labour in accordance with Articles 48 to 51 was approached in stages and was supported by parallel measures such as those which allowed for transferability of social security entitlements. The treaty also sought to enable enterprises and self-employed professional persons to set up in business in other member states. This right of establishment was covered by Articles 52 to 57. Whilst restrictions on grounds of nationality had been swept away (a point confirmed by the Court of Justice) there still remained the regulatory problem: differing standards of formal qualification and practical experience. The treaty envisaged that this could be dealt with either by mutual recognition of national diplomas and qualifications or by the Community itself devising a common standard of training and experience. In practice this process was approached on a sectoral basis, profession by profession. Doctors, dentists, nurses, midwives, veterinary surgeons and pharmacists were all dealt with this way. This was tedious and in the case of, for example, architects, it took 17 years to reach an agreement.

Steps were also taken to secure the right of establishment for business; again the problem was one of regulation. Thus in the case of non-life insurance the problem had been that in order to protect their citizens member states required insurance companies to be licensed, and a condition of holding a licence was that companies met certain standards in terms of reserves, solvency margins and so forth. These differed between states and therefore the possibility existed that a company wishing to set up a subsidiary in another member state could be debarred from doing so if the conditions demanded by the host government were more stringent than those demanded by the government of the country in which the company had its headquarters. The 1973 directive which finally solved this problem required that the taking up of the business of non-life insurance should be subject to official authorization by each member state. This applied to an undertaking which had its head office in a member state and also to subsidiaries of enterprises which had head offices in other member states. Most important of all, uniform standards were specified in respect of reserves and margins of solvency. But while non-life offices were eventually able to establish themselves they did not manage to secure a parallel freedom to supply services. That is to say, a British insurance company could insure a West German risk from its established subsidiary in Germany (since the subsidiary was underpinned by its British parent which, after the 1973 directive, operated under a uniform licensing system) but could not insure the German risk *direct* from the UK-based parent company. This inability proceeded from the fact that in the direct insurance situation there was always the possibility that the contract might be subjected to foreign law (in this case UK law) whereas insurance contracts concluded in Germany by the UK *subsidiary* would have to be concluded under German law. Germany was not willing, for consumer protection reasons, to expose its citizens to the risk of contracts concluded under foreign (possibly laxer) laws.

The overall picture we have painted is a patchy one. Some progress towards a Common Market was achieved but prior to the Single Act and its single market programme the Community could not claim to have created a unified European market for goods, services and factors.

Common Sectoral Policies

As we indicated earlier, the second main aim of the original EEC was the introduction of common policies in certain sectors. These were (1) the CAP,[3] (2) the Common Transport Policy (CTP) and (3) the Common Energy Policy (CEP). The CAP (called for in Article 3(d)) was an essential feature since countries such as France, with substantial agricultural populations, would not have signed up to the Rome Treaty if agriculture had not been included. The detailed nature of the agricultural support systems was not laid down in the treaty but the policy aims were. High among these was the objective of providing farmers with a fair standard of living. The method of support finally chosen was essentially protective. Cheap food would be prevented from undercutting the European price levels needed to provide farmers with a reasonable living. This was to be accomplished notably by levies imposed on imported foodstuffs. In addition, if at the higher target prices EEC farmers produced more than the market would absorb – that is, if they produced surpluses – either specially created intervention bodies would step in, buy up and store the excess or farmers would be paid a subsidy to sell their unwanted surpluses on the world market at a loss. All this was bound to cost money and so a fund (fed from the Community budget – see above and Chapter 8) was created. This was the famous European Agricultural Guidance and Guarantee Fund. Simultaneously with the establishment of the various *common* mechanisms of price support, the barriers to intra-Community trade in agricultural products were removed with the anticipation that this would in turn lead to *common* prices over the whole of the Community. However the latter was significantly thwarted by exchange rate fluctuations.

The Achilles' heel of this system was the open-ended commitment which the Community originally entered into. That is to say, the intervention agencies would buy up or provide export subsidies for whatever the internal market could not absorb. Given the ability of farmers to produce more and more (thanks to technological progress and so on) and the relatively sluggish increase in demand (since the income elasticity of demand[4] for food is quite low), the size of the surplus problem was likely to get bigger and bigger as time went by. The resulting support expenditure in turn began to overwhelm the Community budget. Although suggestions for structural reform were made as early as 1968, nothing really significant emerged until 1984. We will discuss this and later reforms in Chapter 8, when we come to discuss the structure and role of the Community budget.

The Rome Treaty also explicitly recognized the need for a CTP (Article 3(e)) since earlier experience in the ECSC had indicated that transport could be manipulated in ways which would produce barriers to trade and in any case an efficient, flexible and coordinated transport system would be a positive aid to the integration process. Unfortunately the Rome Treaty did not specify in any great detail the nature of the policy and in any case it only applied in the first instance to road, rail and inland waterway. Maritime and air transport were left for later deliberation. Some progress was made towards a more competitive, less regulated transport system, notably in areas such as road haulage. However, as Kenneth Button has observed, until the late 1980s the CTP 'was really little more than a "will-o-the-wisp"' (Button, 1992, p. 147). In road haulage, for example, some price flexibility was established and some harmonization was achieved. The latter was essential if intermodal competition in transport was to be fair (the 'level playing field' idea). But in certain areas, where the Rome Treaty had actually been explicit in its aims, little or nothing had emerged. Thus the treaty had specifically focused on the topic of international road haulage licences but the council had been extremely reluctant to agree to a liberal quota. The treaty had also called for a system by which non-resident carriers could carry out some domestic haulage as part of an international trip. This is referred to as cabotage. Here the council had been entirely resistant. Small wonder then that in 1983 the parliament should take the council to the court for its failure to act!

In regard to the so-called CEP, it has to be said that neither the Rome Treaty nor indeed any other treaty had envisaged such an arrangement. This, allied to the fact that energy was a divided responsibility as between the three communities and that energy was a highly regulated area, may explain why little was achieved. The little which was achieved, thanks in part to a boost given by the 1972 Paris summit, was set against a background of attempts to reconcile the sometimes conflicting aims of cheap energy and a secure supply of it. Much later on the environmental impact (global warming) also became a major concern in policy formulation. The achievements consisted of the creation of emergency measures designed to cope with a sudden cutting off of energy supplies; the implementation of policies concerned with the rational use of energy; the adoption of Community balance sheets to monitor the Community's supply and demand for energy and the likely trend of its import dependency; and finally the use of the Community's budgetary and financial instruments (discussed above) to reduce import dependency.

Common Policies on Particular Issues

The summit meeting in Paris in 1972 was extremely important in this context. In ebullient mood, it encouraged the launching of a series of initiatives which exploited the existing aims and properties of the Rome Treaty without, at least immediately, requiring any modification to it. One was a Community industrial policy. The Rome Treaty made no mention of such a development and indeed France and Germany had very different views on this matter. In Chapter 6 we will see that the Maastricht Treaty has modified this gap in treaty competences. Central to the industrial policy was the need for a European industrial base. This was very much a call for the kind of single market which the Common Market was in any case designed to achieve. We have therefore got to conclude that, up to the signing of the Single Act, only modest progress was made on this aspect of the policy. The industrial initiative also called for the creation of instruments which would facilitate cross-frontier business organization and collaboration. We have to report that here little was achieved until the build-up to the Single Act began to exert its influence. Although not part of the original industrial policy blueprint, the commission also found itself having to formulate *ad hoc* responses to industries in difficulties. In textiles, for example, this involved steering the use of subsidies towards rationalization rather than mere support, together with quantitative protection from imports while restructuring took place. A common policy on science and technology was also launched thanks to the Paris summit.

The Paris summit was also influential in setting in motion a Community policy on the environment, an extremely interesting development in the light of the fact that the original Rome Treaty never mentioned the word 'environment'! As we shall see, this deficiency was remedied by the Single Act. The summit also gave a new impetus to social policy by calling for an action programme. Social policy did feature in the original treaty blueprint but, whilst a wide range of social issues were identified as matters for Community concern (see Article 118), powers to compel action were largely absent. However the power to harmonize under Article 100 could be applied to any matter *which interfered with the establishment of the Common Market*. Social matters could have fallen into this category. However we have to appreciate that the unanimity principle of Article 100 would have enabled any state to veto proposals for action. Nor, it would appear, would any such harmonization have had to have an upward bias. This is why the Social Charter and in particular the Social Policy Protocol and Agreement of the Maastricht Treaty are so important (see Chapter 6). Limited progress was made, notably in respect of matters relating to equal treatment such as equal pay for equal work, which the French had insisted should go into the treaty as an obligation upon members. Also we must note the existence of the European Social Fund (ESF) with its objective of assisting in the retraining and re-employment of workers. It was expressly envisaged in Article 3(i) and was fed by funds from the Community budget.

Regional development did not feature in the original main text objectives of the Rome Treaty. This is a little odd since the *preamble* to the treaty did see the EEC as seeking to achieve a reduction in 'the differences between the various regions and the backwardness of the less favoured regions'. Indeed in some degree the treaty was potentially opposed to such a policy since Articles 92–4 enabled the commission to oppose the giving of state aids. However subsequent developments led to a change of stance. At the Hague summit, in 1969, the heads of state and government met at the end of the original transition period. It would have been possible for them to conclude that the aim of setting up the Common Market had been significantly achieved and that matters should be brought to a conclusion at that point. In fact they decided quite otherwise, since they embraced the idea of developing the EEC further, to the stage of an EMU. In a subsequent report on the process of creating such a union, Pierre Werner (the prime minister of Luxembourg) and others had recognized the need for a regional fund as part of the exercise (the logic was in line with our earlier thinking in Chapter 1). In addition, at the Paris summit of 1972, the British, then about to become new members, pressed for the establishment of a European Regional Development Fund (ERDF) since they were anxious to structure budget spending in a way which would provide a return flow of funds to the UK to balance her budget contributions. The result was the establishment, in 1975, of the ERDF, fed by revenues from the Community budget. The EIB had of course from its inception channelled loans (but not grants) into the development of the backward regions.

It was emphasized earlier that the Rome Treaty provided for the creation of a Common Market but not an EMU. Hence the significance of the Maastricht Treaty. However monetary provisions were built into the Rome Treaty (Articles 103–9) which clearly recognized that, since member states were likely to become increasingly interdependent, there would be a need for consultation and cooperation. A Monetary Committee was duly established and other specialist committees emerged in due course. Nevertheless at the end of the day member states retained their freedom to act in respect of the money supply, interest rates and exchange rates. The attempt to create an EMU by 1980, which was formally launched in the early 1970s, did not succeed. This involved the 'snake in the tunnel' mechanism whereby member states were supposed to keep their exchange rate fluctuations within limits in the run up to a possible common currency. However, later in the 1970s, the idea of limited monetary union was revived and indeed in 1979 the EMS with its famous ERM was set up, *but outside the framework of the Rome Treaty*. It embodied the European Currency Unit (ECU), a composite currency unit made up of prescribed amounts of each national currency. Each member state currency was linked to the ECU and exchange rates were to be kept within a $2^1/4$ per cent band on either side of the central rate against the ECU. Some states were allowed a 6 per cent swing either side, while the UK chose not to join. The whole system was quite flexible since, apart from the $2^1/4$ per cent or 6 per cent swings, periodic devaluations and revaluations against the ECU were allowed and it was possible for individual members to leave the scheme. Increased exchange rate stability was the modest aim: the arrangement was not formally declared to be the first step on the road to a full EMU. For the system to achieve the desired exchange rate stability it was recognized that there was a need for a *parallel* coordination of national macroeconomic policies so as to achieve a convergence of inflation rates and so on. However a *formal* mechanism of policy coordination never emerged. Member states were not willing formally to give up their real or imaginary economic sovereignty, although they had to dance to the Bundesbank's tune.

Trade Relations with Third Countries

The Rome Treaty embodied three key provisions governing its relationships with third countries. The first element was the Part Four (Articles 131–6) association provisions. These were designed to deal with the problem posed by the colonial dependencies of the Six (the overseas countries and territories). The adhesion of the UK and other countries of course added to the list. Quite simply they could not be locked out by the common external tariff. Indeed, under the terms of Part Four, the original Six agreed to reduce their tariffs on goods coming from the overseas territories in line with their own internal tariff disarmament. The Territories for their part had to progressively reduce their tariffs on goods coming from the EEC, but the treaty provided an escape clause since it went on to say that they could retain their tariffs if they were necessary for industrialization, development or revenue raising. This preferential arrangement was accompanied by the creation of the EDF which, as we indicated earlier, was a vehicle for aid giving to the overseas territories. Arrangements on these lines were continued in the succeeding Yaoundé and Lomé Conventions, the detailed arrangements being concluded under Article 238.

The second element was provided by Article 238, which allowed the EEC to conclude association agreements with third countries, groups of countries or international organizations. In due course the EEC proceeded to conclude a range of agreements as diverse as, on the one hand, the reciprocal free trade arrangements with EFTA and, on the other, the largely cooperative pact with the Association of South East Asian Nations.

Finally, under Article 237, any *European* state could apply for full membership. This required unanimity in the Council of Ministers. In due course the UK, Denmark, Ireland, Greece, Spain and Portugal successfully took advantage of this possibility and at the beginning of 1995 they were joined by Austria, Finland and Sweden.

THE POLITICAL SPILLOVER

In Chapter 1 we considered the neofunctionalist expectation that there could be a political spillover – that economic integration could lead on to political integration. This did in fact happen, to a limited degree. Its historical evolution goes back to the early 1960s. We will not pursue that matter here but merely observe that, at the pathbreaking summit at The Hague in 1969, the heads of state and government agreed to instruct their foreign ministers to study the best way to achieve progress in respect of political unification. The resulting 1970 report inaugurated the Davignon (named after the Belgian diplomat involved) or European Political Cooperation (EPC) Procedure.

With a minimum of bureaucracy the member states agreed to cooperate on foreign policy issues (defence was excluded). The aim was to achieve an identity of view on various international issues and, if possible, common action. This was essentially a mechanism for intergovernmental cooperation; there was no majority voting of the kind provided for in the Rome Treaty. We will return to this issue in Chapters 4 and 6.

NOTES

1. Not all issues were subject to qualified majority voting. For example, harmonization directives under Article 100 had to be adopted unanimously and the admission of new members to the Community was also subject to national veto. Some issues were subject to simple majority, such as the calling of an intergovernmental conference under Article 236.
2. This is only partly true. If a member state fails to implement a directive within the time limit laid down, it is possible (under certain circumstances) for individuals to seek to enforce their rights against the negligent state. In such circumstances directives become directly effective.
3. The CAP also embraced the idea of a Common Fisheries Policy. For details of this, see Wise, M. (1984), *The Common Fisheries Policy of the European Community* (London: Methuen).
4. Income elasticity of demand measures the responsiveness of quantity demanded to increases in real income. Typically the demand for most basic agricultural products grows relatively sluggishly; for example, a 1 per cent increase in income will lead to much less than a 1 per cent increase in quantity of milk consumed.

REFERENCES

Button, K.J. (1992), 'The liberalization of transport services', in D. Swann (ed.), *The Single European Market and Beyond* (London: Routledge).

CMLR (1973), Europemballage Corporation and Continental Can Company Inc. *v*. E.C. Commission, *Common Market Law Reports* [1973], 199.

CMLR (1979), Rewe-Zentrale A.G. *v*. Bundesmonopolverwaltung Für Branntwein, *Common Market Law Reports* [1979] 494.

3.   The emergence of the Single European Act

INTRODUCTION

We have seen that the Community of Six made steady and determined progress in the transition period between the beginning of 1958 and the end of 1969. By 1969, the outlines of a Common Market were recognizably in place – notably internal tariff and quota disarmament and the common customs (external) tariff – and some limited steps had been taken to liberalize factor movements. The basic mechanisms of the CAP, in terms of both market intervention and financing, had been established, the French having been extremely pressing on this issue. Arrangements in respect of the Community's colonial inheritance were also in place. Between 1969 and 1973, the Community was indeed in ebullient mood. We have seen that at the Hague summit in 1969 there had been no question of the Community resting on its oars. Proposals for developing the EPC procedure, for providing a firm financial basis for Community operations and, most adventurous of all, for transforming the Common Market into an EMU, were all actively contemplated. The actual nature of EPC, and its successor the Common Foreign and Security Policy (CFSP), are discussed in Chapters 4 and 6 whilst the own resource-based Community budget and the CAP, which has always been intimately connected with it, are covered in Chapter 8. The Paris summit of 1972 was really the high point in this period of expanding horizons. As we have seen, the heads of state and government formally committed themselves to achieving the goal of EMU by 1980; agreed to develop a number of new policy competences concerned with the environment, science and technology, industry and energy; resolved to give social policy a boost and decided to create a ERDF before the end of 1973. Actually it did not see the light of day until 1975. Interestingly the idea of transforming the three communities into a European Union was also entertained. The heads of state and government anticipated that this would happen by the end of the decade (EC Commission, 1972, pp. 6–16) but in fact they had to wait until the 1992 Treaty on European Union had come into operation, that is, until 1 November 1993.

EUROSCLEROSIS

However this optimism proved to be short-lived and ill-founded. Indeed the period from 1973 to 1984 has been characterized as a period of Eurosclerosis – a hardening of the European arteries – that is, a lack of dynamism and flexibility. Two forms of Eurosclerosis have been identified. Moravcsik, in a stimulating study of the negotiation of the Single Act of 1986, refers to Eurosclerosis as a decline, during the late 1970s and early 1980s, in European competitiveness combined with high unemployment and low economic growth as compared with other members of the OECD (Moravcsik, 1991, pp. 72–3). Certainly the EC economy was not performing well in the early 1980s. The average annual percentage growth rate of GDP in Community states between 1980 and 1986 ranged from 0.7 to 2.8, compared with figures of 3.7 and 3.1 for Japan and the USA, respectively. This induced various transnational business groups to exert pressure for a Community response to the need to bolster European competitiveness. More will be said on this topic below.

However Eurosclerosis is usually taken to refer to the general lack of progress in the development of Community policies and institutions. Indeed by 1975, when Belgian Prime Minister Leo Tindemans produced his report on European Union (Mitchell, 1976), much of the steam had gone out of the system. Ominously he referred to the idea of a two-tier Community in which those who had the will and ability to forge ahead with EMU could do so while the rest would lag behind, though they would not be released from the obligation to come into line ultimately. The Europessimism to which Eurosclerosis gave rise reached its apogee in the early 1980s when, as Moravcsik observes, ideas about splitting the EC into subgroups (*Europe à deux vitesses*) proliferated. As we shall see, a variable speed Europe also came to be a device employed by France and Germany to force a reluctant UK to make a move forward.

Before we endeavour to explain why relative stagnation occurred, it is important to keep things in proportion. There was some progress in the 1973–84 period. Notable among these was the negotiation of the

Lomé Convention of 1975. This was hailed by the then British Minister of Overseas Development, Judith Hart, not noted for her enthusiasm for the European cause, as a major milestone in the evolution of relations between the developed and the developing countries. Also the Community was able to take in four new members, although at least two (the UK and Denmark) subsequently proved to be relatively unenthusiastic about further economic integration and one (Greece) has on occasions been the cause of severe embarrassments. Finally although the 'EMU by 1980' plan had run into the ground by 1974, in 1979 the Community recovered some momentum when it introduced the EMS. This, as we have noted, was a rather limited exercise in monetary union, stronger in respect of the exchange rate than of the formal policy convergence aspect. As noted earlier, it centred on a loose exchange rate union in which margins of fluctuation were allowed around the central parities, devaluations and revaluations were permitted and exits from the scheme were not excluded.

While we have described the period from 1958 to 1969 as one of a steady and determined progress, we have to concede that one of the seeds of future difficulty had been sown during this period. As David Allen has pointed out in an extremely penetrating study of the origins of the Single Act, from 1958 to 1965 the EC institutions set about the tasks given them under the original treaty *using the procedures which it prescribed.* However that period came to an end in 1965 with the French boycott. This was finally resolved early in 1966 in terms of the Luxembourg Compromise. According to Allen:

> In essence this represented an agreement to disagree between France and the other five EC member states over how far the Council should go towards seeking unanimous agreement (even where the treaty provided for majority voting) on issues that individual states regarded as vital to their national interests. Although the Compromise was just that and had no legal standing in the EC system, it had important impact on decision making in the Council; it has been interpreted as meaning that any member state could in fact exercise a veto on any issue that it determines will affect its vital national interests. In consequence decision making in the Council slowed down dramatically; for though the veto has only rarely been formally used, its existence ensured that decisions were endlessly postponed until unanimous agreement could be reached. (Allen, 1992, p. 29)

The significance of the Luxembourg Compromise in the context of this chapter was that it created a decision-making deadlock which had to be broken if a single market by the end of 1992 (see below) was to become a reality. That task of rectification was to be accomplished, as we shall see, in the Single Act.

It is not without significance that the onset of Eurosclerosis is usually regarded as being detectable from 1973 onwards – the date when the UK became a full member of the Community! Dean Acheson's famous remark about UK foreign policy in the postwar period, to the effect that she had lost an Empire but had not found a role, could be at least partially refuted in 1973 when the decision to join the Community (first taken in 1961) finally became a reality. Yet it was not a permanently enthusiastic role. It is true that the UK was involved in the heady 1972 Paris summit deliberations but the UK was then led by a dedicated European – Edward Heath – and that situation has never recurred. In due course, as we shall see, France began to take a more relaxed stance on majority voting and was replaced by the UK as the leader of the pack (which included Greece and Denmark) which during the years prior to the Single Act was determined to uphold the right to a veto when important national interests were at stake (Moravcsik, 1991, p. 59).

We turn now to the specific origins of the Eurosclerosis problem. The reasons for this were various. One was that the recessions which followed in the wake of the oil price increases of 1973 and 1979 led to the emergence of protective responses which inhibited the drive to open up national markets. By 1981, when the commission addressed a Communication to the Council of Ministers on the state of the internal market, what it had to say was far from flattering:

> The customs union, the implementation of which is intended to ensure the internal market, is proving to be increasingly inadequate for the achievement of this aim. The substance of what has been achieved is instead being jeopardized and undermined by the fact that old barriers have survived for too long and new barriers have been created. (EC Commission, 1981a)

But recession was not the only cause of Eurosclerosis. Others were associated with quite bitter conflicts between the member states. A major factor was the UK budget problem. When the British accession conditions were negotiated, it was recognized that the Community budget (the details of which had by then been hammered out) might give rise to difficulties for the UK. Libations of soothing language were therefore liberally dispensed by the Community, which pointed out that, if unacceptable situations arose, 'the very survival of the Community would demand that the institutions find equitable solutions' (HMSO, 1971). This may have mollified the Conservatives when negotiating accession but it did not satisfy the succeeding Labour government. It sought a renegotiation on this and other issues. The Labour administration secured what it thought was an adequate budget correction mechanism. In reality this mechanism was never triggered into operation and even if it had been it would have been inadequate. By 1980, when the Conservatives under Margaret Thatcher were once more at the helm, the impact of the Community budget on the UK was apparent for all to see. The details are discussed in Chapter 8. Suffice it to say that in 1980 the UK found itself facing the prospect of paying a good deal more into the budget than it was likely to get out. In short, it was destined to be a net contributor, although not the only one. However, given that the UK had slipped down the European standard of living league table, this could be regarded as doubly inequitable. It prompted the formidable British prime minister to demand 'her money back'. This in turn gave rise to much acrimony and diversion of energies and led to a series of *ad hoc* annual rebates, although the UK wished for a more permanent arrangement.

Another major distracting factor was the continuing conflict over the CAP. As part of the renegotiation, referred to above, the Community had committed itself to a 'stocktaking'. But this proved to be of little benefit. By the early 1980s, the illogicalities of the CAP were increasingly evident. High prices, well above world levels, together with technological changes leading to increased yields, caused domestic supply to outstrip the relatively slow advance of demand. As a result the Community became not just self-sufficient but more than self-sufficient. Surpluses mounted and the Community's open-ended guarantee system presented it with a rapidly growing financial commitment. Excess supplies had to be bought up and stored or export subsidies had to be made available so that the butter, beef and cereal mountains could be dumped abroad. This was bound to cause increasing irritation among outside agricultural producers (such as the USA) and was to culminate in the late 1980s in a full-scale attack on the CAP in the context of the Uruguay GATT Round. However during the early 1980s the major problem was the growing *internal* financial burden, which of course inflamed the opposition of net contributors to the budget. By 1984, the budget was in danger of running out of resources but the response of the UK was that it would not sanction any more resources until the rebate issue had been properly addressed and a decision to reform the CAP had been taken.

Yet another cause of internal tension in the period before 1984 was the issue of further enlargement. Greece had joined in 1981 but Spain and Portugal were also clamouring for admission. However, French farmers, fearful of Iberian competition in the form of cheap vegetables and wine, had encouraged the French government to stall on this issue (Moravcsik, 1991, p. 55). The UK tended to adopt an entirely different stance. It supported a widening of the Community partly on the grounds that this would slow down the process of deepening. Deepening of course refers to the development of new policy competences, the increased use of majority voting and less stress on the kind of intergovernmentalism which afflicted the Community after the 1965 French boycott. David Allen has pointed out that this continued to be the approach adopted by the UK. Thus in the lead-up to the Maastricht Treaty the UK championed the admission of EFTA and some Eastern European countries as a way of preventing EMU and political union (Allen, 1992, p. 29). In the post-Maastricht era the UK fully supported the admission of Norway, Sweden, Finland and Austria, at least in part on the grounds that this would take some of the steam out of the pressure for yet closer economic integration, more majority voting and a federal structure. Having on this latter occasion achieved its objective of widening (see Chapter 9), the UK government then proceeded to make a fool of itself by entering into a conflict over the size of the blocking minority in the Council of Ministers, a battle it was bound to lose.

RELAUNCHING THE COMMUNITY

Institutional progress was clearly an important ingredient if the Community was to restore its momentum and there were some encouraging signs in the late 1970s. In 1979, two reports were submitted relating to the reform of Community institutions. In 1978, French President Giscard d'Estaing suggested that a group of eminent persons should be charged with the task of considering what adjustments in machinery and procedures might make the Community more effective and whether progress could be made towards economic union. This task was remitted by the European Council to Barend Biesheuval, Edmund Dell and Robert Marjolin – the so-called 'Committee of Three Wise Men'. Early in 1979, the commission set up an independent review body, under the chairmanship of Ambassador Dirk Spierenburg, consisting of Karl Buschmann, Paul Delouvrier, Giuseppi Petrilli and Dick Taverne. Its task was to consider possible reforms of the Commission and its services. Of the two, the former was certainly the most important. Most of the criticism of the Three Wise Men was reserved for the Council of Ministers. In particular its activities were too intergovernmental in character. The supranational element in the Rome Treaty had been lost sight of. Despite the Luxembourg Compromise, more use should be made of majority voting (Swann, 1978, pp. 315–17).

The European Parliament too was concerned about the shortcomings of the institutional structure and if we are to look for a turning point, when the tide began at last to flow in the direction of a more dynamic Community, then it seems reasonable to select 1979. As we noted in Chapter 2, in the first instance the European Parliament (originally the Assembly or Common Assembly) had no legislative or budgetary powers. The Council of Ministers made the laws but only *in consultation* with the parliament. All that parliament could do by way of showing its teeth was to pass a motion of censure (relevant voting rules having been satisfied) on the commission but it could not nominate or renominate commissioners. As we have seen, in earlier days parliament consisted of unelected delegates drawn from national parliaments. However in 1979, for the first time, it was directly elected by the people and consequently came to enjoy a greater legitimacy in European affairs.

David Allen has pointed out that the first signs of significant movement out of stagnation came from the newly elected body and in 1981 the direction it was likely to move in was revealed when it adopted a resolution submitted by the so-called 'Crocodile Club'. They were a group of pro-federal MEPs who took their collective name from the Strasbourg restaurant where they first met. The leader of the group was Altiero Spinelli, who recognized that the parliament needed to strike out in a new direction. As will become clearer in Chapter 8, parliament had been granted additional powers in connection with the own resource-based Community budget. In particular the budget only became law when parliament voted to adopt it. Flexing its muscles, it had on more than one occasion refused to adopt the budget, but this had brought some bad publicity. Thus Spinelli concluded that parliament would be wiser to direct its efforts towards increasing its legislative as opposed to its budgetary powers. (Allen, 1992, p. 30). It was as a result of this that in 1984 it brought forth its Draft Treaty Establishing the European Union.

Parliament also included a Kangaroo Club, apparently because such animals can hop over barriers. They tended to focus on economic issues and in particular on the need to abolish the remaining barriers to the free movement of goods, services and factors. Moravcsik points out that these two groups respectively represent the maximalist and minimalist positions in the lead up to the Single Act. If we compare their aspirations with the achievements of the SEA, then the inescapable conclusion must be that, while the maximalists made some gains, the Single Act was really a victory for the minimalist position. *However we should not underestimate the importance of the Spinelli initiative since its ideas remained on the table and, as we shall see in Chapter 5, were influential in the negotiations which led to the Maastricht Treaty.*

What then did Spinelli and, indeed, the parliament propose? The aim of the draft treaty was to turn the Community into a European Union. Although the word 'federal' was not employed in it, it being anathema to some of the Ten (Lodge, 1984, p. 383), the draft treaty had a broadly federal thrust. This interpretation is supported by reference to two key ingredients. First, there should be dual citizenship, of the Union and of the individual member states. Second, the Union should respect the principle of subsidiarity. This latter feature will be discussed in Chapter 6. At this point all we need to note is that subsidiarity suggests the need for a method of determining what powers and competences ought to remain with the member states and what powers and competences are more appropriately invested in the Union. The draft treaty envisaged an expanded role for both the commission and the parliament. The commission was to be sole executive of the Union, a number of tasks which it had previously shared with the council were to be assigned exclusively to the commission. Whereas previously the commission had enjoyed the sole right of initiative, and the council was largely the legislator, under the new arrangements parliament would also enjoy a right of initiative and would colegislate with the council. The council would take decisions by qualified majority voting. The European Council would become a Union institution. It would appoint the president of the commission. Parliament would share the investiture of the commission with the council. The EPC mechanism would cease to be a separate arrangement: it would be brought within the Union system (Allen, 1992, p. 35).

But new initiatives did not emanate solely from the European Parliament. In October 1981, the French government submitted to its partners a memorandum on the revitalization of the Community (EC Commission, 1981b, pp. 92–100). However its emphasis was wholly on the need to reinvigorate the Community's efforts in the fields of economic, social and cultural policy and it contained no proposals for institutional innovation. It was followed by the German–Italian (Genscher–Colombo) initiative for November 1981 (EC Commission, 1981b, pp. 87–91), which proposed the adoption of a European Act; drafts of this, together with a declaration on European integration, were addressed to the European Council and Parliament. The draft act was centrally concerned with institutional matters and looked to the creation of a European Union. The European Council submitted this to the foreign ministers for study and the results of these studies were picked up at the European Council in Stuttgart in 1983; upon that occasion the heads of state and government signed the Solemn Declaration on European Union (EC Commission, 1983, pp. 24–9). This latter sounded very promising but closer inspection reveals that the main body of the declaration consisted largely of a somewhat cautious reaffirmation of the need to make progress on European Union. The final provision, where concrete action might have been expected, was characterized by hesitancy: it declared that European Union was already being achieved by deepening and broadening the scope of existing European activities. The European Council would subject the declaration to a review when progress towards European Union justified it, and such a review would take place not later than five years from the signing of the declaration. In the light of such a review, a decision would be made as to whether the progress achieved should be incorporated in a Treaty on European Union: in short, member states could sign the declaration without committing themselves to any immediate radical change.

In addition, as Moravcsik has pointed out, transnational business groups were pressing for change, particularly in respect of the need to create a single European market and to make greater use of majority voting as a method of speeding up the European legislative process. In 1981, Viscount Etienne Davignon, the commissioner responsible for the EC internal market, brought together a group of information technology firms and they proceeded to develop proposals for technological collaboration and market liberalization. In 1983, Pehr Gyllenhammer, chief executive of Volvo, and Wisse Dekker, chief executive officer of Philips, set up the Roundtable of European Industrialists. Dekker went on to produce plans for the creation of a single market which were in many ways anticipations of the famous Cockfield 1985 White Paper (see Chapter 4). In 1984, the leading EC industrial interest group UNICE (Union des Confédérations de l'Industrie et des Employeurs d'Europe) came out in favour of increased use of majority voting (Moravcsik, 1991, p. 44).

So far the formative pressures have been viewed as emerging from internal sources – the commission, individual states, collaborations between states, the parliament and transnational business groups. External sources of influence have not figured in the analysis except insofar as an internal market could be viewed as an economic response to outside competition. But in addition there were external political influences at work. These have been admirably reviewed by David Allen and we shall not endeavour to detail them here (Allen, 1992, pp. 33–4). Basically they boil down to saying that European states were beginning to wonder how long they could rely on the American security guarantee. They were not always comfortable with the stance adopted by the USA, such as the anti-Soviet hostility of the Reagan administration. They were also alarmed at the prospect that their interests might be bargained away in their absence. This latter seemed to be the message to be derived from the Reagan–Gorbachev exchange in Reykjavik in 1986. Such concerns were bound to heighten Community interest in developing its own foreign policy stance and thus the future shape of EPC was likely to figure in the negotiations leading up to the Single Act.

FONTAINEBLEAU, DOOGE AND THE IGC

The first really concrete step forward occurred in 1984 at the Fontainebleau summit. It was significant for two reasons. First, it made a major contribution to solving the bitter disputes which had plagued the Community for several years. In particular, real progress was made towards reforming the agricultural surplus problem and therefore curbing excessive budget spending, and this was to be achieved by instituting milk quotas and tighter financial controls. The UK also secured a more durable settlement of its own budget dispute. These bold decisions paved the way for an increase in the own-resource base of the Community budget. Second, with the atmosphere significantly improved, member states were willing to contemplate further progress to a European Union. Indeed after the summit President Mitterrand (France was holding the presidency of the council and European Council in the first half of 1984) observed: 'There is not a single dispute left to settle' (EC Commission, 1984, p. 12). The heads of state and government had in fact also agreed to set up a committee to study the creation of a Peoples' Europe (the Adonnino Committee) and an Ad Hoc Committee on Institutional Affairs (the Dooge Committee). The Dooge discussions were the more important, but the Adonnino Committee did make important recommendations on the need for the free movement of people. The Fontainebleau agreement was not achieved without a tussle which in substantial measure involved putting pressure on the UK to settle its disagreements with the Community. The tactic adopted by France in alliance with Germany has already been alluded to. It consisted of threatening the British with the prospect of a two-tier Europe: France, Germany and others would forge ahead and Britain would be marginalized. This seems to have done the trick, since the British were anxious to stay in the game. To have been relegated to a second division would not only have involved a loss of status but could have been economically damaging. A semi-detached UK would be a less attractive base for inward investment from the USA, Japan and so on. This latter consideration continued to be a major UK concern after the Maastricht Treaty had been signed, since the UK had by then the lion's share of such investment flows. The idea of a two-tier monetary union, which as we shall see is a possibility under Maastricht, was thus an extremely distasteful prospect.

This technique of persuasion highlights the important role which France, and in particular President Mitterrand, came to play when France assumed the presidency in 1984. French policy had indeed changed in the direction of a positive pro-European stance. The socialist government of the early 1980s had adopted an expansionist macroeconomic policy and had urged upon Mitterrand a policy of protectionism and autarky. However Germany in particular made it clear to France that such expansionism was incompatible with continued membership of the EMS – a point which was underlined by a mounting balance of payments deficit and devaluations of the franc. The failure of the policy, together with a change in the balance of political forces which enabled Mitterrand to ally himself to more moderate elements, paved the way for a change of stance. The way forward for France lay in Europe.

In all this, we cannot avoid noting the role played by individuals. Mitterrand's Euro-enthusiasm has attracted the attention of commentators. Apparently at Fontainebleau he kept the other heads of state and government waiting for the best part of a couple of hours while he regaled the press and television with his dreams of Europe. Was this a long-standing and deep-seated conviction or was it, as Moravcsik speculates, a case of making a virtue out of necessity? The temptation of politicians to seek to turn themselves into visionary statesmen by playing the European card is strong. Whatever the true motives, a change had indeed occurred.

The Dooge (and Adonnino) Committees duly reported in March 1985. Dooge recommended the establishment of an Inter-Governmental Conference (IGC) to negotiate a European Union Treaty. In July 1985, the heads of state and government met in Milan and decided to do just that. However this was by no means a unanimous decision: Britain, Denmark and Greece were opposed but Article 236 (which provides for treaty-modifying IGCs to be called) merely requires a simple majority. Margaret Thatcher is reported to have been furious but no doubt was persuaded to join in by being reminded that, whilst IGCs can be called by simple majority, the Rome Treaty can only be modified by unanimity, that a two-track solution could not therefore be thrust upon the UK and that the federalist-inclined parliament was not to be directly involved in the deliberations.

Once again personalities played a key role. By Milan, Jacques Delors was firmly in the presidential chair and brought to the commission an enthusiasm and effectiveness which had been markedly absent in the case of his immediate predecessors. David Allen has drawn a contrast between Delors and Thorn, Ortoli and Jenkins. In fairness it has to be pointed out that Roy Jenkins did manage to set the ball rolling towards the EMS at a time when it was thought extremely unpropitious to launch a new monetary union adventure. A measure of the effectiveness of Delors is the fact that, while the European Council in 1982 instructed the council to decide before March 1983 on the priority measures needed to reinforce the single market, it was only when Delors was on the scene, ably assisted by fellow commissioner Lord Cockfield, that the matter achieved the high profile associated with the famous 1985 single market White Paper (Allen, 1992, p. 37). By the time of the Milan summit, Delors had also thrown into the discussion a proposal for an intensified R&D programme.

The Dooge Committee and the IGC itself highlight the role played by the three big players: France, Germany and the UK. What, if anything, came out of these deliberations depended on finding a formula which they in particular could agree to. Some side payments to other parties might also be necessary and this included the two Iberian aspirants. Moravcsik puts his finger on the matter when he describes the IGC process, which as we noted rests on unanimity, as least common denominator bargaining. In the end, and not therefore surprisingly, it led to a victory for the minimalist position.

The role of the parliament was, for reasons given earlier, bound to be a limited one. Moravcsik notes that one of the first actions of Dooge was to reject the parliament's draft treaty, but this tends to underestimate the influence that parliament exerted. David Allen perceptively draws our attention to the implicit answer which Jacques Delors was hinting at in 1989 when, at Bruges, he asked, 'Do you think it would have been possible to convene the IGC that produced the SEA had Parliament not thrown its weight behind the idea on the basis of the draft European union treaty which it had adopted at the initiative of that great European, Altiero Spinelli?' (Allen, 1992, p. 35). Nonetheless we have to admit that the result was bound to be a disappointment to the parliament – the cooperation procedure which finally emerged (see Chapter 4) was a substantially watered down version of the role it had envisaged for itself in the draft treaty. Moravcsik may be correct in not assigning any preponderant influence to the transnational business groups.

In the search for lowest common denominators, the liberalization of the internal market was bound to be high on the list of probable final ingredients since it had enjoyed fairly general support (certainly among the Ten) since at least 1982 and was something which the commission had been agitating about for several years. Procedural reform exhibited fewer prospects of substantial agreement. France and Germany were broadly in favour of majority voting; the UK was initially very reluctant, looked for informal ways round but was *selectively* persuadable on the grounds that some procedural modifications were necessary if the single market, about which she was extremely enthusiastic, was to be achieved. Increased powers for the parliament enjoyed the support of Germany but not of France and the UK and, given that parliament was not present at the bargaining table, this did not bode well for dramatic progress on this issue. Significant progress on monetary union was almost certainly a dead duck since Germany had ruled it out until capital flows had been liberalized and it is reported that, at the Luxembourg summit late in 1985, Chancellor Kohl and Prime Minister Thatcher had agreed to oppose the inclusion of a monetary dimension in the final agreement (Lodge, 1986, p. 212). As for political cooperation, the view of major players centred around codifying existing practice although France did envisage the creation of a secretariat. All this does not suggest that a dramatic leap forward was in prospect. However, as we shall see in the next chapter, the Single Act proved to be a major milestone not only for what it provided but also for what it presaged.

The details of the future SEA, largely a modification of the Rome Treaty, together with a formal recognition of EPC, were hammered out in the IGC during the autumn of 1985. Issues were also dealt with at the European Council in Luxembourg in December 1985 and at an EC foreign ministers meeting that December. The Act was formally adopted at Luxembourg and The Hague in February 1986. In then had to be ratified before it could come into operation.

REFERENCES

Allen, D. (1992), 'European union, the Single European Act and the 1992 programme', in D. Swann (ed.), *The Single European Market and Beyond* (London: Routledge).

EC Commission (1972), *Sixth General Report on the Activities of the Communities* (Brussels: Office for Official Publications of the European Communities).

EC Commission (1981a), COM(81) 313 final, 17 June 1981.

EC Commission (1981b), *Bulletin of the European Communities*, no. 11 (Brussels: Office for Official Publications of the European Communities).

EC Commission (1983), *Bulletin of the European Communities*, no. 6 (Brussels: Office for Official Publications of the European Communities).

EC Commission (1984), *Bulletin of the European Communities*, no. 6 (Brussels: Office for Official Publications of the European Communities).

HMSO (1971), *The United Kingdom and the European Communities* (London).

Lodge, J. (1984), 'European Union and the First Elected European Parliament: The Spinelli Initiative', *Journal of Common Market Studies*, **22**, (4) (June).

Lodge, J. (1986), 'The Single European Act: Towards a New Euro-Dynamism', *Journal of Common Market Studies*, **24**, (3) (March).

Mitchell, J. (1976), 'The Tindemans Report: Retrospect and Prospect', *Common Market Law Review*, **13**.

Moravcsik, A. (1991), 'Negotiating the Single European Act', in R.E. Keohane and S. Hoffman (eds), *The New European Community* (Boulder: Westview Press).

Swann, D. (1978), *The Economics of the Common Market* (Harmondsworth: Penguin).

4. The Single European Act

INTRODUCTION

As we indicated in Chapter 3, the IGC of 1985 finally led to the Single Act. It was duly ratified by national parliaments and entered into force on 1 July 1987. In what follows we will first identify the competences, powers and institutional changes which flowed from the Single Act and we will then discuss in some detail the implementation of its most important aspect – the completion by the end of 1992 of the single market.

COMPETENCES, POWERS AND INSTITUTIONAL CHANGES

The provisions of the Act had implications for all three economic communities and for EPC. However the implications for the ECSC and Euratom were of no great significance and we will not concern ourselves with them. By contrast the implications for the EEC Treaty were considerable and this was also true for European Political Cooperation and we discuss both of these below.

Rome Treaty Economic Policy Competences

The overwhelmingly most important feature of the Single Act was the single market commitment. We have seen in Chapter 3 that the EEC had failed in its aim of creating a true Common Market. Substantial NTBs continued to exist. Freedom to supply services was not a reality. Factors of production were not free to move in an undistorted fashion. It was this failure to act which had been highlighted in a series of reports by the Commission and which culminated in Lord Cockfield's White Paper of 1985. What the Single Act did was to set the Community the target of completing the internal market by the end of 1992.

Moreover it aimed to create a market without internal frontiers. This implied not just free movement of goods, services and factors, with an end to border controls, but also the free movement of people.

The latter was very significant. It should be added that a General Declaration was attached to the Act which stipulated that the single market provisions did not affect the right of member states to take such measures as they considered necessary to control immigration from third countries, and to combat terrorism, crime, the traffic in drugs and illicit trading in works of art and antiques. The actual way in which the Community set about the task of completing the internal market we leave for treatment later in this chapter.

The Single Act was also extremely important for Community regional development and policy. We noted earlier that, whilst the preamble to the Rome Treaty did draw attention to the desirability of reducing the differences between the regions, the main text of the Treaty did not contain any relevant competences other than that it called for the creation of the EIB. (The latter, however, was a lending institution and was not in the grant-giving business.) Indeed, as we noted earlier, state aid for regional development could actually be prohibited. What the Single Act did was to insert into the Treaty a new section or title concerned with economic and social cohesion. It declared that the aim of the Community should be to reduce disparities between the regions and the backwardness of the less favoured regions. In effect what the Single Act did was to import into the main text of the Rome Treaty what had originally merely been a grand aspiration in its preamble. The new title saw the task of reducing disparities as being accomplished through the agency of the structural funds, whose existence was thus formally recognized, in concert with, amongst others, the EIB. The structural funds are of course the ESF, the ERDF and the guidance section of the European Agricultural Guidance and Guarantee Fund (EAGGF). Guidance grants are for structural improvements to farms as opposed to guarantee monies which are allocated for the purpose of dealing with farm surpluses. Therefore, while the Single Act was significant because it formally recognized that the Community had a regional development role to play, we are of course aware that prior to the Act the Community had not been entirely idle in this respect. The ERDF had been dispensing grants since 1975 and the EIB had been in existence since 1958 and had had loan-based assistance to backward regions at the top of its list of priorities for action.

It is perhaps worth mentioning at this point that the new economic and social cohesion competence was a response to pressure exerted by the new members, Spain and Portugal. Both only became new members in 1986 but were nevertheless involved in the 1985 IGC. They, as relatively poorer countries, were particularly concerned about their ability to survive in the increasingly competitive atmosphere which the 1992 commitment would create. They indicated that their condition for acceptance of the Single Act was that there should be a transfer of resources to the weaker economies of the EEC. When in Chapter 8 we come to consider the Community budget we will see how that commitment was discharged.

The Single Act also modified the Rome Treaty by inserting a new section or title concerned with the environment. This was significant because the task of protecting the environment did not feature in the original treaty. As a result, the Community was now formally endowed with a competence to adopt measures concerned with preserving and improving the quality of the environment. For a measure to be adopted the Council of Ministers had to act unanimously; the usual requirement of consultation with the European Parliament and Ecosoc of course applied. In should be noted, however, that in practice some environmental measures could be subject to majority voting. This derived from the fact that the Article 100 harmonization powers were modified by the Single Act (see below) so as to allow for majority voting *in certain instances*. These harmonization powers were of course designed to deal with national laws and practices which affected the setting up of the Common Market. Quite clearly differing standards as between the member states in matters such as pollution could distort cross-frontier trade. It therefore followed that an environmental measure might be designed to harmonize environmental standards so as to eliminate competitive distortions and thus the majority voting system would be applicable. In 1991, this approach was confirmed by a Court of Justice ruling.

However, the reader will be aware that, from the 1972 Paris summit onwards, the Council of Ministers had been adopting directives in matters as diverse as the quality of drinking water, the noise emitted by lawn mowers and air pollution, and three Environmental Action Programmes had been agreed. On the other hand, as we have just noted, the task of protecting the environment did not feature explicitly anywhere in the treaty. What, then, was the authority upon which the Community had based its actions? The answer was apparently twofold. Environmental issues sometimes arose as an incidental by-product of the standards harmonization process. For example, inter-state trade in cars could be inhibited if various member states adopted different national rules about the acceptable level of pollution that could be emitted from car exhausts. Directives on standards therefore might involve the Community in reaching agreement on acceptable levels of pollution. But this hardly explained how the Community could make laws about the quality of drinking water or, perhaps more mysteriously, the cleanliness of seaside bathing facilities! Here a second justification could be invoked. Article 2 of the Rome Treaty declared that the Community should seek to achieve 'an accelerated raising of the standard of living'. One way to do that was to improve the quality of the environment. It was an interpretation which could have been challenged, but no one successfully sought to do so. We can therefore conclude that the true significance of the Single Act was that it finally removed any doubts on this issue: the Community was formally endowed with a competence to make policy in the area of the environment.

The motivations which lay behind this development were various. It was expected that the single market programme would lead to an acceleration in the growth rate of the Community economy. This carried with it the possibility that pollution, if it grew *pro rata* with the growth of the economy, would become an even greater problem. Moreover increased competitive pressures might lead to firms seeking to achieve cost savings by adopting less environmentally safe technologies and practices. On the other hand it was recognized that, if increased competition led to a more rapid pace of technological change, it would also increase the rate at which opportunities would occur when firms could opt to adopt more environmentally friendly processes. This was clearly the preferred course of events.

A number of other concerns were apparent. For example, the removal of barriers to trade might lead to more transportation of wastes as the more efficient processors undercut the less efficient ones. This was seen as a problem because of the risks inherent in transporting particularly hazardous wastes. Concern was also felt over the prospect that a lack of border controls could lead to a growth in the illegal trade in endangered animals and birds. The free and less costly movement of people (thanks to airline deregulation – see below) was also viewed by some as presaging yet more tourism and yet more environmental degradation.

The modifications to the Rome Treaty brought about by the Single Act, together with the various action programmes, gave rise to a series of environmental policy principles. The first was the prevention principle, which was particularly appropriate where there was a prospect of irreversible damage to the environment. The second was at-source rectification based on the 'polluter pays' principle – in other words it was desirable to *internalize* the avoidance and damage cost in order to obtain a more cost-efficient application of Community environmental policy. The third was the subsidiarity principle to which we referred earlier. Thus the Community should take action relative to the environment to the extent that the objectives of policy could best be attained at Community level. Other than that, it was desirable that competence should rest at the lowest possible level in the political hierarchy. The fourth principle was that of economic efficiency; that is, actions in the fields of the environment should be based on an assessment of the costs and benefits of action or lack of action.

The Single Act also explicitly granted to the Community institutions a competence to make laws relating to health and safety at work. In the Act this comes under the general heading of Social Policy. In the Social Policy title of the original Rome Treaty, Article 118 indicated that working conditions and protection against occupational accidents and diseases were to be regarded as matters of Community concern. However when it came to action the emphasis was on consultation and collaboration. The normal treaty mechanism whereby the Council of Ministers could make laws either unanimously or by qualified majority vote was conspicuously absent. What the Single Act did was to enable the Council of Ministers to adopt directives which were designed to improve the working environment with respect to health and safety at work. Moreover this was to take place on a qualified majority voting basis.

The Single Act also declared that the commission would endeavour to develop the dialogue between the two sides of industry – management and labour – at the European level. This could, if the two sides considered it desirable, lead to relations based on agreement. The role of Jacques Delors in this context is discussed below, in Chapter 5. The Act also added a new title to the Rome Treaty, concerned with research and technological development. This was designed to address the need to strengthen the scientific and technological base of the Community and to enable the Twelve to become more competitive at the international level. Here the Community was required to act in ways which complemented the activities of the member states. Apart from specific actions, such as opening up public contracts to competition and defining common standards, the Community would identify priority research programmes and would assist in their funding. Again this was not entirely new. The Community had been in the R&D business since the 1972 Paris summit and had also been engaged in scientific collaboration with third countries. Nevertheless the new title was important because it formally recognized that contributing to R&D excellence was a priority function for the Community.

Mention must also be made of consumer protection policy. While it is true that, prior to the Single Act, some enactments of the Council of Ministers had had a consumer protection dimension, that dimension was always incidental, as in the case of the 1985 directive on product liability which was really dictated by internal market considerations rather than the protection of the consumer *per se*. Under the Single Act, consumer protection was given formal recognition under the Rome Treaty since the modified harmonization provisions of Article 100A required that not only health and safety and environment, but also consumer protection, measures should take as a base a high level of protection (Lane, 1993, pp. 959–60).

The macroeconomic provisions *of the main text* of the Single Act were, by contrast, of no great significance. We anticipated this in Chapter 3. Although they were prefaced by a reference to EMU, they did not specifically call for, or contribute to any great extent to, the realization of such a goal. Rather the new provisions which were inserted into the Rome Treaty recognized the need for cooperation in the conduct of national macroeconomic policies in order to ensure the convergence necessary for the further development of the Community. The EMS and the ECU (products of a previous and separate intergovernmental agreement) were, however, specifically mentioned and the Act required that experience in connection with them should be taken into account.

Rome Treaty Economic Decision-making Powers

The Single Act was extremely important not only for the competences it provided or confirmed but also for the decision making powers it conferred on various Community policy-making bodies. At this point the focus is on two of them, the Council of Ministers and the European Parliament.

One of the impediments to progress in completing the internal market was the unanimity requirement of Article 100. The reader will recollect that Article 100 is concerned with the harmonization (approximation) of national laws. Much of what needed to be done in order to create a single market was bound to proceed through the agency of directives which sought to bring national laws and adminis-trative practices into line and thus to eliminate the obstacles to cross-frontier flows of goods, services and resources. What the Single Act did was to recognize that, notably in the light of the increased number of member states and the greater disparity of national interests and prac-tices, unanimity (other than at the very lowest common denominator) was bound to be difficult to achieve. It was therefore decided that on a range of single market issues a qualified majority vote would suffice to achieve an agreement to harmonize. As we have noted, it was also agreed that harmonization relating to health and safety, environmental protection and consumer protection would be based on a high level of protection. The decision to switch harmonization to a majority voting basis was, however, subject to certain exceptions. These exceptions related to fiscal matters, the free movement of people and the rights and interests of employed people. More will be said on this issue in Chapter 5. These exceptions were almost certainly pressed for by the UK.

In the case of the European Parliament, significant extra powers were conferred and indeed the Single Act represented yet another lim-ited step on the path to giving the parliament real legislative influence. These new powers are generally referred to under the headings of the assent procedure and the cooperation procedure. The assent procedure applied to both the admission of new members to the Community and the conclusion of trade agreements (association) with third countries, groups of third countries and international organizations. The Act pro-vided that such admissions and agreements were only valid if they had received the assent of the European Parliament acting by an absolute majority of its component members. The parliament in due course exerted these powers; for example, it rejected the trade agreement with Israel on the grounds that it disapproved of Israeli action in connection with the Intifada.

The cooperation procedure modified the role of the parliament, in relation to the commission and Council of Ministers, in the legislative process. Under the old system the reader will recollect that the commis-sion proposed legislation. Parliament gave an opinion and might suggest amendments. The council finally adopted the legislation – possibly in amended form. Under the new cooperation procedure, the commission continued to propose legislation but a first and second reading system emerged. At its first reading, parliament adopted an opinion by simple majority. The council for its part adopted a 'common position' by quali-fied majority. Then came the second reading when parliament could approve, amend or reject the common position; an amendment or rejection could only be made by majority vote of those entitled to vote. If parliament approved the common position then the council could go ahead and adopt the act in question. If, however, parliament amended the common position then the commission would review its proposal and might revise it accordingly, in which case the council could only change the revised proposal by unanimity. Equally if parliament rejected the common position the council could only agree to the common position by unanimity. While the final decision continued to rest with the council, the parliament had the ability to send a powerful message to the commission and council, telling them to think again. Thus if the commission agreed with the parliament they could collectively put considerable pressure on the council since, as we have seen, the council could only change the revised proposal by obtaining a unanimous vote.

Institutional Changes

Three other institutional developments of the Single Act are also worthy of note. The first relates to the European Court of Justice, which had attached to it a new Court of First Instance. In 1988, it was decided that the new court should be empowered to hear cases involving Community officials and actions against Community institutions in the context of competition policy. There is an appeal to the principal court but only on points of law. The new court is debarred from hearing actions brought by member states or by Community institutions or from hearing questions referred for a preliminary ruling under Article 177. The reader will recollect that by this latter means the Court of Justice gives guidance to member state courts as to the proper interpretation of the Rome Treaty and acts deriving from it.

The second development relates to the European Council. As we indicated earlier, in Chapter 2, the heads of state and of government had been holding summit meetings from the very earliest days of the Community. However it was only in 1974 that they decided to dignify their collective deliberations with the title of European Council. This body was of course not specifically referred to in the Rome Treaty. What the Single Act did was to formally recognize the overarching role of this body in relation to the two pillars of European Union – the Economic Communities on the one hand and EPC on the other.

This conveniently brings us to the third development, the formal recognition of EPC in the search for a European Union. As we noted earlier, in Chapter 2, the participants at the Hague summit of 1969 agreed to instruct their foreign ministers to study ways of achieving progress in respect of political unification. The foreign ministers duly reported in July 1970, and their 'Luxembourg Report' (EC Council of Ministers, 1970), inaugurated the Davignon (named after the Belgian diplomat) or Political Cooperation procedure.

The political cooperation procedure was separate from the institutions of the European Community. Its membership was however, identical with that of the Community. It did not compel the member states to agree on any issue. There was no majority voting. It was essentially an exercise in intergovernmental cooperation in which the member states endeavoured to work out common positions and to agree on common actions in foreign policy matters. In the words of the Luxembourg Report:

> The objectives of this cooperation are as follows:
> — to ensure, through regular exchanges of information and consultation, a better mutual understanding on the great international problems;
> — to strengthen their solidarity by promoting the harmonization of their views, the coordination of their positions, and, where it seems possible and desirable, common actions.

Not all foreign affairs matters came within the purview of this system. Defence was excluded; for the most part that was a NATO function. However, after 1980, significant moves took place, encouraged by the UK, France and West Germany, to introduce discussion of security matters regardless of the sensitivities of some smaller states. Disarmament, on the other hand, was frequently discussed. The main focus was on foreign policy towards non-member countries, and so issues which divided members, such as Northern Ireland, were taboo. There were a number of other topics which were out of bounds, of which West Berlin prior to German reunification was one instance.

As we have already noted, at the top of the political pyramid was the European Council. The heads of state and of government met three times a year, and foreign policy matters as well as European Communities matters came within the ambit of their consideration. The Paris summit communique of 1974 also provided for them to meet as often as necessary in the context of political cooperation. In practice, the major burden of cooperation fell on the foreign ministers, and it should be noted that they were the original focus of activity when the system first began to operate in 1970. The presidency of these foreign ministerial meetings rotated alphabetically and ran for a term of six months, in parallel with the presidency of the Council of Ministers. Theoretically such meetings were supposed to take place twice in each six-month presidency, but in fact they occurred more often, frequently being held at the same time as the Council of Ministers' meetings in Brussels or Luxembourg.

The system worked with the minimum of bureaucracy. Originally there was no permanent secretariat. Meetings of ministers and officials were organized by the foreign ministry of the country which provided the presidency. In order to pave the way for such ministerial meetings, a steering body, called the Political Committee, was established. It consisted of the senior foreign policy civil servants of the Community countries. These political directors, as they were called, met once a month. In addition to preparing for the meetings of the foreign ministers, the Committee acted in a similar way for other meetings, including the European Council and the UN General Assembly. There was indeed something of a parallel between the roles of Coreper and the Political Committee. A series of expert working groups was established to cover geographical areas and particular issues. They comprised national civil servants and operated under the jurisdiction of the Political Committee and reported to it. The hammering out of common positions was very much in the hands of the foreign ministers and their senior civil servants in the Political Committee. The instruments of cooperation, however, were diverse. The cooperating partners kept in touch with each other via a special coded telex network known as COREU (after the French, *correspondance européenne*). Although there were no common embassies abroad, member state ambassadors in the foreign capitals often worked together.

Originally there was a lot of opposition to the involvement of the commission in the political cooperation mechanism. However it came to be realized that Community policy and political cooperation were capable of being at cross purposes, and so a liaison system came to be established. Apparently the position of the EC commission was satisfactory: the president and members of the commission were able to attend meetings of the foreign ministers without restriction.

The Single Act was of considerable significance for political cooperation. In most significant fashion it declared that the High Contracting Parties would endeavour jointly to formulate and implement 'a European foreign policy'. They undertook to inform and consult each other on foreign policy matters so that their combined influence was exercised as effectively as possible through the convergence of their positions and the implementation of joint action. The European Parliament was to be kept informed and its views were to be taken into account. It was once more recognized that the external policy of the European Communities and EPC should be consistent, and to this end the commission should be 'fully associated' with the proceedings of political cooperation. A secretariat in Brussels (on the margins of the council secretariat) was created to assist the presidency in preparing and implementing the activities of political cooperation.

THE SINGLE MARKET PROGRAMME

We will not attempt to discuss in detail all the measures which the single market commitment gave rise to. Rather we will concentrate on a range of key issues which also indicate the procedural innovations which the Community introduced in order to tackle this formidable task.

A key area for further progress was standards. We have already noted that, to the extent to which they differed from state to state, trade was either prevented and choice restricted or else goods had to be modified to meet the different standards of each member state, with a consequent loss of scale economies. The original approach had been one of harmonization or approximation of national laws under Article 100: a Community standard would be embodied in a directive and this standard would be adopted by all the member states and as a result goods manufactured in one member state would automatically be acceptable in all the others.

Up to 1985, the Council of Ministers had adopted approximately 180 directives relating to industrial products as well as a number concerned with foodstuffs. The industrial products included motor vehicles, metrology (measuring instruments), cosmetics, solvents (and other dangerous substances) and electrical equipment. In the case of foodstuffs, directives governed their labelling (durability, additives used and so on), packaging (restriction on the use of PVC), presentation, advertising and composition. Additives were subject to provisions specifying maximum levels. Much had therefore been achieved, but there was still a long way to go. Moreover the harmonization process is very time consuming. Not only that, but technological progress rendered existing standards obsolescent, and therefore effort had to be diverted into bringing them up to date. The Community was in fact forced to adopt a speedier process in respect of amendments to standards.

What was needed was a new more streamlined approach to the problem, which built on the implications of the *Cassis de Dijon* case. In the Cockfield White Paper of 1985, the commission noted that in 1984 the Council of Ministers had recognized the essential equivalence of the objectives of national legislation. That being so, freer trading conditions could at least in part be achieved by making use of the principle of mutual recognition. Thus the mere fact that countries had different views about the appropriate ingredients for making ice cream could hardly be invoked as a defensive argument for not importing from each other: no harm was likely to ensue to consumers. It was true that if the Community wished to take full advantage of the scale economies available in a continental sized market then standardization had its virtues. But to proceed exclusively down that path would be over-regulatory. There would, however, be some situations where the need to have particular rules was inescapable and goods not conforming to them could be excluded. In such cases the only solution was to harmonize. Several changes were therefore necessary. First, and as we have already noted, thanks to the Single Act such harmonization activity would require a qualified majority vote. Second, the council would not get bogged down in the detail but would merely seek in its directives to identify the objectives to be attained, such as the essential safety requirements with which products would have to comply in order to qualify for free movement. Third, the detailed process of standard setting would be off-loaded onto special European standards bodies. Fourth, governments would be obliged to presume that if a good was manufactured according to such standards then it complied with the fundamental objectives stipulated in the directive and had to be granted free access. Fifth, in the absence of European standards, conformity to national standards carried the same benefit.

It is perhaps worth reiterating that the Single Act stipulated that, in the process of following this new procedure, proposals concerning health, safety, environmental protection and consumer protection would 'take as a base a high level of protection'. In respect of food, the commission totally rejected the idea that it should be subject to standardization. Rather the culinary riches of Europe should remain. Therefore, instead of a host of recipe laws being produced, consumers would be protected by being advised as to what they ate by means of labelling. Of course where there were dangers to health – for example from additives and packaging – some harmonization of standards would still be needed. By as early as 1990 much of this food harmonization programme had been accomplished (Swann, 1992, pp. 53–9).

National public procurement practices were, as we have seen, a major inhibitor of cross-frontier trade. Quite simply, member states directed their purchases towards their national champions rather than allocating contracts on the basis of the lowest tendered price or the best overall offer. This was a significant problem because public procurement constituted a large component of total spending. Spending by central, regional and local governments, plus that of public enterprises, constituted about 45 per cent of total spending. Of course some of this was wages, salaries and transfer payments, but, even when allowance was made for this, public spending on goods and services was still, as we noted earlier, about 15 per cent of total spending. The plain truth was that there was no common market in such public purchasing. The Community had devised rules in respect of certain types of procurement, specifically public works contracting (OJ, 1971) and public supply contracts (OJ, 1977), but, to quote Shakespeare, these rules were often honoured in the breach rather than the observance. The following indicates the kinds of evasions which were evident. Community purchasing procedures identified three main forms of contract – open, restricted and negotiated. Open contracts were those in which any potential suppliers could bid. In restricted contracts the tendering authority identified a limited list of eligible bidders. In negotiated contracts only one bidder would be approached. There was an unjustified tendency for public authorities to adopt the latter procedure, that is to select 'the firm down the road'. Community rules only applied to contracts above a certain threshold value. The obvious way round this was to subdivide contracts so that each fell below the threshold value. Provision was made for emergency procedures whereby the notice-to-bid period could be shortened. The commission was of the view that this provision was sometimes employed without justification and it tended to favour the local supplier. These were not the only problems. Significant areas of public procurement had not been brought within the scope of Community public purchasing rules. Notable among these were public utilities, such as water, transport, energy and telecommunications, and services. In addition flexible and quick-acting procedures were necessary so that legal restraints or redress could be quickly instituted where there was evidence of malpractice.

In due course the Council of Ministers took action to deal with all of these problems. First, the existing directives were tightened up. For example, under the revised rules on public supply contracts the open tender was made mandatory; the use of other procedures had to be justified to the commission (OJ, 1988a). Second, areas not covered by specific rules were addressed. Public procurement rules were agreed for public utilities in 1990 (OJ, 1990a) and for services in 1992 (OJ, 1992a). Third, each member state was required to establish a system of legal redress so that, where a contract was going to be let, or had been let, in ways which breached Community rules, the disadvantaged parties could either halt the letting of the contract or seek damages if it had already been let. The emphasis was laid on quick acting, on-the-spot remedies, although this did not prevent the commission from itself initiating actions in cases of malpractice (Weiss, 1992, pp. 307–35).

While the problems posed by standards and public procurement implied a significant legislative task for the Council of Ministers, this was less apparent in the case of state aids: that is, subsidies. The basis for action was already provided in Articles 92–4 which indicated that state aids which distorted competition by favouring certain enterprises or industries, and also affected inter-state trade, were prohibited. However certain forms of aid were capable of exemption. The actual task of enforcing these principles was delegated to the commission and it had produced a series of guidelines which indicated what types and levels of aid were acceptable. The real task was therefore primarily one of effective enforcement.

To this end the commission concluded that more information was needed about the amount of state aid which was being given. The result was a series of surveys of the volume and direction of aids given in the various member states, notably in the manufacturing sector.[1] Apart from providing the commission with additional evidence upon which to found corrective action, this was also part of an attempt to make member state governments more aware of the demands of the Rome Treaty. This was accompanied by specific actions, as for example in 1991, when the commission addressed a communication to the member states relating to state involvement in the financing of public enterprises (OJ, 1991a). Apart from pointing out that some forms of financial assistance were not being notified, the commission sought to remind member states of the market economy investor principle. The reader will recollect from Chapter 2 that the commission regarded the provision of capital to public enterprises at less than commercial rates of interest or return as potentially an illegal state aid. The commission also decided to tighten up the rules. Previously it had not been able to investigate aid until it had been given. In its 1991 communication, the commission indicated that each government would have to notify the commission of its financial relationship with its state-owned companies and of any aid given before it was paid.

The commission also let it be known that it intended gradually to move to a position where aids would be declared illegal for purely procedural reasons: in other words, aids which might otherwise be acceptable under the treaty rules would be declared illegal if member states did not follow the proper procedure, for example in respect of notifying the commission in advance. In addition, the commission followed a policy of requiring the repayment of aid which had been granted illegally. This was not a new departure but it was one which the commission followed systematically after the Single Act came into force. The *Renault* case was a spectacular instance.

Renault was a state-owned company which was also in considerable financial difficulty. However its régie (public enterprise) status meant that it could not go bankrupt. The clash between the commission and the French government over Renault originally centred on equity injections and loans going back to 1984. The commission maintained that these capital contributions contained aid elements and decided to proceed against them. The French government for its part did not see these as notifiable aids but as transactions to be reported under the 1980 directive relating to financial relationships between governments and public undertakings. The case came to a head when in 1987 the French government notified the commission of its intention to pay off Renault's FF12 billion debt to the Crédit National. This was to be part of a package whereby Renault would change its status from régie to a legal entity under normal commercial law.

Ultimately what appeared to be a settlement was reached and this was published as a formal Commission Decision in 1988 (OJ, 1988b). First, certain earlier loans were deemed to be illegal; they had to be repaid or would have to bear a normal commercial rate of interest, and any interest subsidy up to the date of the decision also had to be recouped. Second, a capital contribution of FF8 billion and the FF12 billion debt write-off were declared to be compatible with the Common Market. Third, and this was a crucial element of the settlement, the debt write-off had to be preceded by a change in the legal status of Renault.

Additionally, Renault had to complete a restructuring plan involving significant cuts in car and truck production capacity.

The subsequent controversy arose because the commission alleged that neither of these latter terms had been met. A change of government had led to backtracking on the legal status issue. Also Renault had undertaken to cut car production capacity by 15 per cent and truck production capacity by 30 per cent, but the commission reckoned that the cuts had only amounted to 5 and 9 per cent, respectively and therefore decided to demand the repayment of FF8.4 billion by Renault. This the French government opposed; intensive bargaining then occurred. Ultimately, in May 1990, the commission and the French government came to an amicable settlement (ECC, 1990). In the light of the fact that some capacity cuts had taken place and that Renault was in the process of becoming a public limited company (with an involvement by Volvo) the repayment was scaled down to FF6 billion. FF3.5 billion was to be repaid, the remaining FF2.5 billion was to stand as a long-term debt on Renault's balance sheet.

While enforcement was the prime requirement, some legislative changes were required. In 1986, the commission published a framework for state aid for R&TD (OJ, 1986) and in 1989 did the same in respect of assistance to the motor vehicle industry (OJ, 1989a). The research and technological development (R&TD) provisions were particularly interesting. The commission is broadly sympathetic to such aid since it helps to strengthen European competitiveness. The general principle is that aid for basic industrial research should not exceed 50 per cent of the gross cost of a project or programme. As the activity gets nearer to the market-place, the commission will look for progressively lower levels of assistance.

In 1988, the commission also redefined its approach to regional aid (OJ, 1988c). Regional aid could be justified under the exemptions prescribed in either Article 92(3)(a) or 92(3)(c). Article 92(3)(a) related to more serious situations where the standard of living is abnormally low or there is serious underemployment. By contrast, Article 92(3)(c) merely referred to aid designed to facilitate the development of certain economic regions. Apparently, in approving regional aid in the past, little use has been made of Article 92(3)(a); now, however, with the accession of three more Mediterranean countries and the SEA's emphasis on economic and social cohesion, this had to change. The 1988 regional aid communication identified the areas or regions which could benefit under Article 92(3)(a) and established for them a uniform and relatively high aid ceiling. It also specified generally lower and differential aid ceilings for other regions which could benefit on the basis of Article 92(3)(c). The height of these aid ceilings depended on the region's relative socioeconomic position within its own country, though the better off a country was relative to the Community average the more serious the region's socioeconomic position had to be to qualify for any given aid ceiling.

Fiscal factors were high on the list of areas for priority action. The Cockfield White Paper focused on indirect taxes – VAT and excise duties. No reference was made to the possibility of fundamentally changing the direct tax system, although the commission had proposed a harmonization of national corporation tax structures and rates as far back as 1975. However, in 1990, the commission announced that it had set up a working party to assess the severity of the problems arising in connection with corporation taxes. The working party reported in 1992 in favour of harmonizing the corporation tax base, together with uniform maximum and minimum rates of 40 and 30 per cent, respectively (Ruding Committee, 1992). Matters have not progressed beyond that point, except that the commission did not welcome the idea of a maximum rate and felt that the minimum of 30 per cent could be too high.

We will focus on VAT, in respect of which the commission proposed, in 1987, a standard band of 14 to 20 per cent, together with a lower band of 4 to 9 per cent. Subsequently the idea of the upper rate of 20 per cent was dropped. In 1991, the Council of Ministers reached a *political* agreement. The UK was resistant to the adoption of a directive on this issue and was in a position to oppose it since majority voting on single market measures did not apply in the case of fiscal matters. The agreement raised the minimum standard rate to 15 per cent. It also allowed member states to apply one or two lower rates, provided they were not lower than 5 per cent. *On an interim basis* it also allowed very low rates and zero rating to continue. In principle it is assumed that, as from 1 January 1997, sufficient rate harmony will exist for the Community to switch over to the origin system. The zero rating of exports would then cease and goods would be exported bearing the tax of the country of origin.

In all this the commission showed some flexibility. Identical rates of VAT were not necessary. All that was needed was that national rates should be brought closer together so as to prevent any significant distortion of trade and competition. Approximation rather than harmonization would suffice. US experience supported this view. Also the commission recognized that competition would tend to bring rates into line. That being so, upper rates, such as the original 20 per cent limit, were not necessary.

The single market programme had a noticeable impact in the field of services. We will illustrate this with respect to three sectors – transport, financial services and the professions. In the field of scheduled air passenger transport the commission was faced with the problem that basic Rome Treaty principles – competition and the freedom to supply services – still did not apply. Within the context of a series of bilateral air services agreements, member states rubber-stamped cartel arrangements on air fares concluded by their airlines, many of which were publicly owned and in receipt of state aid. Traffic between any two states was typically reserved for one national flag carrier from either end (single designation), the traffic being shared on a 50/50 basis. In some cases revenue was also pooled and divided up likewise. Access to the market by other airlines from the two countries was restricted and access for airlines from other member states (fifth freedom carriers) was largely debarred. In 1987, the Council of Ministers introduced the first of three liberalizing packages (Button and Swann, 1989). They initiated a progressive move towards rate freedom, in that airlines could seek to introduce more competitive fares on routes between the two countries. Originally both national regulatory bodies had to approve fares. In the first package, if one country approved but the other disapproved, the disapproving country could not veto the fare proposal since a system of arbitration was provided for which might approve the rate proposal. Later packages, however, moved the system to one of double disapproval: an airline was entitled to introduce a fare unless both regulatory bodies disapproved. Freer access to the inter-country markets was also progressively introduced since the 50/50 traffic sharing rule was modified by stages so as to allow the airline (airlines) from the other bilateral partner to capture a bigger share of the inter-country traffic. In the final stage the traffic sharing system in inter-country agreements was dropped. In parallel each country was allowed to permit additional national airlines to fly on the inter-country routes between the two partners (that is, multiple designation was allowed) and airlines from other member states were allowed to enter and compete: that is, fifth freedom operations were permitted (Button, 1992).

In international road transport of goods and passengers (and we confine our analysis to these two activities) the Community had made disappointing progress in implementing the CTP. As part of a policy of opening transport up to competition, obligatory fixed *haulage* rates had been replaced either by reference rates, where the officially published price was purely a recommendation, or by rate brackets, in respect of which the upper and lower rates were mandatory but, since the spread was considerable, it was reasonable to conclude that actual rates were determined by market forces. In addition certain measures of harmonization (working hours, rest periods and so on) had been agreed in order to provide a 'level playing field' for competition. However two major gaps remained. The Rome Treaty had called for action in respect of access to the market for international road transport (goods and passengers) and also in respect of cabotage (goods and passengers). The latter referred, for example, to the ability of a road haulier, as part of an international journey, to carry goods from point A to point B in another member state. In respect of the first problem the commission had sought to persuade member states to drop their bilateral quotas of international road haulage licences in favour of a generous quota of international licences, to be called a Community quota. But member states were disinclined to drop their country-to-country licence arrangements and had only agreed to a miserable Community quota.

However, as part of the single market initiative, they were eventually persuaded to drop the bilateral licensing system. They also agreed to radically increase the size of the Community quota. Later they also agreed to drop the quantitative limit and to replace it with a qualitative licensing system (OJ, 1992b). Hauliers of good repute, financial standing and professional competence could qualify automatically. In respect of the second problem, member states agreed to introduce an experimental and very limited cabotage authorization system. However complete liberalization was blocked by lack of agreement on common charges for lorries using motorways and principal roads. In 1993, this latter problem was overcome and, as a result, cabotage licences will be progressively increased and unrestricted cabotage has also been agreed in respect of international coach and bus operations.

There was no common market in financial services prior to the SEA. The kind of changes which the Single Act brought about can be best be illustrated by two cases – banking and non-life insurance. In banking the key development was the Second Banking Directive of 1989 (OJ, 1989b). This laid down common rules for banking supervision, what is called prudential control. These rules involve minimum requirements in regard to matters such as capital and capital/asset ratios. These rules are based on the principle of home country control combined with mutual recognition. In other words, if a bank meets the requirements for licensing in the home country (which, as we have just seen, have a common minimum base) then it must automatically be recognized by any other member state. That is to say, the bank can lend money across the frontier to an individual company and so on in the other state (freedom to supply services) or it can set up a *branch* in the other state and lend from there (right of establishment). However, if the bank seeks to set up a *subsidiary*, the regulatory process will be performed by the host state.

In the case of non-life insurance, the basis for providing for the right of establishment had been agreed in 1973. However, as we noted earlier, a freedom to supply services in this sector had been much more difficult to achieve because of different views about how best to protect the smaller consumer. Where a company established in, say, Germany insured a German risk, the relevant legal basis of the insurance contract would quite clearly be German law. But if a German risk was insured by a company located in, say, the UK the situation was potentially more complicated. Here we are contemplating a transaction which falls under the heading of freedom to supply services. Originally the commission had contemplated a choice of law solution. The insured person or company could choose the law which should apply. It could be the law of the state of the insurer, the law of the state of the insured or the law of a third country. This the German government was not willing to accept, since it regarded some national laws as too lax and 'the man in the street' would not be in a position to protect himself. In the end the solution adopted was that the supervision of large risks (such as jumbo jets) would occur in the country where the head office of the insurer was located. Mass risks (the 'man in the street') would broadly be regulated by the country where the risk was situated (OJ, 1988d).

In the case of professional services, the Community's original approach to professional mobility had been a *sectoral* one. Profession by profession (doctors, dentists, veterinarians and so on) mechanisms for the mutual recognition of diplomas, harmonization of training requirements and so on had been devised. However this was a tedious and time-consuming business. Nowhere was this more obvious than in the case of architects. It took 17 years to achieve agreement in respect of the architectural profession; the directive was adopted in 1985, with 1987 as the date for implementation. The agreement allowed architects who were nationals of any member state to practise in other member states, provided they possessed an approved qualification. A system of mutual recognition of qualifications was agreed. The approved qualification might or might not include a period of practical training. Once registered in a member state, an architect had to abide by the regulations governing that country's profession. For example, some countries required compulsory indemnity insurance.

What was needed was a speedier process and, in 1988, the Council of Ministers took a step in that direction when it adopted a directive which established a *general* approach to the professions (OJ, 1989c). It applied to all those professions in which access was restricted by the state and required at least three years' university training or its equivalent, such as lawyers, accountants, engineers, teachers and surveyors. It enabled a qualified professional in one member state to become a member of the equivalent profession in another member state without having to requalify. If the length of training was shorter than that in the country receiving a professional, then the receiving country could demand evidence of an additional period of professional experience. If the content of the training was deficient, examinations or supervised practice could also be required.

The process of creating and maintaining competition requires the existence of a policy which addresses the issue of market power. In other words, the activities of cartels and dominant firms must be brought under control. As we indicated in Chapter 2, the Rome Treaty contained provisions to this end. However there was a notable gap in the armoury since the treaty contained no explicit power to regulate mergers. It is true that, in the celebrated *Continental Can* case, the Court of Justice did declare that Article 86 was in principle applicable to mergers. However Article 86 was a far from perfect instrument and, despite its success in establishing that Article 86 could be applied, the Commission never employed it in any *formal* merger decision, although it was deployed in a number of *informal* cases.

It should be added that, whilst the failure to equip the commission with a formal and effective power to control mergers was a serious omission, the Cockfield White Paper of 1985 did not identify it as a topic for action. However, in 1989, the Council of Ministers was finally persuaded to act and a regulation was adopted which enabled the commission to control mergers (OJ, 1989d). These are referred to as concentrations with a European dimension. Some member states were anxious to reduce the commission's scope for action. Quite high thresholds were therefore prescribed (in respect of the combining firms' turnover worldwide and in the Community) and mergers which largely affected only one state were excluded. Subject to these restrictions, the commission could investigate, and if necessary ban, mergers which either created or strengthened a dominant position in the Common Market and thereby impeded effective competition. In due course the commission was to make use of this new power, as when in 1991 it forbade the Aérospatiale–Aleni/de Havilland merger (OJ, 1991b).

In respect of the free movement of factors, a major step under the single market programme was taken in 1988 with the adoption of a directive liberalizing capital movements (OJ, 1988e). Some temporary safeguard clauses were allowed. The impact of this on the stability of the ERM will be discussed later.

The Single Act called for the complete free movement of people, a matter about which there has been considerable controversy. Margaret Thatcher was forthright on this subject. In her famous, to some infamous, speech at Bruges in 1988 she declared, 'it is a matter of plain common sense that we cannot totally abolish frontier controls if we are also to protect our citizens from crime and stop the movement of drugs, or terrorists, and of illegal immigrants' (Thatcher, 1988, p. 7). The UK argued that, though the Single Act envisaged easier passage for nationals of member states, it did not intend this to apply to nationals of third countries; therefore it could maintain border controls, if only to control third-country nationals. This may have been a convenient piece of logic chopping, but nevertheless there is no doubt that the act did provide support for UK resistance since one of the declarations at the end guaranteed that nothing in it should prevent states taking such measures as they considered necessary to control third-country immigration, terrorism, crime, drug-trafficking and illicit trade in art and antiques.

There was a serious problem here since, before removing border controls, member states did need to be assured that adequate alternative safeguards existed. These required developments such as adequate policing at the common external frontier by all the other member states and arrangements which guaranteed that the ability to apprehend criminals, terrorists and drug-traffickers was not undermined. Two approaches were followed. First, some countries sought to develop a comprehensive treaty abolishing all frontier controls on the movement of people between them. The now famous Schengen Treaty, signed in June 1990, began life in 1984 as a Franco-German endeavour, which the Benelux countries joined in 1985. Eventually all the Community countries became signatories except for Denmark, Ireland and the UK. Second, and in the light of the Adonnino Committee's aspirations, ministers of justice and international affairs have sought agreement on a piecemeal basis on subjects such as the right of asylum. An important agreement on this latter subject was reached in Dublin in June 1990, with the result that asylum-seekers were guaranteed that at least one state would process applications, and situations where individuals were shuffled from state to state would not arise.

Under the Schengen agreement the parties agreed to shift controls away from their internal borders to their external frontiers. To this end they agreed on a common list of countries whose citizens required visas to enter the zone; a common right of asylum policy; to pool their crime data in a giant computer; to let their police forces pursue criminals on each other's territories; and undertook to narrow national differences in narcotics policies. There would be no border controls for people travelling between the signatories and passport controls on flights between the Schengen Treaty partners would be scrapped. The attempt to eliminate passport controls was, however, repeatedly delayed.

NOTES

1. It should not be assumed that the existence of Articles 92 to 94 has eliminated state aids as a major problem. When the commission reported on state aids to manufacturing and certain other sectors, it drew attention to a still substantial volume of aid. This amounted to 89 billion ECUs in the years 1988–90. On the plus side, this had fallen from an average of 93 billion ECUs in the years 1986–8. The commission drew attention to the worrying feature that the four largest economies (Germany, France, Italy and the UK) accounted for a growing share of aid. This threatened the capacity of the weaker economies to catch up with the stronger ones. Italy was a particular culprit. Aid to Italian manufacturing as a percentage of value added was three times as high as in the UK. Greece apparently failed to cooperate with the commission in this study and the latter had to rely on a list of aids compiled by a consultant. See EC Commission (1992), *Third Survey on State Aids in the European Community in the Manufacturing and Certain other Sectors* (Brussels).

REFERENCES

Button, K.J. (1992), 'The liberalization of transport services', in D Swann (ed.), *The Single European Market and Beyond* (London: Routledge).

Button, K.J. and D. Swann (1989), 'European Community Airlines – Deregulation and its Problems', *Journal of Common Market Studies*, June.

EC Commission (1990), *Nineteenth Report on Competition Policy* (Luxembourg: Office for Official Publications of the European Communities).

EC Council of Ministers (1970), *The Problem of Political Unification* (Brussels).

Lane, R. (1993), 'New Community Competences under the Maastricht Treaty', *Common Market Law Review*, **30**.

OJ (1971), *Official Journal of European Communities*, L185, 16 August 1971.

OJ (1977), *Official Journal of European Communities*, L13, 15 January 1977.

OJ (1986), *Official Journal of European Communities*, C83, 11 April 1986.

OJ (1988a), *Official Journal of European Communities*, L127, 20 May 1988.

OJ (1988b), *Official Journal of European Communities*, L220, 11 August 1988.

OJ (1988c), *Official Journal of European Communities*, C212, 12 August 1988.

OJ (1988d), *Official Journal of European Communities*, L172, 4 July 1988.

OJ (1988e), *Official Journal of European Communities*, L178, 8 July 1988.

OJ (1989a), *Official Journal of European Communities*, C123, 18 May 1989.

OJ (1989b), *Official Journal of European Communities*, L386, 31 December 1989.

OJ (1989c), *Official Journal of European Communities*, L19, 24 January 1989.

OJ (1989d), *Official Journal of European Communities*, L395, 30 December 1989.

OJ (1990a), *Official Journal of European Communities*, L297, 29 October 1990.

OJ (1991a), *Official Journal of European Communities*, C273, 18 October 1991.

OJ (1991b), *Official Journal of European Communities*, L334/42, 5 December 1991.

OJ (1992a), *Official Journal of European Communities*, L209, 24 July 1992.

OJ (1992b), *Official Journal of European Communities*, L95, 9 April 1992.

Ruding Committee (1992), *Report of the Committee of Independent Experts on Company Taxation* (Brussels: Commission of the EC).

Swann, D. (1992), 'Standards, procurement, mergers and state aids', in D. Swann (ed.), *The Single European Market and Beyond* (London: Routledge).

Thatcher, M. (1988), *Britain and Europe* (London: Conservative Political Centre).

Weiss, F. (1992), 'Public Procurement Law in the EC Internal Market 1992: The Second Coming of the European Champion', *The Antitrust Bulletin*, Summer.

5. Onwards to Maastricht

INTRODUCTION

The purpose of this chapter is to try to identify the forces which led to the emergence of the Maastricht Treaty on European Union. Before we address that question, it is important to stress that the strategy adopted by the leading actors in the Community in the search for closer union proved to be well-founded. More precisely, our argument is that, had the Community in the 1985 IGC sought to address the single market, EMU and political union issues simultaneously, it is likely that it would have failed and jeopardized the prospect of even limited progress. Metaphorically it would have been trying to digest too much at one sitting. Instead, as matters transpired, it ended up approaching the ultimate goal of closer union in stages. The completion of the single market was the main objective of stage one. Below we argue that, by adopting the Single Act and committing itself to the market completion process, the Community gave a stimulus to, and provided a rationale for, moves forward on other fronts – to stage two or Maastricht.

CHANGE FACTORS REVIEWED

The specific change factors which were at work were as follows. First, in Chapter 3 we saw that the European Parliament had in its draft European Union Treaty committed itself to a plan for a radical reshaping of the whole Community decision-making system. In practice the Single Act fell far short of its ambitions and was bound to be a disappointment. It was therefore inevitable that parliament would press for further change if and when the opportunity presented itself.

Second, while the attitudes of the member states as to the way to progress varied considerably, there was considerable enthusiasm for a variety of relatively radical initiatives. These we will discuss later in connection with the Maastricht negotiating positions. Third, the UK proved to be a significant change factor. This was not because it was an enthusiastic advocate of further integration, particularly if it had a federal flavour. Rather its influence arose from its opposition to change. This is well illustrated by the case of the Social Charter which, as we shall see, it refused to sign. The fact that it was opposed to the kind of social programme which the charter envisaged, and had helped to arrange matters in the Single Act so that it had a veto in respect of harmonization powers applied to social issues, served to reinforce the point that the Rome Treaty was an inadequate vehicle for action on the social front and was in need of a radical overhaul. Hence the Social Protocol and Agreement of the subsequent Maastricht Treaty.

Fourth, the Single Act itself, and all it foreshadowed (see below), helped to give an impetus to the process which the neofunctionalists, in their analysis of spillover, had described as the expansive logic of integration. For example, the completed single market would yield even greater benefits if the Community could achieve a parallel move forward on the monetary front. Then again the intensified competition unleashed by the single market gave rise to the need to guarantee a minimum platform of workers' rights which could not be eroded by competitive pressures and the increased fluidity of investment.

Fifth, it is important to note that the Single Act *specifically* looked forward to progress on two issues, namely EMU and what ultimately came to be associated with the Social Charter and the Social Protocol and Agreement. We can indeed argue that in these two connections the Single Act contained what may be called delayed-action devices. These were to be found in the preamble to the act. In due course they were to be triggered into action. This we discuss below.

Finally, we have to take account of the fact that change and instability abroad demanded a strengthening of the Community's capacity to deal with foreign policy issues. By the time the Maastricht Treaty came to be negotiated this was very obvious, since the break-up of the Warsaw Pact, and particularly ethnic tensions in Yugoslavia and the reunification of the two Germanies, together with hostilities in the Gulf, were demanding powerful and united responses (Laffan, 1993, p. 48).

THE BRITISH ATTITUDE

Given that we are arguing that the British attitude to further developments was of considerable significance, it is appropriate to review what
exactly that attitude consisted of. Perhaps it would be more appropriate
to describe it as the attitude of the then Prime Minister Margaret Thatcher.
(It was substantially taken over by her successor John Major.) Her
views, which were clearly dominating, were trumpeted loud and clear
in 1988 in an address to the College of Europe at Bruges (Thatcher,
1988). Some points were quite explicit, others could be inferred.

Margaret Thatcher's central message was that the single market was
a development which the UK wholeheartedly supported. A Europe-
wide market was an essential base upon which enterprises could hope
to complete with the USA, Japan and the newly emerging economic
powers in Asia. But the single market needed to be a competitive free
enterprise market and not a regulated one. Britain had not set in motion
a domestic programme of deregulation only to have regulation reintro-
duced at the European level. In particular Europe did not need new
regulations which increased the cost of employment and made its labour markets less flexible and less competitive with those of competi-
tors overseas. This clearly signalled the nature of the coming conflict
over the Social Charter and indeed it was an argument which was to run
and run as Europe plunged into recession and high unemployment in
the first half of the 1990s. While not explicitly rejecting EMU and,
specifically, a European central bank (ECB), Thatcher's lack of enthusiasm was clearly implied by her remark that what Europe really needed
was a single market for capital and financial services. Here again the
seeds of future conflict had been exposed.

By contrast, her views on political union were quite explicit. Federalism was rejected in favour of willing and active cooperation between
sovereign states. In other words, her aim was an intergovernmental
Europe. Her anti-federalist sentiments were underlined by scornful re-
jections of the prospect of a European super-state exercising a new
dominance from Brussels and imposing an identikit European personality on countries with otherwise diverse customs and traditions. On the
external relations front it was NATO and Western European Union
(WEU) which should be nurtured and strengthened. Here further seeds
of conflict were sown.

Thatcher's view, therefore, was broadly that the completion of the
single market was a sensible and practical step. It was folly for the EC

to entertain arcane and utopian goals about political and monetary union when it has not even created the single market which the Rome Treaty had identified as long ago as 1957. To Thatcher the Single Act was the end of the line. Others, however, saw it as a staging post on the road to greater things.

EXPANSIVE LOGIC AND THE SINGLE ACT PREAMBLE

The Social Charter and After

The idea that the EC ought to make a distinctive social impact was not new. It had been emphasized at the Paris summit in 1972, when the heads of state and government had recognized that the existing social potential of the Rome Treaty needed to be given greater prominence. A Social Action Programme was subsequently adopted (Swann, 1992, pp. 295–301). The idea of a European social area (*L'Espace social*) was put forward by the French president in 1981 and was subsequently taken up by EC Commission President Jacques Delors. This was complemented by the idea of social dialogue, a dialogue between the two sides of industry; here too Delors was much to the fore when, in 1985, he organized at Val Duchesse, a chateau in Belgium, a series of discussions on socioeconomic issues, in which the major participants were the European Trade Union Confederation, the Union of Industries of the European Communities and the European Centre of Public Enterprises. The concept of social dialogue was duly incorporated in the Single Act. In addition there was the concept of a Peoples' Europe: here the emphasis was on the need to develop the kind of policies which had real practical significance for the average citizen and would bring home the contribution which the European Community could make to their well-being. The task of developing these was assigned to the Adonnino Committee, which we referred to in Chapter 3 when discussing the origins of the Single Act. It covered a variety of topics and high on its list for future action was the need to provide greater freedom of movement for individuals.

The role of the Single Act in contributing to the emergence of the social component of the Maastricht Treaty derives partly from the expansive logic (spillover) factor but also from the fact that there was an explicit provision relating to social matters in the Single Act preamble. We will treat them in that order. The prospect of a single market with an intensification of cross-frontier competition stimulated a concern as to its social implications. Various arguments were put forward as to why the Community should therefore forge ahead on the social front. One argument pointed to the possibility that increased competition could erode working conditions generally throughout the Community. Therefore there was a need for a platform of basic social rights which could not be eroded by competition and by the increased ability of enterprises to seek out low-cost locations. A somewhat more populist version of this argument emphasized the idea that the Community should provide a prospect that economic improvement would be paralleled by social improvement. This could be dressed up politically as an attempt to guarantee that greater market opportunities for business would be accompanied by better conditions for labour. More divisively countries with relatively high levels of social protection (which placed burdens on business enterprises) were obviously likely to be concerned about social dumping – that poorer countries with lower levels of social protection would provide attractive low-cost locations for footloose investment. In short the conditions of competition should be equalized. Given that this was undoubtedly a reason why some countries viewed the Social Charter with approval, it is odd that some of the poorer countries were nevertheless enthusiastic supporters of the charter proposal. Curwen has suggested that their support may have stemmed from the knowledge that, conveniently, they would be unable to enforce any regulations which emerged as a result of the charter (Curwen, 1992, p. 158).

While we are arguing that the process of further integrating markets was forcing the EC partners to contemplate further extending integration in the social field, it is also important to note that the preamble to the Single Act *specifically* emphasized that the signatories were determined to work together in developing the social dimension of building Europe. The actual wording in the preamble ran as follows:

> Determined to work together to promote democracy on the basis of the fundamental rights recognized in the constitutions and laws of the Member States, in the *Convention for the Protection of Human Rights and Fundamental Freedoms* and the *European Social Charter*, notably freedom, equality and social justice. (Italics added)

Both the documents referred to were products of the quite separate Council of Europe. The first entered into force in 1953 and the second in 1965.

The actual emergence of the Social Charter began with the 1987 Belgian presidency of the Council of Ministers. The then Belgian minister for labour stressed the need 'to establish a platform of basic rights which would give the two sides of industry a stable common basis from which they could negotiate to guarantee that the internal market has a real social dimension' (Soisson, 1990, p. 10). However the major impetus for change came from a succession of European Council declarations, starting in Hanover in June 1988, when the heads of state and government stressed 'the importance of the social aspects of progress towards the objectives of 1992'. This was sufficient encouragement for Commission President Jacques Delors, a self-confessed advocate of a maximalist Social Charter, to set the Community wheels in motion. The Rhodes summit later that year went further in emphasizing that the completion of the internal market should not be regarded as an end in itself but seen as part of a larger design which involved maximizing the well-being of all within the European tradition of social progress. The summit communiqué also indicated that the heads of state and government should look to the commission for proposals based on the social charter of the Council of Europe. At Madrid, in 1989, they went yet further by declaring that the same emphasis should be placed on the social as on the economic aspects of the single market and that they should be developed in a balanced manner; a preliminary draft of the Social Charter was also discussed. Matters came to a head at Strasbourg later that year, when the Social Charter was tabled and approved by 11 of the 12 member states, though the UK, reflecting Margaret Thatcher's Bruges declaration, declined to subscribe.

The charter enshrined the rights and freedoms of Community citizens – in particular for workers, whether employed or self-employed – shown in Table 5.1 below. It was something of a compromise document. On the one hand, the commission was anxious to bring the UK on board and at one stage it seemed possible that she might sign up (Teague and Grahl, 1991, p. 214). On the other hand, within the European Parliament and the Workers Group of the Ecosoc, strong criticism was directed at the draft charter because it was proposed that it should take the form of a declaration which would not be made binding under Community law.

In the end the document did indeed take the form of a declaration. At first sight it appeared not to be capable of being made binding under Community law. Rather, if it was to be implemented, the initiative would have to come from each member state acting individually within

Table 5.1   Fundamental rights of the Social Charter

(a)   The right of freedom of movement. Here the emphasis is on the right to move to other countries and take up occupations on the same terms as nationals. The right of freedom of movement would be restricted only on grounds of public order, public safety or public health.

(b)   The right to employment and to fair remuneration for that employment. Protection would be given to part-time workers. There would be limits on the withholding of wages, and workers would have free access to job placement services.

(c)   The right to improved living and working conditions. Here the emphasis is on the idea that the completion of the internal market should be accompanied by harmonization of social conditions while the improvement is being maintained. There should be an improvement particularly in terms of limits on working time, minimum annual paid leave and weekly breaks from work. Particular mention is made of the need for improved conditions for those not on open-ended contracts (for example, part-time or seasonal workers).

(d)   Social protection. Workers, including the unemployed, should receive adequate social protection and social security benefits.

(e)   Freedom of association and collective bargaining. This involves the right to organize trade unions and to choose whether or not to join them, to conclude collective agreements and to take collective action. Such action includes the right to strike, except where existing legislation stipulates exceptions (including the armed forces, the police and government service).

(f)   The right to vocational training. Every worker has a right to continue vocational training right through his or her working life.

(g)   The right of men and women to equal treatment. This extends beyond pay to access to jobs, education, training, career opportunities and social protection.

(h)   Information, consultation and participation for workers. This should apply especially in multinational companies and in particular at times of restructuring, redundancies or the introduction of new technology. Worker participation would be developed 'in such a way as to take account' of existing rules and traditions.

(i)   The right to health and safety protection at the workplace.

(j)   The right to the protection of children and adolescents. This includes a minimum working age of 16 and rights to such things as vocational training after leaving school.

(k)   The right of the elderly to retirement pensions which provide a decent standard of living. Those not entitled to a pension should nevertheless be entitled to a minimum of social protection.

(l)   The right of the disabled to take advantage of specific measures, especially in the fields of training and occupational and social integration and rehabilitation.

Source: House of Lords Select Committee on the European Communities, *Third Report, 1989–90* (London: House of Lords, Paper 6–1).

its own legislature. However the situation was more complicated than that, for three reasons. Some charter topics did fall within the competence of the Community. Also in some cases the commission could endeavour to argue so. In addition the principle of subsidiarity enabled the Community to act when the aims to be achieved could be more effectively attained at Community as opposed to member state level. Having said that, it was necessary to recognize that the commission in its proposals could not exceed the powers which were laid down in the Rome Treaty as amended by the Single Act.

The real problem is summed up in the last sentence. The commission followed up by proposing an Action Programme which would set in motion the task of putting the charter into operation. But here it was bound to encounter the problem that the Rome Treaty (as amended by the Single Act) was inadequate to the task, particularly in the light of continued British hostility. Thus, when it put forward a draft proposal on working hours, it was constrained to argue that this was really a health and safety measure, thus enabling it to take advantage of the majority voting procedure which applied in that area of policy. This was bound to provoke the opposition of the UK. Equally, old Article 100 did enable the harmonization power to be applied when laws, regulations and administrative actions in member states directly affected the creation of the single market. Since such laws and so on could be social in character, it followed that the harmonization process could be applied to social matters. But we also have to remember that new Article 100A (introduced under the Single Act) excluded from the new majority voting arrangement matters relating to *the rights and interests of employed persons*. Thus unanimity was still required and the UK could impose a veto, or water down, as the case demanded.

As a result, relatively little progress was made in implementing the charter. As Phillipa Watson has pointed out, the crux of the problem was a lack of adequate powers to fulfil the objectives of the charter (Watson, 1993, p. 486). In a working paper addressed to the subsequent IGC (which gave rise to the Maastricht Treaty) the commission blamed the lack of progress on 'the wide gap between the powers available under the current legal bases and the ambitions set out in the Charter and the new constraints arising from the completion of the internal market'. What was needed was a basic revision of the social policy section of the Rome Treaty: hence the ultimate Protocol and Agreement on Social Policy of the Maastricht Treaty. This course of events was dictated by lack of adequate treaty powers but was also at least in part a product of UK hostility to Community endeavours in the social sphere.

Economic and Monetary Union

This, like the Social Charter, was a product of the expansive logic of economic integration – a spillover fact was at work – together with the fact that monetary union was explicitly foreshadowed in the preamble to the Single Act. The spillover motivation was based on the proposition that the benefits of removing the residual barriers to the free movement of goods, services and factors (central aims of the 1992 single market programme) were likely to be all the greater if businesses could be assured that there would be currency stability, indeed if a single currency could be established. In addition to the removal of inhibitions caused by uncertainty, there was the greater transparency which would arise when cross-frontier economic operations could be evaluated in terms of one currency. There were of course other benefits of monetary integration which were trade enhancing such as the elimination of the transaction costs which arise when different currencies have to be exchanged.

The foreshadowing of EMU in the Single Act preamble consisted of a recollection of the fact, noted in Chapter 2 above, that the heads of state and government had approved the progressive realization of EMU at the Paris summit in 1972. That commitment had never been formally revoked. It was not therefore entirely surprising that, at the Hanover summit in 1988, the European Council should, recalling the 1972 commitment, ask the president of the EC Commission, Jacques Delors, together with the central bank governors, another member of the commission and three others, to examine the process and stages by which EMU might be achieved. They reported back to the Madrid summit in June 1989, where the now famous Delors Report (Delors, 1989) was considered.

The report recommended a three-stage approach to EMU. In the early part of the report the adoption of a single currency was not seen as strictly necessary for EMU but irrevocably fixed exchange rates were and, indeed, this needed to be accompanied by a common monetary policy. Considerable stress was laid on the need for convergence of macroeconomic policies and performance and it was recognized that this should proceed in parallel with the development of the necessary policy and institutional arrangements. The report also laid considerable stress on the subsidiarity principle. Centralization would be confined to those areas where collective decision making was necessary. Wherever possible policy functions, which could be carried out at national level without adverse repercussions on cohesion and the functioning of the EMU, should remain in the competence of the member states. Although reference was made to the need for fiscal and budgetary, as well as monetary, coordination, the fiscal and budgetary implications were not spelled out in the same detail as was the case in the subsequent Maastricht Treaty (see Chapter 6).

The actual movement to EMU was to be achieved as follows. Stage one was to be characterized by the coordination of national monetary policies in the interests of greater economic convergence. Also all member states were to be involved in the ERM of the EMS. Some members also advocated the setting up of a European Reserve Fund in which member states would pool some of their reserves. The Fund would

1. serve as a training ground for implementing a better coordination of monetary analysis and decisions;
2. facilitate, from a Community point of view, the concerted management of exchange rates and possibly intervene visibly (in third and participating currencies) on the foreign exchange market at the request of the participating central banks;
3. be the symbol of the political will of the European countries and thus reinforce the credibility of the process towards EMU.

In stage two the European System of Central Banks (ESCB) would be set up. Its main task would be to effect a transition from the coordination of *national* monetary policies to the formulation and implementation of a *common* monetary policy. The latter would lie exclusively in its hands in stage three. In stage three the exchange rates would be irrevocably locked and would eventually be replaced by a single currency. The ESCB, independent and committed to price stability, would be responsible for (a) the formulation and implementation of monetary policy, (b) exchange rate and reserve management and (c) the maintenance of a properly functioning payments system.

The Madrid summit agreed to proceed to stage one of EMU and agreed that preparatory work should begin on organizing an IGC to determine the subsequent stages. An IGC was necessary since the Rome Treaty as it stood did not expressly envisage the creation of an EMU (it will be recollected that it provided powers which were sufficient only to carry the process of economic integration to the stage of a Common Market). Even the rather limited EMS was of course the product of a separate intergovernmental agreement and not of the Rome Treaty.

We have just noted that stage one of the Delors Plan required members to participate in the ERM of the EMS. Notably the UK had not done this, as it was far from happy about the prospect of EMU, though it had agreed to meet the ERM requirement when certain conditions were satisfied. These included a reduction of the UK inflation rate, the abolition of exchange controls by other member states and the completion of the internal market. In fact, the UK jumped the gun and joined the ERM in October 1990, while the rate of inflation was still high.

The monetary preparations culminated in the Strasbourg summit decision of December 1989 that the IGC on EMU should indeed start in December 1990. It of course reached its conclusion a year later at Maastricht. The monetary details of that agreement are discussed in Chapter 7.

Political Union

What we have termed the 'expansive logic' of economic integration also played a role in the decision to convene a separate and parallel IGC on political union, the results of which were incorporated in the subsequent Maastricht Treaty. A major ingredient of this development was concern about the 'democratic deficit' in the Community. At one point Jacques Delors let slip the speculation that, by the mid-1990s, perhaps 80 per cent of economic legislation would derive from Brussels. In other words, in addition to the legislative implications of the original Rome Treaty, it was necessary to add in the effects of the new and confirmed economic competences of the Single Act and to contemplate the further possible implications of the Social Charter and EMU. Even if Delors' estimate was only half true, it pointed to the emergence of a democratic gap. Since Community law is supreme, national parliaments would necessarily be consigned to rubber stamping the actions of the Council of Ministers. The European Parliament, on the other hand, was largely consultative. It did not provide a substitute for national parliaments, in that the Council of Ministers did not legislate through it and was not accountable to it in the way typical of representative democracies. Some change, possibly a redefined role for the parliament in relation to the Council of Ministers, would be needed.

Not surprisingly, all kinds of ideas were ultimately canvassed. Here we were witnessing a neofunctionalist spillover effect, proceeding from economic and social integration, which was helping to force the pace of political integration. Jacques Delors' ideas on the need for constitutional reform won the support of both the French president and the German chancellor. In April 1990, they issued a joint appeal for political union. The two Dublin summits which followed decided that a parallel IGC should be convened in December 1990, to be devoted to political union.

Apart from the spillover affect discussed above, it is also necessary to take account of the major role played by external forces. The changes in Eastern Europe and in the general international atmosphere had several implications. The changes were of such a magnitude that it was increasingly felt that the EPC mechanism was inadequate to bear the weight of the new challenge. The changes also implied the possibility of new members, but a larger Community would slow down decision making in the absence of institutional reform. The increasing prospect of German reunification was another powerful influence. The rest of the Community felt that German unity would be a safer and more acceptable prospect if it was to take place within a Europe which was more united. The Germans too were increasingly warm towards European unity, and, where previously there was always the fear that Community membership would debar them from following the path to German reunification, after 1990 this was no longer a concern.

NATIONAL AND INSTITUTIONAL POSITIONS

The two IGCs were initiated in December 1990, towards the end of the Italian presidency of the European Council and Council of Ministers. The subsequent negotiations were handled by Luxembourg, which held the presidency in the first six months of 1991, and finally by the Dutch, who wound up the proceedings. The final tying up of loose ends occurred at a meeting of the European Council in Maastricht in December 1991 – hence the title often given to the resulting Treaty on European Union. The terms of the agreement are discussed in Chapters 6 and 7.

The draft treaty proposals relating to EMU were extremely controversial. The great majority of the EC states were, in varying degrees, in favour, while the UK was basically opposed to making a commitment in this area of policy and looked for an opt-out clause. When the possibility of a general opt-out was tabled, the Danes too saw some virtue in the idea, since they envisaged that the final movement to a common currency might require the approval of a referendum. Germany, supported by the commission, was undoubtedly the keenest advocate of EMU – indeed the German government favoured an arrangement which would automatically and irreversibly lead to monetary union. However the German commitment was conditional. Stiff convergence criteria would have to be applied and thereafter adequate safeguards for future good financial behaviour would be needed. Without a continued converged performance, countries which fell out of line in competitive terms would suffer from mass unemployment, and migration from poor to wealthy regions would occur. The alternative would be that the poorer countries would demand big financial transfers. Germany was likely to be a major paymaster. Coupled with this was the German view that a European central bank would have to be based on the Bundesbank model; that is, it would have to be independent and be dedicated to the achievement of price stability. Additionally monetary union would have to be accompanied by greater political union. In November 1991, Hans Tietmeyer, the then vice-president of the Bundesbank, argued vigorously for the widest possible political union as an essential underpinning of a common currency. This he maintained would be necessary in order to cope with the strains that a single monetary area would cause among the different regions of Europe. During the negotiations Germany indicated, and in this it was joined by Belgium, that it would be prepared to block monetary union if no satisfactory deal could be reached.

Differences also arose among supporters on the more technical issues concerning the transition to full monetary union. These turned on issues such as (a) when the second stage (as envisaged in the Delors Report) should begin; (b) whether the proposed central bank should emerge in stage two or only make its appearance when full union was achieved in stage three; (c) what functions would be performed by the institution which emerged in stage two (notably in respect of transfers of reserves and currency support operations); (d) what criteria should be satisfied in order to move to full monetary union (Sandholtz, 1993, pp. 132–7).

The views which underlay the varying positions are of considerable interest. Perhaps the most interesting was that of Germany. German enthusiasm, more specifically enthusiasm on the part of Helmut Kohl and the leadership of the German CDU (as opposed to the Bundesbank), demands an explanation. That explanation has to confront the problem that Germany was in effect contemplating ditching the Deutsche Mark. This was a remarkable decision when we recall the German hyper-inflation experience of the 1920s. The memory of that traumatic experience (and that of the suppressed inflation between 1945 and 1948) undoubtedly lingered on through the postwar period and emphasized in German minds the cruciality of monetary stability. Moreover the enormous success of the German economy and its monetary strength clearly owed much to the price stability presided over by the Bundesbank. How, then, do we explain this commitment to EMU? Undoubtedly part of the explanation must lie in the deep German commitment to European integration. After all, it was the ECSC which initiated the readmission of Germany to the comity of nations and it had to be admitted that the Common Market had been good for German exports and industry. Additionally German enthusiasm for the cause of European union must in some degree be related to a desire on the part of the German political elite to wipe out the memory of the past. Coming closer to the present, a major factor was undoubtedly a desire to generate support for German unification. The reunited Germany, for its part, would still be committed to the EC and the EC, for its part, was anxious to bind it in. A former chancellor, Helmut Schmidt, has also suggested another motivation. This was related to the growing economic strength of Germany. This he welcomed, but he was concerned that it might give rise to a growing antagonism within the rest of the EC: for example, that everybody else had to dance to the Deutsche Mark tune. Submerging Germany monetarily within a larger entity would in his view help to preclude a damaging growth of hostility. Finally we have to recognize that Germany was only prepared to contemplate a European central bank if it was in effect the Bundesbank writ large: independence and a commitment to price stability were essential.

The hostility of the UK to monetary union had been implied by Margaret Thatcher at Bruges. Her view was that the single market was essential but, for the rest, Europe should be based on the intergovernmental model. John Major, who took over the helm, was hardly in a position to change course, even if he had wanted to. This opposition to federalism clearly implied a rejection of the idea of a single currency controlled from the centre. There were, however, more technical arguments that could be deployed in favour of retaining sovereignty in monetary matters. The UK still believed that the power to devalue was meaningful, even if in the medium to long term its effect in restoring export competitiveness might be dissipated. Under a single currency that power disappeared. What could be put in its place as a means of combating a loss of competitiveness? A downward readjustment of wages and prices was one possibility, but there was no confidence that the UK economy yet exhibited the necessary degree of inbuilt wage–price flexibility which alone would do the trick. The alternative was that, if the UK was uncompetitive and unemployment increased, this latter problem could be alleviated by labour mobility. In other words, the unemployed British workers would decamp across the English Channel and find jobs elsewhere. Quite simply, the objection was that British workers were not that mobile. Third, while in theory it was tempting to contemplate that an uncompetitive economy might qualify for a compensating transfer of resources from the rest of the union, in practice the relative smallness of the Community budget (see Chapter 8) did not suggest that this was a realistic prospect.

The UK could no doubt justify its reluctance to be involved by referring to the fact that previous monetary exercises did not suggest that the chances of success were very high. The 'EMU by 1980' plan quickly ran into the ground and the EMS, like the 1980 plan, indicated that, in the end, the member states were not willing to surrender their economic sovereignty to the extent necessary if formal policy convergence was to be achieved (Kruse, 1980, p. 193). Post-Maastricht ministerial statements tended to avoid saying that the plan would never work and preferred to dwell upon the idea (which history may judge correct) that the timetable of transition to EMU was too short and thus unrealistic.

France, unlike the UK, was favourable to a single currency and indeed was reported to be prepared to accept (if reluctantly) greater powers for the European Parliament in return for German commitment to EMU. French support for EMU (which initially appears to have been stronger than that of the Germans) could be seen as a response to German monetary hegemony within the context of the EMS. The Bundesbank dictated the monetary conditions which France had to live with and live up to if she was to remain competitive. This policy stance of the Bundesbank was outside French influence. However it was possible to imagine that a European central bank would be more amenable to adopting the more accommodating monetary stance that French economic conditions required. This was clearly possible if the European central bank was dependent. Since Germany wished for central bank independence, such a French position was less credible, although it had to be admitted that a European central bank would have to take account of a wide range of economic interests which could include those of countries less dedicated to a strategy of price stability above all.

The enthusiasm of countries such as Belgium and the Netherlands was explicable on similar lines. They were so economically bound up with the German economy that monetary union did not really carry with it a loss of economic sovereignty but rather the prospect of regaining it.

Considerable controversy also emerged over the ultimate objective to be assigned to the new treaty. In other words, was it to be assigned a federal goal? Apart from the president of the commission, the ardent federalists included Germany, Italy, the Netherlands and Belgium. France was described as 'happy in principle but ambiguous in practice'. Other countries expressed various degrees of reluctance. The position of the European Parliament has been spelled out by Juliet Lodge. Whilst the words 'federalism' and 'federation' appear nowhere in the parliament's Draft European Union Treaty (see Chapter 3) its provisions 'evoke and embrace traits that typify federal arrangements' (Lodge, 1984, p. 383).

The UK was wholly opposed: the dreaded 'F word' should not appear. Phraseology such as 'an ever closer union of peoples' was acceptable. This was essentially the status quo since it is what the Rome Treaty preamble declared. The UK took its stand on a maximized role for intergovernmental arrangements, opt-outs and a writing into the treaty of the subsidiarity principle. The latter point emphasizes a basic difference of opinion over what federalism implies. Germans could interpret it as a weak central authority combined with substantial devolution of powers. To the UK it implied overcentralization and little devolution. Hence the emphasis on subsidiarity and Prime Minister Major's assurance to the British House of Commons that 'the sovereignty of this House is not a matter that is up for grabs'.

The political union element, *broadly defined*, had four main strands (a) the powers to be assigned to the European Parliament; (b) the new competences to be assigned to the Community and the decision making arrangements relating thereto; (c) the idea of a Common Foreign and Security Policy (CFSP); (d) the EC role in defence. The existence of a democratic deficit had been signalled by Jacques Delors and the idea of granting greater powers to the European Parliament was enthusiastically supported by Germany, Italy, Belgium and the Netherlands. In Germany the opposition SPD, which was as enthusiastic as the federal chancellor, indicated that it and a majority of the Bundestag would vote against any treaty which failed to strengthen substantially the parliament's role. Greater powers centred on proposals which would enable the parliament to initiate legislation, to colegislate with the Council of Ministers (including a power to veto) and to play a role in the appointment of the commission. France was less keen but was prepared, once assured that the predominant role of the European Council would be strengthened (de la Serre and Lequesne, 1993, p. 148), to rebalance the institutional system in favour of the parliament as a means of securing German commitment to EMU. Other states (apart from the UK) were reported to be willing, with varying degrees of reluctance, to go along with a strengthening of parliament's role.

The kind of powers proposed for the parliament had of course all featured in its Draft European Union Treaty (see Chapter 3) and the parliament indicated that it would oppose a draft treaty which failed adequately to meet its aspirations. Constitutionally the parliament could not block revisions to the Rome Treaty made by the Twelve. However it was conscious that it could exert significant influence indirectly, since in the past national parliaments had held up treaty ratification until the proposed changes had won the assent of members of the European Parliament (MEPs) (as with the Italian parliament in relation to the Single Act) and there was evidence that this could happen on this occasion.

The UK was unenthusiastic and, while not totally opposed, nevertheless aimed to circumscribe concessions tightly. Its preference was to give the parliament more power to act as a financial watchdog – notably in relation to commission spending – and to approach the democratic deficit problem by giving national parliaments a more effective role in the Community law-making process. New competences and beefed-up decision-making powers in the Council of Ministers were another area where the UK was at odds with its fellow members. While the idea of adding new areas of policy to the Community's competence and extending the role of majority voting (even to the extent of making it the general rule) were variously supported by the rest, the UK was distinctly unenthusiastic. The UK reacted strongly to the Dutch draft treaty on political union, notably for its implication that majority voting should apply to social policy (where, as we have seen, the UK had already dug in its heels) and to environmental policy and taxation where (as we have also seen) the Single Act had settled on unanimity.

The negotiations also threw up the idea of a CFSP and also the view that closer cooperation was needed on justice and home affairs (including immigration). The need for a CFSP was generally supported but on this issue, and that of justice and home affairs, France and the UK supported the earlier Luxembourg approach to the treaty's architecture, namely that there should be three pillars: EMU should be part of the EC pillar (this was certainly the French view) but foreign and security policy and justice and home affairs would be subjects of separate pillars which would continue to be based on intergovernmental cooperation. While some countries wished to see foreign and security policy brought within the scope of the majority voting system, the French and British view was supported by Denmark, Ireland and Portugal. At a late stage in the negotiations the UK showed some flexibility by conceding that it might be possible to allow majority voting on the detailed *implementation* of the foreign and security policy.

While the UK and France were at one on the broad approach to foreign and security policy, the issue of the EC role in defence was one which divided them. A Franco-German plan envisaged the creation of a European defence force and that eventually the CFSP and security policy would also extend to common defence. The European defence force would be created under the aegis of Western European Union (WEU) which in turn would be brought under the umbrella of the EC. The UK and Italy, however, were concerned about the effects of this plan in undermining NATO and the US commitment to Europe. The possible threat to NATO also concerned the Dutch. Italy and the UK preferred to see European efforts centring on the nine-country WEU which would act as a bridge between the EC and NATO. The UK and Italy were also urging WEU to develop a rapid reaction force which could operate outside the NATO area. It should be added that Greece indicated that it would veto the proposed union treaty unless it was admitted to WEU membership.

Almost inevitably the issue of the need for a further transfer of resources from the richer to the poorer countries reared its head. This demand was spearheaded by Spain and was echoed by other poorer states including the Irish Republic. The position of Spain in relation to the Community budget and the details of its demands will be discussed in Chapter 8.

REFERENCES

Curwen, P. (1992), 'The Economics of Social Responsibility in the European Community', *Economics* (Winter).

De la Serre, F. and C. Lequesne (1993), 'France and the European Union', in A.W. Cafruny and G.G. Rosenthal (eds), *The State of the European Community*, vol. 2 (London: Longman).

Delors Report. Report on economic and monetary union in the European Community (1989) (Brussels: EC Commission).

Kruse, D.C. (1980), *Monetary Integration in Western Europe: EMU, EMS and Beyond* (London: Butterworth).

Laffan, B. (1993), 'The Treaty of Maastricht: Political Authority and Legitimacy', in A.W. Cafruny and G.G. Rosenthal (eds), *The State of the European Community,* vol. 2 (London: Longman).

Lodge, J. (1984), 'European Union and the First Elected European Parliament: The Spinelli Initiative', *Journal of Common Market Studies*, **22**, (4) (June).

Sandholtz, W. (1993), 'Monetary Bargains: The Treaty on EMU', in A.W. Cafruny and G.G. Rosenthal (eds), *The State of the European Community*, vol. 2 (London: Longman).

Soisson, J.-P. (1990), 'Observations on the Community Charter of Basic Social Rights for Workers', *Social Europe*, **1**.

Swann, D. (1992), *The Economics of the Common Market* (Harmondsworth: Penguin).

Teague, P. and J. Grahl (1991), 'The European Community Social Charter and Labour Market Regulation', *Journal of Public Policy*, **11**, (2).

Thatcher, M. (1988), *Britain and Europe* (London: Conservative Political Centre).

Watson, P. (1993), 'Social Policy After Maastricht', *Common Market Law Review*, **30**.

6. Maastricht: principles, competences and powers

INTRODUCTION

The Maastricht Treaty on European Union is a complex document consisting of a preamble and a series of new and modifying substantive treaty articles which in turn are rounded off by a list of 17 protocols and 31 declarations, together with one agreement. Their declared effect, in conjunction with the three original economic community treaties, is to create a European Union. That in turn has been portrayed as an edifice supported on three pillars, namely the provisions concerning (a) the economic, social and cultural policy competences and powers, (b) the CFSP and (c) cooperation on judicial and home affairs. The first are in the main based on the decision-making powers contained in the Rome (EEC) Treaty including supranational qualified majority voting. The last two are essentially intergovernmental in character and reflect the reluctance, notably of France and the UK, to allow Rome Treaty supranational powers to spread to other issues. In short the Maastricht Treaty embodies differing decision-making systems. But then this is not new since, as we have seen, the Single Act gave a boost to majority voting but also formally recognized the essentially intergovernmental EPC.

While the three pillars model has much to commend it, if we wish to understand the Maastricht Treaty we need to break it down further into its eight main components:

1. the general principles of the Union Treaty;
2. the general principles relating to the key Rome (EEC) Treaty;
3. the new, modified and enlarged economic, social and cultural competences provided under the Rome (EEC) Treaty;
4. the intergovernmental provisions relating to the CFSP;
5. the intergovernmental provisions relating to cooperation on judicial and home affairs;

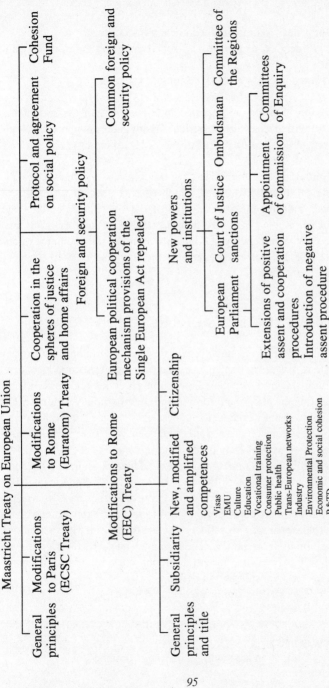

Figure 6.1 Maastricht Treaty on European Union

6. the new decision-making powers and institutions;
7. the protocol on economic and social cohesion and the Cohesion Fund;
8. the protocol and agreement relating to social policy.

These various aspects are depicted in Figure 6.1. In the rest of this chapter we will discuss the Maastricht Treaty under these headings, but will reserve a detailed treatment of the EMU aspect of (3) above until Chapter 7.

It is important to emphasize that the Maastricht Treaty does not supersede the founding treaties. Much of it is devoted to modifying rather than replacing the original Rome Treaty which created the EEC. To a much lesser extent it also modifies the ECSC and Euratom treaties. The provisions relating to cooperation on judicial and home affairs and the CFSP are not amendments to the founding treaties but stand separately from them.

GENERAL PRINCIPLES OF THE UNION TREATY

By the treaty the High Contracting Parties seek to establish a European Union which, as we have seen, is a collective term for economic, social and cultural integration under the founding treaties together with the judicial and home affairs and foreign and security policy elements. The European Union is declared to mark a new stage in the process of creating an ever closer union among the peoples of Europe. This wording is the same as was embodied in the preamble to the Rome (EEC) Treaty. In short, the attempt to incorporate a federal aspiration (features of the earlier Luxembourg draft and the later Dutch draft) had failed. Here the UK played a major role. The treaty also goes on to couple the ever closer union concept with the need to take decisions as closely as possible to the citizen. This reflects a desire for subsidiarity (see below) – another aim high on the UK negotiating agenda. The federalists were defeated on this occasion but will no doubt return to the fray when the treaty is up for reconsideration in 1996.

The objectives of the Union are declared to be:

1. the promotion of economic and social progress which is balanced and sustainable;
2. the creation of an area without internal frontiers;

3. the strengthening of economic and social cohesion;
4. the establishment of an EMU, including a single currency;
5. the assertion of the identity of the Union on the international stage by means of a CFSP which will eventually lead to the framing of a common *defence* policy which in turn might in time give rise to a common defence;
6. the maintenance in full of the 'acquis communautaire' – the existing body of Community laws and practices.

The Union Treaty also highlights the guiding role to be played by the European Council. It will provide the Union with the necessary impetus for its future development and will define the general political guidelines of that development. In this context the European Council will consist of the heads of state and government and the president of the commission. They are to be assisted by the ministers of foreign affairs and a member of the commission. The European Council will meet at least twice a year.

Interestingly the activities of the heads of state and government are not justiciable. That is to say, the legitimacy, or lack of it, of their activities is not capable of being tested before the Court of Justice.

GENERAL PRINCIPLES OF THE EC TREATY

Four main changes need to be highlighted. They relate to a change of the title of the EEC, changes to its stated aims and specific objectives, the emphasis on the subsidiarity principle and the introduction of citizenship (of the Union) rights. Following the Maastricht Treaty, the European Economic Community is now called simply the European Community. This is a reflection of the fact that the growing social, cultural and citizenship dimensions of the Community meant that exclusive reliance on the word 'Economic' would have been misleading.

While the SEA amended the original Rome Treaty quite significantly, it did not modify Article 2, which sets out the broad aims of the Community. Nor did it amend Article 3 which, as we noted in Chapter 2, lists the specific objectives (there will be a CAP, a ESF, and so on). By contrast, the Maastricht Treaty has, as Lane observes, shown no timidity in this respect (Lane 1993, p. 843). A new Article 2 has been introduced and the list of specific objectives in Article 3 has been considerably lengthened. Article 2 now runs as follows:

The Community shall have as its task, by establishing a common market
and an economic and monetary union and by implementing the common
policies or activities referred to in Articles 3 and 3a, to promote throughout
the Community a harmonious and balanced development of economic activities, sustainable and non-inflationary growth respecting the environment, a high degree of convergence of economic performance, a high level
of employment and of social protection, the raising of the standard of living
and quality of life, and economic and social cohesion and solidarity among
Member States.

Two points are particularly noteworthy. First, the European Community now seeks to move forward from a Common Market to the new
destination of EMU. Second, gone is the old unqualified objective of
continual expansion and an accelerated raising of the standard of living. Instead emphasis is laid on sustainable development, non-inflationary growth, respect for the environment and the need for social
protection.

Article 3, which descends from the general to the specific, now
indicates that the activities of the Community shall include the following:

1. the elimination, as between member states, of customs duties and
    quantitative restrictions on the import and export of goods, and of
    all other measures having equivalent effect;
2. a common commercial policy;
3. an internal market characterized by the abolition, as between
    member states, of obstacles to the free movement of goods, peo-
    ple, services and capital;
4. measures concerning the entry and movement of people in the
    internal market as provided for in Article 100(c);
5. a common policy in the sphere of agriculture and fisheries;
6. a common policy in the sphere of transport;
7. a system ensuring that competition in the internal market is not
    distorted;
8. the approximation of the laws of member states to the extent
    required for the functioning of the common market;
9. a policy in the social sphere comprising a ESF;
10. the strengthening of economic and social cohesion;
11. a policy in the sphere of the environment;
12. the strengthening of the competitiveness of Community industry;
13. the promotion of research and technological development;

14. encouragement for the establishment and development of trans-European networks;
15. a contribution to the attainment of a high level of health protection;
16. a contribution to education and training of quality and to the flowering of the cultures of the member states;
17. a policy in the sphere of development cooperation;
18. the association of the overseas countries and territories in order to increase trade and promote jointly economic and social development;
19. a contribution to the strengthening of consumer protection;
20. measures in the spheres of energy, civil protection and tourism.

Most of this is not strictly new. One *absolutely* new element is Article 3(d) which relates to Community competence in respect of the movement of third country nationals. The rest are either elements which were present in old Article 3 or concern activities which have crept in often piecemeal or tangentially, alongside the main activities of the Community. However, as Lane points out in admirable style, 'Their formal inclusion in Article 3, and in greater detail in subsequent provisions of the Treaty, not only broadens quantitatively and qualitatively the pantheon of Community competences; it also confers upon them legitimacy, coherence, new direction' (Lane, 1993, p. 944). Article 3 is complemented by Article 3(a) which emphasizes the principle that the Community will be based on an open market with free competition and that the open economy will in turn give rise to an EMU with a single currency, the ECU. The objective of transforming the Common Market into an EMU is of course the other fundamentally new element.

Most significantly new Article 3(b) incorporates within the Rome Treaty the principle of subsidiarity. Laffan has pointed out that subsidiarity originated in Catholic social teaching in the 1930s as a method of restricting the reach of public policy and the role of the state in social matters (Laffan, 1993, p. 43). Subsidiarity was, as we saw in Chapter 3, keenly debated in the discussions leading up to the European Parliament's Draft European Union Treaty (Lodge, 1984, p. 383). It did not feature in the original Rome Treaty but made an isolated appearance in the environmental provisions which were added to the treaty following the SEA. Subsidiarity is a political concept which is particularly relevant in a federalist context since it is generally regarded as meaning that competence should be exercised at the lowest level – as near to the citizens as possible. The approach adopted by Article 3(b) is based on the proposition that, in policy areas where the Community does not have exclusive competence, the Community will only act in circumstances where policy objectives cannot be sufficiently achieved by the member states acting independently and can be better achieved by common action (that is, by Community action). Commentators argue that subsidiarity is justiciable – that the Court of Justice can and will interpret it. It is however a vague principle. Brave indeed is the man or woman who could claim to be able to draw a firm line of distinction between those things which can be best done independently and those which are best done collectively. No doubt reflecting that fact, the president of the European Court of Justice has declared publicly that the court cannot apply it (Nicholl, 1993, p. 23).

At the Birmingham European Council in 1992 it was agreed that an attempt to flesh out the meaning of the principle would be aided by the commission itself reviewing pending legislation to see which proposals could, in the spirit of subsidiarity, be dropped.[1] At the subsequent Edinburgh summit the fruits of this exercise were reviewed and at the same time the European Council went on to identify the general approach which should be adopted. This took the form of a series of guidelines, the general flavour of which was as follows. The Community institutions should begin by asking (a) whether a draft measure could be justified by reference to the objectives of the Rome Treaty and (b) whether the necessary legal basis for its adoption existed. If the answer to both was in the affirmative, then the next question to ask was this: was the situation such that it would not be possible for the objectives of the proposed action to be sufficiently achieved by member state action and therefore could be better achieved by Community action? If the latter was true then the question of the nature of the proposed action should be considered. Here flexibility and national discretion should be maximized. Action involving the harmonization of national laws and practices should only be resorted to where it was clearly necessary to do so. The consequent burdens, financial and administrative, falling on national and local governments and businesses and individuals should be minimized and be *proportionate* to the objectives to be achieved. Community measures should leave as much scope as possible for national discretion. Directives were preferable to regulations. Framework directives were better than detailed measures. Voluntary codes of conduct should be chosen wherever appropriate. Cooperative arrangements were preferable to compulsion (European Council, 1992, Annexe 2 to Part A).

Two other points are worthy of note. First, the Edinburgh Council communiqué declared that, while the principle of subsidiarity could not be regarded as having direct effect, the interpretation of the principle, and review of compliance with it, were subject to control by the Court of Justice. We shall see! Second, while the British were keen advocates of the principle, its practical impact in the UK context is to be limited. Closeness to the citizens means closeness to London but not to Edinburgh, Cardiff or Belfast.

Finally new Articles 8 and 8a to 8e established the principles of Union citizenship, a concept which, it will be recollected, featured in the European Parliament's Draft European Union Treaty. Citizenship of the Union is enjoyed automatically by all nationals of member states. Member states, however, remain responsible for determining who their nationals shall be. Citizens' rights and duties are those already conferred by the Treaty of Rome and subsequent legislation, such as rights of residence in other member states plus some new rights. Citizens resident in another member state may vote and stand as a candidate in municipal and European elections in that state (but not in national elections); they have the right of consular protection in third countries where their government is not represented; and they have the right to petition the European Parliament and to make applications to the EC ombudsman. Under the Maastricht Treaty, no further rights can be granted to citizens without the unanimous agreement of the European Council and ratification by national procedures.

NEW MODIFIED AND ENLARGED POLICY COMPETENCES

By far and away the most important of these competences is the commitment to transform the EC into an EMU. This involves a staged transition to a single currency, the ECU, together with institutional developments, notably a transitional European Monetary Institute (EMI) which will ultimately be replaced by a European central bank (ECB) as part of a European System of Central Banks (ESCB). The detailed nature of this programme will be addressed in the ensuing chapter. It should be added that the UK was reluctant to commit itself to an automatic process of transition to EMU. It obtained an opt-out whereby it was not obliged or committed to move to the third and final stage of monetary union (for a discussion of which see Chapter 7) without a separate decision to that effect being made by the UK government and parliament. This was embodied in a protocol attached to the treaty. Denmark too was the subject of a protocol since it was recognized that, under its constitution, a referendum might be necessary before it could proceed to the third stage.

The other absolutely new competence is, as indicated above, concerned with the movements of third country nationals; specifically it relates to visas. While the Maastricht Treaty deals with a range of subjects which are typically the concern of the central authority of a federation, it does so in a variable fashion. As we have seen, foreign and security issues are almost totally consigned to the intergovernmental category. But citizenship is part of the Rome Treaty system. By contrast, matters such as immigration and rights of asylum are regarded as falling into the intergovernmental justice and home affairs category. As we saw in Chapter 4 these have been dealt with outside the Community framework by means of a series of separate conventions, such as Schengen. But thanks to Maastricht, new Article 100(c) of the Rome Treaty empowers the Community to determine the third countries whose nationals will require a visa to enter the Community. Such decisions will be made unanimously up to 1996, but thereafter they will be decided by qualified majority vote.

The remaining competences range from those which already existed but were deemed to be in need of amplification or modification to those which, while not absolutely new to Community processes, have hitherto been largely peripheral but are now firmly established within the pantheon of Community competences.

Two features of these competences are worthy of note. First, it is quite evident that they represent a (not entirely tidy) resolution of a conflict between those political actors who wished to add significantly to the Community's policy-making armoury and those who wished to safeguard national sovereignty and diversity. Indeed a significant degree of emasculation has been incorporated. Second, the range of decision-making processes has been widened yet further. The Single Act introduced the *cooperation mechanism*, which enabled the European Parliament to play a more effective role than one of mere consultation as envisaged in the original Rome Treaty. However the parliament's amendments could ultimately be overridden by unanimous vote in the council. This is now referred to as the Article 189(c) process. A further power has now been provided, namely the 'co-decision' or negative assent procedure, under Article 189(b). Here a more protracted dialogue involving conciliation is envisaged. The parliament cannot impose its amendments on the council, but it can, in a case of unresolved conflict, refuse to adopt a proposal, with the result that it does not pass into law. In at least one policy area (the environment) it is now apparent that, depending on the nature of the particular environmental issue, the council may act in consultation with the parliament, may act in cooperation with it or may act in codecision with it.

Before we leave the decision making issue, it is as well to note that both the cooperation procedure (Article 189c) and the negative assent procedure (Article 189b) envisage that in the absence of differences between the council and the parliament the proposal will be decided by qualified majority vote in the council. In short, the additional processes envisaged in both these mechanisms only arise when the parliament wishes to amend rather than to accept the initial common position taken by the council.

Culture is one of the competences which comes close to being brand new. The original Rome Treaty did not confer on the Community institutions any express competence to make laws and policy in this respect. However cultural considerations crept in peripherally in at least two ways. Under Article 36, one of the grounds for imposing quantitative restrictions on trade was the desire to protect national treasures possessing artistic, historic or archaeological value. Also ministers of culture have met from time to time within the context of the Council of Ministers. For example, in 1985 they agreed to institute a European sculpture competition, although in doing so they invoked no specific treaty article (OJ, 1985). Under Maastricht, culture now formally becomes a Community competence, by virtue of new Article 128 which declares that 'The Community shall contribute to the flowering of the cultures of the Member States.' However a host of safeguards have been inserted. Community action has to respect national and regional diversity. Action by the Community will aim at encouraging cooperation between member states and, if necessary, will support and supplement their action. Action through the Council of Ministers will exclude harmonization of national laws and will take the form of either incentive measures (that is, no compulsion involved) or recommendations. Incentive measures will be based on the Article 189(b) procedure but, while that process normally holds out the possibility that in uncontroversial situations *(vis-à-vis* the parliament) a majority vote will suffice, in this case unanimity is required.

Education likewise comes close to being a new competence. The Rome Treaty makes no reference to education but it does quite explicitly refer to vocational training. In the past the Court of Justice has been happy to blur the distinction and we know that the national ministers of education have introduced various Community-financed education programmes, such as the Lingua programme which was designed to improve the teaching and learning of foreign languages (of the Community). Under Maastricht, education is formally declared to be a Community competence. By virtue of new Rome Treaty Article 126, 'The Community shall contribute to the development of quality education.' Again certain limitations on competence are apparent. Community action will contribute to encouraging cooperation between member states and if necessary will support and supplement such action. The responsibility of member states for the content, organization, cultural and linguistic diversity of national education systems is acknowledged. Action by the Council of Ministers will exclude harmonization of national laws and will be confined to incentive measures and recommendations. Incentive measures will be based on the Article 189(b) procedure. The restrictions on Community competence in this area of policy are not surprising since typically in federal systems education is regarded as a matter to be devolved to lower levels.

By contrast, vocational training was, as we have noted, an explicit Community competence under the original Rome Treaty: Article 118 required the commission to promote collaboration in this area and Article 128 empowered the council to lay down the principles for carrying out a common vocational training policy. New Article 127, which relates to this area of activity, cannot therefore be regarded as a new development. There is, however, a contrast between the education and the vocational training implications of Maastricht. In education the Community is essentially concerned with encouraging cooperation; in the case of vocational training it is called upon to adopt a policy (Lane, 1993, p. 949). Council action will be based on the Article 189(c) procedure and will exclude the harmonization of laws.

Consumer protection is another development which is not entirely new to the Rome Treaty. For example, from the inception of the Community the protection of the consumer provided a justification for the imposition of quantitative restrictions on trade under Article 36. It also featured in directives such as that of 1985 concerning product liability, but of course the central object of that directive was the creation of the internal market and not the protection of consumers *per se*. The significance of new Article 129(a) of the Rome Treaty is that the Community now has a consumer protection competence *which is centrally con-*

cerned with that issue as well as being incidental to other issues such as the single market. The council, in legislating on consumer protection, will follow the Article 189(b) procedure. The requirement, introduced under the Single Act, that consumer measures should aim at a high level of protection only applied to those which were incidental to internal market completion activities. Now the high level of protection requirement also applies to consumer protection measures *per se*.

The position on public health under the original Rome Treaty was very similar to that of consumer protection. It did not feature as a mainstream policy competence but could be invoked for protection purposes under Article 36 and in connection with the free movement of labour, freedom to supply services and right of establishment. It was also *incidentally* involved by virtue of the single market process. By contrast, health and safety at work had been an ingredient of Community social policy from the start and, as we saw in Chapter 4, a power to legislate cooperatively on a qualified majority voting basis had been inserted into the Rome Treaty, thanks to the SEA. The Maastricht Treaty marks a positive step forward by declaring (new Article 129) that henceforth the Community has an express competence in the field of public health and that it will contribute to ensuring a high level of human health protection. It will do this by encouraging cooperation between member states and if necessary by lending support to their actions. The council will be excluded from harmonizing national laws and will be restricted to incentive measures and recommendations. Incentive measures will proceed via Article 189(b), while in respect of recommendations the council will merely act in consultation with the parliament.

The Maastricht Treaty also identifies trans-European networks as an area of Community activity. These are to be encouraged because they contribute to the freedom of movement of people and greater economic and social cohesion and also facilitate the more effective operation of the internal market. The Community will contribute to the development of such networks in the fields of transport, telecommunications and energy. The aim is to build up cross-frontier systems and interconnections. The Community will produce guidelines for priority action, will implement measures which ensure interoperability (such as standardization) and will be able to assist financially. Notable in the latter context is the new Cohesion Fund, which we discuss later and in Chapter 8. This, of course, is not an entirely new idea. Under Article 92, aid for projects of common European importance could be exempted from the prohibition on state aids and the EIB was empowered to lend money in such cases. Also under the aegis of the CTP, coordination of transport infrastructure investments had been agreed as early as 1966 and, in 1982, the council declared that in principle budget monies could be used to aid priority Community transport networks.

An industrial policy competence, focusing on the goal of competitiveness, is also provided by virtue of new Article 130. Formally there was no provision for an industrial policy under the original Rome Treaty and therefore, on the face of it, we have a new development. However the absence of a specific mandate did not, as we saw in Chapter 2, prevent the heads of state and government from agreeing in 1972 to the development of such a policy. This followed from the Colonna initiative of 1970. The policy which emerged, very slowly indeed, was essentially a cobbling together of a variety of treaty powers. But it lacked any real edge by dint of the fact that Germany was not willing to contemplate a dirigiste approach, favouring instead a free market philosophy. That general qualification is still apparent in Article 130, although on this occasion it probably owes most to the influence of Thatcher (Major) free market thinking. To that end the Article stipulates that Community industrial activities must be in accordance with a system of open and competitive markets and at the very end of the Article this general posture is reinforced by the injunction that they must not lead to a distortion of competition. In short, pro-competition Article 3(g) (previously 3(f)) continues to reign supreme. The new Article envisages actions designed to speed up adjustment to structural change, to foster better exploitation of new technology and so forth. On such issues member states will consult each other and the commission's role is confined to coordinating any actions which result. The council for its part is restricted to acting unanimously, in consultation with the parliament and the Ecosoc.

The remaining competences highlighted in the Maastricht Treaty are not new. New Article 130(r) relates to the environment, an issue which, as we noted in Chapter 4, was formally addressed in the Single Act. Significantly Community *policy* will aim at a high level of protection. The Single Act, by contrast, referred to *action* and did not stipulate a high level. The reference to subsidiarity is dropped but this is not significant since, as we saw above, subsidiarity is now a general principle and does not require reiteration within particular substantive competences. Community policy will be based on the precautionary principle and on the principles that preventive action should be taken, that environmental damage should be rectified *at source* and that the polluter should pay. Mainstream environmental actions will be based on the Article 189(c) procedure. However provisions of a fiscal nature, measures concerning town and country planning, land use (with the exception of waste management) and the management of water resources and measures affecting member state choice of energy resources will be decided unanimously and in consultation with the parliament and Ecosoc. Programmes of action in other areas will be decided via the Article 189(b) procedure, but in respect of the actual legislation the council will act under 189(c) or in consultation according to the nature of the issue involved. Reflecting changes already apparent in more recent environmental action programmes (see in particular EC Commission, 1992), Article 130(r) now requires that the protection of the environment should cease to be a separate consideration and must be accepted as a central formative component in all other Community policies.

As we noted in Chapter 4, economic and social cohesion as an objective was clearly taken on board when the Community adopted the SEA. Articles 130(a) to (e) effectively restate its role and point to the assistance which is provided by the structural funds, the EIB and other financial instruments. The really new aspect is found in Article 130(d), where the creation of the Cohesion Fund is indicated. This will be discussed in Chapter 8. Likewise a Community R&TD policy, designed to render European industry more competitive at the international level, had been formally embodied in the Rome Treaty via the Single Act. New Articles 130(f) to (p) replace old Articles 130(f) to (q) but these essentially constitute a tidying up operation and do not represent any really significant new development.

Lane points out that a common policy in the field of development cooperation was considered in the lead-up to the Single Act but was not proceeded with for lack of consensus (Lane, 1993, p. 974). Such a policy has now been incorporated in the Rome Treaty: Articles 130(u) to (y) relate. Again the fostering of development in the third world, notably by the granting of aid, is not new. It proceeded initially through the Part IV association provisions and culminated in the Lomé Conventions agreed under Article 238, the beneficiaries being the African, Caribbean and Pacific group of countries. Similar assistance has been given to the as yet dependent overseas countries and territories. In addition the Community has channelled aid to countries outside the colonial and ex-colonial category, the funds being provided from the

Community budget. The declared aim of the policy is to foster sustainable economic and social development, and the integration of the developing countries into the world economy and to combat poverty. Allied to this, the policy seeks to develop and consolidate democracy, the rule of law and respect for human rights and fundamental freedoms.

It will have been noted that the objectives laid out in new Article 3 are rounded off by a reference to measures in the spheres of energy, civil protection and tourism, but nothing appears in the substantive text by way of amplification. However a declaration was attached to the Maastricht Treaty which indicated that the possibility of introducing specific provisions into the Rome Treaty relating to these issues would be examined in 1996, when the Union treaty is re-examined. The declaration goes on to state that, in the view of the commission and as an interim arrangement, Community action in these spheres will be pursued on the basis of the present European Community treaties. This obviously includes those founding the ECSC and Euratom, as well as the EC.

While these are the really significant developments in policy competence, the Maastricht Treaty adds a number of other detailed changes. For example, under Article 92(3) the grounds upon which state aid *may* be validated are now extended to include the promotion of culture and heritage conservation.

INTERGOVERNMENTALISM: FOREIGN AND SECURITY POLICY

This area is covered by Maastricht Treaty Article J. It therefore stands on its own and is not a modification to the Rome (EC) Treaty. To a large extent it codifies the practices and procedures of EPC which go back to 1970 and were formally recognized in the SEA. The EPC mechanism is transformed into a CFSP. Security is thus now explicitly involved. By contrast, the Single Act referred merely to cooperation in foreign policy, although aspects of security were actually brought into the picture. The objectives of the CFSP are as follows:

1.	to safeguard the common values, fundamental interests and independence of the Union;
2.	to strengthen the security of the Union and its member states in all ways;

3. to preserve peace and strengthen international security, in accordance with the principles of the United Nations Charter as well as the principles of the Helsinki Final Act and the objectives of the Paris Charter;
4. to promote international cooperation;
5. to develop and consolidate democracy and the rule of law, and respect for human rights and fundamental freedoms.

The policy will operate upon the following lines. The European Council will define the principles and draw up general guidelines for the policy. The actual implementation will be with the Council of Ministers. Here a distinction is made between defining a *common position* on an issue and adopting *joint action* in respect of it. When it comes to defining a common position any member state, or the commission, may raise a question or submit a proposal. It will, however, be the Council of Ministers which actually defines the common position with respect to such questions or proposals. This is in contrast to the previous EPC system where member states were regarded as acting in political cooperation (House of Lords, 1993, p. 11). Common positions defined by the council will be binding under *international* law. Member states are required to ensure that their national policies conform to them and that they uphold them in international conferences and organizations. The Council of Ministers will also decide (on the basis of general guidelines from the European Council) whether a matter should be the subject of a *joint action*. It will also decide the details of the joint action and these too will be legally binding on member states. In its proceedings, both in defining common positions and in adopting joint actions, the Council of Ministers will act unanimously. The only exception to this is that the council, when adopting a joint action, and at any stage in its subsequent development, may define those matters where decisions can be made by qualified majority vote. The reader will recollect that, in the run-up to Maastricht, considerable differences arose over the issue of whether political cooperation should be based on the Rome Treaty supranational model or should be intergovernmental in character. Quite clearly the intergovernmentalists won the main battle, but the supranationalists made a limited gain.

The old Political Committee, consisting of political directors from the member states, survives. Its task is continuously to monitor the international scene and to provide appropriate inputs into Coreper and the Council of Ministers. The small secretariat set up by the 1986

Single Act has been quadrupled in size and fully incorporated into the council secretariat.

The vexed question of the appropriate arrangements in relation to defence, in which France and Germany were ranged against Italy, the UK and the Netherlands, is resolved in Article J4. It requests WEU, which is declared to be an integral part of the development of the Union, to implement decisions and actions of the Union which have defence implications.[2] Under Article J4, the policy of the Union must respect NATO obligations. We noted earlier that Maastricht looks ultimately to a common defence policy and eventually a common defence.

The European Parliament's role in relation to all this is limited. It will be consulted, kept informed and may question the Foreign Affairs Council and make recommendations – but that is all. These arrangements also pose problems for national parliaments. Thus the UK House of Lords, noting that ministers are responsible to parliament for the conduct of international relations, has expressed some concern as to how that can be effected. The Select Committee on the European Communities put the matter thus:

> We think it essential that work under the inter-governmental pillars of the European Union should be supervised by national parliaments. By comparison with Community legislative procedures, the Commission will have a smaller role, there will be no automatic publicity for proposals and governments will tend to prefer for their negotiations the secret ways to which they are accustomed. This lays a greater responsibility on national parliaments each to hold their own ministers to account. The European Parliament's formal powers under the Maastricht Treaty are limited in regard to foreign and security policy and justice and home affairs, and the Parliament is less able to influence the outcome of inter-governmental negotiations through the Commission whose role is limited. As with Community legislation, the work of the European Parliament and the work of national parliaments are complementary, but we see national parliaments as having the stronger potential in regard to the inter-governmental pillars. We note the determination already shown by the Dutch and Danish Parliaments to hold their ministers to account in these areas, and we intend under our own constitutional procedures and traditions of scrutiny of European matters to be equally vigilant. (House of Lords, 1993, p. 22)

INTERGOVERNMENTALISM: JUDICIAL AND HOME AFFAIRS

Cooperation on justice and home affairs is covered by Maastricht Treaty Article K, which, for the first time, places intergovernmental cooperation in these fields on a formal treaty basis. In the interests of achieving the objectives of the Union, and in particular the free movement of people, the member states have agreed that the following topics are to be regarded as matters of common interest:

1. asylum policy;
2. rules governing the crossing by people of the external borders of member states;
3. immigration policy;
4. the combating of drug addiction;
5. the combating of fraud on an international scale;
6. judicial cooperation in civil matters;
7. judicial cooperation in criminal matters;
8. customs cooperation;
9. police cooperation for the purposes of preventing terrorism, drug-trafficking and serious forms of international crime, combined with an information exchange system (to be centred on a European Police Office or Europol).

There is specific commitment to deal with these matters in compliance with the European Convention on Human Rights and the Convention Relating to the Status of Refugees. All member states are in fact already parties to these undertakings.

The emphasis is on the coordination of national actions in the fields referred to above. The focus of decision making is once again the Council of Ministers and there is now a single Council of Interior and Justice Ministers to replace the previously more diverse arrangements. This council adopts both joint positions and joint actions. Joint positions, like common positions under the CFSP, are binding under international law. Proposals, which may lead to joint positions or joint actions, will come from the member states and the commission, except that the latter is debarred from making proposals relating to (7), (8) and (9) above. In addition a Coordinating Committee of Senior Officials has been set up to prepare council work and the commission is fully associated with that activity. The general rule is that council decisions will be based on unanimity. However the council may decide that the implementation of joint actions may be decided on a qualified majority basis. The role of the European Parliament is effectively the same as in the case of the CFSP.

NEW DECISION-MAKING POWERS AND NEW INSTITUTIONS

The bones of contention which were highlighted in the pre-Maastricht negotiations were concerned with the desire of some political actors to give the European Parliament a more effective voice in Community affairs and to increase the scope of qualified majority voting. Did this happen?

As far as the parliament is concerned, the answer is yes, but to a modest extent. A glance at Table 6.1 indicates that the Positive Assent Procedure, which figured in the Single Act, made yet further headway at Maastricht. Likewise the scope of the Cooperation Procedure (Article 189(c)), introduced under the Single Act, was extended. Of particular significance is the *new* Negative Assent Procedure (Article 189(b)) which now applies over a wide range of issues. We should not of course exaggerate the significance of all this. The parliament does not thereby enjoy a right of initiative. That still remains with the commission. Nor can the parliament impose amendments on a united Council of Ministers. However under Article 189(b) it can ultimately block a measure when conciliation between the two has not resolved differences.

On the qualified majority voting front, some progress is also apparent. Thus, in the case of environmental protection, the Single Act required unanimity but Maastricht has shifted the emphasis so that mainstream environmental measures can be decided by qualified majority. Also in relatively new areas, such as consumer protection *per se*, qualified majority voting decisions are possible. But in other areas, such as public health, some of the steam has been taken out of the change by virtue of the fact that action is confined to incentive measures and recommendations. The harmonization of laws and practices also tends to be precluded.

The parliament has made some gains on other fronts. One is in relation to the appointment of the commission. Under Article 158, the member states by common accord will nominate the person they wish

Table 6.1   Decision-making changes flowing from the Maastricht Treaty

Areas where negative assent procedure (Article 189(b)) applies

Article 49	Free movement of workers
Article 54(2)	Right of establishment
Article 56(2)	Treatment of foreign nationals
Article 57(1)	Mutual recognition of qualifications
Article 57(2)	Right of establishment
Article 100a(1)	Single market legislation
Article 124(4)	Education incentive measures
Article 128(5)	Culture, but on the basis of unanimity
Article 129(4)	Public health
Article 129a(2)	Consumer protection
Article 129d	Trans-European networks
Article 130i	R & TD framework programmes (but on the basis of unanimity)
Article 130s(3)	Environment multinational action programmes

Extension of positive assent procedure†

Article 8a(2)	Citizenship: provisions to facilitate rights of free movement and residence
Article 105(6)	European central bank and prudential supervision*
Article 106(5)	Amendments to European system of central banks' statutes*
Article 130d	Organization and structural funds and establishment of Cohesion Fund
Article 138(3)	Uniform European Parliament electoral procedure
Article 228(3)	For conclusion of certain additional international agreements (This procedure already applies to association agreements under Article 238)

Extension of cooperation procedure (Article 189(c))‡

Article 75(1)	Transport
Article 103(5)	Rules for multilateral surveillance*
Article 104a(2)	Defining application of no privileged access rule*
Article 104b(2)	Definition of no bail-out rule
Article 105a(2)	Regulations concerning issue of coins*
Article 125	European Social Fund
Article 127(4)	Vocational training
Article 129d	Trans-European networks (measures other than guidelines)
Article 130e	Implementing decisions on the European Regional Development Fund
Article 130s(1)	Environment (except measures primarily fiscal (etc.) and action programmes)
Article 130w	Development cooperation

Notes:
* Aspects of EMU programme discussed in Chapter 7 below.
† See text for explanation.
‡ The cooperation procedure has been removed from specific R&TD programmes.

to be president of the commission. Then the member states, in consultation with the nominee president, will nominate the other persons to be members of the commission. Finally the whole commission will be subject (as a body) to a vote of approval by the parliament and thereafter will be appointed by the member states by common accord.

The parliament is also permitted, under Article 138(c), to set up temporary committees of enquiry to investigate alleged contraventions or maladministration in the implementation of Community law. This power does not apply when the matter in question is the subject of a proceeding before a court. The parliament, under Article 138(e), is also empowered to appoint an ombudsman to investigate complaints from citizens of the Union concerning maladministration in the activities of Community institutions. The latter do not include the Court of Justice and the Court of First Instance.

The powers of the Court of Justice have also been extended. Under the original Rome Treaty there was a marked contrast between the sanctions which could be imposed on enterprises and so on, as compared with member state governments, in connection with infringements of the Rome Treaty. Substantial fines could be imposed on the former, but if, for example, a government refused to implement a Court of Justice ruling upholding a commission ban on a state aid, no financial sanction could be applied. This has now changed. Under revamped Article 171, the old and extremely tame obligation to conform to judgements has been replaced by a further process. Under this the commission, having given the errant state an opportunity to explain itself, then informs the state of the points upon which it has not complied with the court. If the state still fails to comply, the commission can initiate a case before the court which would, *inter alia,* specify what it considered to be the appropriate lump sum or penalty payment. The court would then rule appropriately. The Maastricht Treaty also raised the Court of Auditors to a status equal to that of the parliament, council, commission, Court of Justice and Ecosoc.

A number of new institutions were also envisaged. These included the ECB, ESCB and the temporary EMI, which will be discussed in Chapter 7. The European Council at Maastricht looked to the conclusion of a convention establishing Europol (the European Police Office). This, as we noted above, is referred to in Article K of the Maastricht Treaty and was conceived as a Union-wide focus for the exchange of information by the police in relation to crime. A Committee of the Regions was also to be established. It was to be made up of representatives of regional and local bodies with an appropriate quota from each state and would be advisory to the council and commission. The committee held its first meeting in March 1993. The objective is to bring the European Union closer to its citizens by providing a channel of influence for regional and local views. The committee has no legislative power, but it has to be consulted on economic and social cohesion, trans-European networks, public health, culture, education and vocational training. It can also make its views known on any issue which it thinks has regional implications.

The seat of these institutions was decided later at a European Council in Brussels on 29 October 1993. The EMI and ECB will be located in Frankfurt. Europol will have its seat in The Hague. At the same time the locations of various other institutions were also decided, as follows:

1. European Environmental Agency: Copenhagen;
2. European Training Foundation: Turin;
3. Office for Veterinary and Plant-Health Inspection and Control: Ireland;
4. European Monitoring Centre for Drugs and Drug Addiction: Lisbon;
5. European Agency for the Evaluation of Medicinal Products: London;
6. Agency for Health and Safety at Work: Spain;
7. Office for Harmonization in the Internal Market (trademarks, designs and models): Spain.

THE COHESION FUND

In our earlier discussion on economic and social cohesion, the Maastricht commitment to create a Cohesion Fund was noted. This, it will be recollected, was something which Spain in particular pressed for in the Maastricht negotiations. The rationale behind the Spanish pressure will become more apparent when, in Chapter 8, we come to discuss the position of Spain in relation to the Community budget. The Cohesion Fund was the subject of a special protocol. It committed the Community to establishing such a fund not later than 31 December 1993. In fact the European Council at Edinburgh in December 1992 identified the main ingredients of a Cohesion Fund regulation (to be adopted by the Council of Ministers) and, as part of the 1993–9 Community budget settlement, allocated funds for the purpose. The financial details are outlined in Chapter 8 below. The Fund is designed to provide financial contributions for projects in the fields of the environment and trans-European networks in member states whose GNP per capita is less than 90 per cent of the Community average. In Chapter 8 we shall see that Spain had also levelled a number of criticisms at the Community budget, alleging that it did not adequately take account of individual member states' contributive capacity and that the counterpart funds provided by a member state when it received aid from the budget ought to take account of the prosperity of the recipient. Both these points were noted in the protocol.

THE PROTOCOL AND AGREEMENT ON SOCIAL POLICY

In Chapter 5 we noted that the UK had refused to sign the Social Charter and that the need to provide appropriate powers if the charter was to be implemented was one of the reasons for instigating the IGC. In the negotiation the UK continued to resist the incorporation of the Social Charter in the Rome Treaty – the idea that the law-making powers contained in the social chapter of the Rome Treaty should be significantly extended and that this should be coupled with substantial use of qualified majority voting. The result was an untidy and very un-communautaire arrangement which essentially granted the UK an opt-out.

Much ink has been spilt in regard to the legal status of the Protocol on Social Policy and the attached Agreement. The general impact has been admirably summarized by Whiteford (Whiteford, 1993, p. 204), who points out that the preamble to the Protocol indicates that the provisions of the Agreement are without prejudice to the Rome Treaty. In other words, the 11 states agreed to exhaust the possibilities of the Rome Treaty before having to resort to the Agreement. The Agreement, however, enables the 11 to make decisions which the 12 (that is, including the UK) would not be able to agree to. Under the Agreement measures are divided into two categories. Category one are those concerned with (a) improvement in particular of the working environment to protect workers' health and safety; (b) working conditions; (c) the information and consultation of workers; (d) equality between men and women with regard to labour market opportunities and treatment at work; and (e) the integration of people excluded from the labour market. These measures will be subject to qualified majority voting under the Article 189(c) process. Category two involves those that relate to (a) social security and social protection of workers; (b) protection of workers where their employment contract is terminated; (c) representation and collective defence of the interests of workers and employers, including co-determination; (d) conditions of employment for third-country nationals legally residing in Community territory; and (e) financial contributions for promotion of employment and job creation. These measures will be subject to unanimous decision, the council acting in consultation with the parliament and Ecosoc. The UK will not take part in the legislative process and will not be bound by the results of it. This UK reluctance is of course a product of Conservative Party thinking and was signalled by Margaret Thatcher in her famous Bruges speech. It is not supported by either of the main opposition parties and it is reasonable to assume that any change in political control in the UK would mean that the opt-out would be dropped.

TITLES OF THE INSTITUTIONS

All this change was not destined to be accomplished without some change of names. We have already noted that the EEC is now simply the EC. The Council of Ministers of the European Community duly reconstituted itself as the Council of Ministers of the European Union. Also the European Communities Commission was to be called the European Commission.

NOTES

1. The attention given to the subsidiarity issue was strongly motivated by a desire to persuade the Danes to reverse their first referendum decision to reject the Maastricht Treaty.
2. Following the second Danish referendum, Denmark became an observer at WEU. It was agreed by the European Council that nothing in the Maastricht Treaty committed it to be a member of WEU and that Denmark would not be involved in the elaboration and implementation of decisions which have defence implications.

REFERENCES

EC Commission (1992), *Fifth European Community programme of policy and action in relation to the environment and sustainable development*, COM (92) 23 final, 27 March.

European Council (1992), *Conclusions of the Presidency* (Edinburgh).

House of Lords Select Committee on the European Communities (1993), *Scrutiny of the Inter-governmental Pillars of the European Union*, 28th Report, Session 1992–3.

Laffan, B. (1993), 'The Treaty of Maastricht: Political Authority and Legitimacy', in A.W. Cafruny and G.G. Rosenthal (eds), *The State of the European Community*, vol. 2 (London: Longman).

Lane, R. (1993), 'New Community Competences under the Maastricht Treaty', *Common Market Law Review*, **30**.

Lodge, J. (1984), 'European Union and the First Elected European Parliament: The Spinelli Initiative', *Journal of Common Market Studies*, **22**, (4) (June).

Nicholl, W. (1993), 'Maastricht Revisited: A Critical Analysis of the Treaty on European Union', in A.W. Cafruny and G.G. Rosenthal (eds), *The State of the European Community*, vol. 2 (London: Longman).

OJ (1985), *Official Journal of the European Communities,* C153/4, 22 June 1985.

Whiteford, E. (1993), 'Social Policy after Maastricht', *European Law Review*, **18**.

7.   Maastricht: the economic and monetary union programme

INTRODUCTION

In Chapter 1 the alternative scenarios which could be described as constituting an EMU were surveyed. It was suggested that the 'economic' aspect could be regarded as referring to the existence of free movement of goods, services and factors of production. The variety of scenarios which could therefore be envisaged inevitably arose from differences in respect of the 'monetary' condition. We also concluded that the monetary condition could itself be divided into monetary and fiscal components. It is possible to identify a minimalist monetary arrangement in which the member states agree to operate a fixed exchange rate system – in fact an exchange rate union. Then there is the maximalist version where the member states decide to get rid of the separate national currencies in favour of one union currency, the supply of which is controlled from the centre. Alongside this, the union money supply authority would also control interest and exchange rates – a currency union. On the fiscal side it was equally possible to point to a range of alternative scenarios. A minimalist arrangement would leave the raising of taxes and the spending of them in national hands. However tax structures and rates would be harmonized, as a necessary condition for the elimination of competitive distortions in connection with the Common Market (or 'economic') aspect of the arrangement. Nevertheless some control over national budget deficits and debt levels would have to be imposed. But in a maximalist arrangement the whole system of taxing and spending would be centralized and, in conjunction with this, there would be a centralized system of borrowing and a federal budget deficit (or surplus). The word 'federal' has just crept in, and justifiably, since it is difficult to conceive of such a fiscal arrangement in the absence of a substantial, though not necessarily total, transfer of political power to the centre. In other words, 'no taxation without representation', to quote our American brethren of long ago.

In practice we will see that the Maastricht model, following quite closely the path mapped out by the Delors Report of 1989, opts for what is essentially a maximalist monetary arrangement, together with what we may term a minimalist fiscal condition.

BACKGROUND

Before we turn to the stages which lead up to EMU we need to review the background condition. Four aspects are worthy of note: the coordination and convergence requirements, the excessive deficit procedure, the 'no bail-out' clause and the free movement of capital obligation. Under new Article 102(a), member states are required to conduct their economic policies with a view to achieving the objectives of the Community as laid down in Article 2. Article 2 includes the need for economic convergence and the establishment of an EMU. In respect of coordination, new Article 103(a) declares that it will be under the direction of the Council of Ministers. The latter will draw up broad guidelines on member state economic policy and these will be discussed by the European Council. On the basis of the conclusions drawn by the heads of state and government, the Council of Ministers will adopt recommendations setting out these broad guidelines. To facilitate coordination a Monetary Committee was set up with immediate effect. Its role was to be purely advisory.

This call for coordination highlights the important role which has to be played by convergence. The reader will recollect that in the 1970s the Community agreed upon the aspiration of achieving EMU by 1980. It failed, but we shall not dwell on that fact. What is relevant is the different views which were then advanced about how best to proceed to the ultimate objective. (As we shall see later, and in the light of the turbulence within the EMS in the post-Maastricht period, this problem has not gone away.) During the 1970s debate, two alternative views were put forward, referred to as the monetarist and economist positions. The monetarists believed in locking the exchange rates at the outset. This, it was felt, would force member states to apply the appropriate monetary discipline and bring into convergence their economic performances. The economists, on the other hand, called for convergence first and the locking of exchange rates and a common currency second. The Maastricht programme clearly adopts the latter approach since it envisages a stage-by-stage transition to the final goal and emphasizes the need to achieve convergence before the final monetary act is accomplished.

The Maastricht Treaty also inserted into the Rome Treaty a requirement (Article 104(a), that governments should avoid excessive deficits. A protocol was attached to the Maastricht Treaty which stipulated that budget deficits as a ratio to gross domestic product (GDP) should not exceed 3 per cent and that government debt in relation to GDP should not exceed 60 per cent. Member states which breached these guidelines would find themselves on the receiving end of council recommendations requiring them to bring the excessive deficit and so on to an end. Failure to come into line would be followed by an order to do so, which could be backed up by financial sanctions. These include invitations to the EIB to reconsider its lending to the errant state, a requirement for the state in question to make a non-interest-bearing deposit with the Community or the imposition of a fine. The excessive deficit procedure of course points up the fact that monetary union has a fiscal dimension and this fiscal dimension is designed to be a continuing feature of the EMU plan. Later we will see that macroeconomic management is a divided responsibility since the Union central bank system will be primarily responsible for handling monetary (narrowly defined) matters while the Council of Ministers will be responsible for the appropriate fiscal (government borrowing) discipline.

New Article 104(b) also imposes a 'no bail-out' condition on member states. In the Maastricht negotiations Germany in particular was concerned to impose this restriction. The problem here is that a government, for example Italy, might continue to run budget deficits and consequently pile up an ever-growing burden of debt. Eventually this could lead to a situation where the capital markets came to doubt the ability of Italy to service and repay its debt. While in the monetary union that debt would be Italian, it would nevertheless be denominated in the Union currency. The fear of that consequence could lead other debtor countries to bail out the Italian government and indeed the Italian government might be tempted to rely on this and to that extent would not be constrained in its borrowing. What Article 104(b) does is to declare that this kind of bribery would not work. The Italian government would be responsible for its debts and moreover would, as we have just seen, be subject to control of excessive deficit.

The final background condition is imposed by new Article 73(b) which states that all restrictions on the movement of capital between member states and between the member states and third countries are prohibited. The reader will of course recollect that, as part of the single market programme, a capital liberalization directive had been adopted in 1988.

THE STAGES

As we noted, the Maastricht Treaty envisaged a stage-by-stage movement to EMU. The second and final stages are detailed in new Article 109(e)–(m) of the Rome Treaty. In stage one the main condition was that all member states should be members of the ERM of the EMS which, it will be recollected, centred on a limited normal margin of fluctuation of ±2$^1/_4$ per cent around the central parities against the ECU.

Stage two opened on 1 January 1994. The avoidance of excessive budget deficits (see above) continued and by the beginning of 1994 the Council of Ministers was required to have introduced detailed rules for the operation of the excessive deficit mechanism. On the monetary side, the significant development was the creation of the EMI. This body was to have a legal personality and be managed by a council consisting of a president and the governors of the national central banks. Alexandre Lamfalussy, a former general manager of the Bank for International Settlements, was the first president and Maurice F. Doyle, a former governor of the Central Bank of Ireland, was appointed as the vice-president.

The Institute (located, as we have seen, in Frankfurt) had three main tasks to perform. The first was to facilitate convergence by strengthening the coordination of national monetary policies. In effect it was to manage a process of transition from a condition of coordinated national monetary policies to a single Union monetary policy. It would seek coordination through the issuing of recommendations to member states on the conduct of their monetary policies. Second, it was to be responsible for overseeing the operation of the ERM. In this connection the European Monetary Cooperation Fund (EMCF) was to be dissolved and its tasks were to be discharged by the Institute.[1] Third, it was to prepare all the procedures, mechanisms of control and so forth which would be necessary when the final stage of monetary union came into existence. For example, an appropriate quantity of paper currency would have to be ready for use. Apparently the physical task of printing all the notes which would be put into circulation when the single currency made its appearance was bound to take several years.

During this second stage the member states were also required to take steps to render their central banks independent. The statute of the ESCB and the ECB defines such independence as a situation where neither a central bank nor any member of its decision-making bodies seeks or takes instructions from a government or any other body. The reason for this move was of course that in the final state of monetary union the Union central banking authority was to be independent and the Maastricht Treaty envisaged a collaborative arrangement involving the national central banks.

Preparations for the entry into final stage 3 were required to begin not later than the end of 1996. According to new Article 109(j), during 1996 the European Commission and the EMI would report to the Council of Ministers on the degree to which member states had achieved a convergence of economic performance. Each member state's performance would be judged against five criteria which were fully set out in a protocol attached to the Maastricht Treaty. Those criteria are shown in table 7.1 below. The assessment would also take account of 'the development of the ECU, the results of the integration of the markets, the situation and development of the balances of payments on current account and ... of the development of unit labour costs and other price indices.' On the basis of these reports the Council of Ministers, acting by qualified majority, would assess which member states fulfilled the conditions necessary for the introduction of a single currency. The Council of Ministers, 'meeting in the composition of Heads of State or of Government', would then by qualified majority make three final

Table 7.1   Maastricht Treaty on European Union: EMU convergence criteria

---

1. In the year prior to examination an inflation rate no more than 1.5 percentage points above the average of the three EC states with the lowest price rises.
2. In the year prior to examination a long-term rate of interest within two percentage points of the average of the three members with the lowest rates of inflation.
3. A national budget deficit less than 3 per cent of GDP.
4. A public debt ratio which does not exceed 60 per cent of GDP.
5. A currency for two years in the normal band of the ERM of the EMS which has not been devalued.

---

decisions: (1) whether a majority of states fulfilled the necessary conditions; (2) whether it was appropriate to enter the third and final stage; and (3) assuming it was appropriate, when the third stage should start.

While it is therefore possible that the third stage could commence in 1997, it is also possible that for one reason or another the member states might choose not to. If by the end of 1997 a date has not been set for the beginning of the third stage, then indeed Article 109(j) declares that the third stage will start on the 1st January 1999.[2] Before 1 July 1998, the convergence assessment procedure will once more be carried out. On this occasion the majority requirement will be dropped. As long as at least two countries satisfy the criteria they will proceed to form a monetary union as from 1 January 1999. In the lead-up to the Maastricht Treaty the German chancellor was keen to see an irreversible process set on foot, and the 1999 provision seems to meet his requirement – but see below.

THE FINAL STAGE

The third and final stage is characterized by the emergence of a single currency, in the form of the ECU, the supply of which is controlled by the ESCB (this institution is discussed below). The reader will recollect that the Delors Report had proposed that the ECB should appear at the second stage, but this was resisted, notably by Germany. At the outset of the final stage, Article 109(i) requires the Council of Ministers to decide the irrevocably fixed conversion rates between the national currencies and the ECU.[3] After that the single currency has to be rapidly introduced. It will only be introduced, however, amongst those countries that are qualified to participate by virtue of having satisfied the convergence criteria. The Maastricht Treaty explicitly recognizes that some countries may not qualify; they are referred to as 'Member States with a derogation'. Thus a 'two-tier Europe' is a potentiality under Maastricht. Countries may also opt out, a subject to which we will return later.

According to Article 105, the ESCB is assigned the task of defining and implementing the monetary policy of the Community. Thus control of the supply of the single currency (the ECU) and interest rates falls under its aegis. Equally the ESCB is charged with the task of conducting foreign exchange operations; in other words, it will carry out support operations in respect of the exchange value of the ECU against the

US dollar, yen and so on. In this connection the foreign exchange reserves of the member states are to be centralized in the ESCB. The ESCB involvement in foreign exchange management is, however, a qualified one and this will be discussed further below. The ESCB is also called upon to promote the smooth operation of the payments system. Oddly the Maastricht Treaty does not specifically refer to the ESCB acting as lender of last resort. Perhaps references to its role in contributing to the smooth operation of the system and to the achievement of financial stability imply such a responsibility. It is also possible that its role in conducting open market operations may be stretched to include rescue operations. It is hoped that, during the second stage, the EMI will flesh out the details of this vital central bank function. Alongside these monetary (narrowly defined) elements, the final stage also continues the system of fiscal discipline associated with the excessive deficit procedure. This of course is in the hands of the Council of Ministers and not the ESCB.

This brings us to the institutional structure. In the final stage the EMI disappears and is replaced by the ESCB. The ESCB is a collaborative structure involving two operating arms, the national central banks (NCBs) – each with separate legal personalities – and the newly created ECB, which is also envisaged as having a separate legal personality. The use of the word 'collaborative' should not, however, disguise the fact that the decision-making centre is the ECB. Thus, in the protocol setting out the statute of the ESCB and ECB, Article 8 enunciates the general principle that 'The ESCB shall be governed by the decision-making bodies of the ECB',[4] and Article 14(3) further reinforces the centrality of the ECB when it declares that 'The national central banks are an integral part of the ESCB and shall act in accordance with the guidelines and instructions of the ECB.' The ECB governing council is made up of the executive board of the ECB together with the governors of the NCBs. The executive board is itself composed of a president, a vice-president and four other members.

In passing we should also note that the acts and omissions of the ECB are open to review or interpretation before the European Court of Justice. Also the ECB may itself institute proceedings before the court. Incidentally this latter possibility includes bringing actions against individual NCBs where the latter have failed to fulfil an obligation under the statute governing the activities of the ESCB and ECB.

We have already identified the central tasks of the ESCB in broad terms, defining and implementing Community monetary policy and so on, but the main text of the Maastricht Treaty and the protocol on the statute assign specific *functions*. The ECB has the exclusive right to *authorize* the issue of notes and a non-exclusive right to *issue notes*. Such notes will be the only notes to have the status of legal tender. The member states may issue coins but subject to control as to volume by the ECB. The ECB will (alongside the NCBs) be empowered to engage in open market operations. It will be able to impose minimum reserve requirements on credit institutions and employ any other method of monetary control which it deems appropriate. The ECB (alongside the NCBs) will be empowered to carry out support operations in the foreign exchange market. By contrast its role in the prudential control of credit institutions is the more limited one of contributing to the smooth operation of the system. However the Council of Ministers has the power to confer specific control tasks on the ECB, insurance undertakings being explicitly excluded from the remit of the ECB. The specific functions of the NCBs can be deduced from the above. Against the general background that they will act in accordance with the guidelines and instructions of the ECB, the NCBs can in particular issue notes and conduct open market and foreign exchange operations.

In the final stage the Monetary Committee is dissolved. It is replaced by an Economic and Financial Committee. Its task is to keep the economic and financial situation of the member states and the Community under review. It is required to report regularly on this issue and may deliver opinions to the commission and council on its own initiative or at their request. The scrutiny of the committee is particularly directed towards the state of affairs in respect of the freedom of payments and the movement of capital.

The Maastricht Treaty opts for central bank independence: more will be said about this later. Article 107 stipulates, and the protocol on the statute reiterates, that neither the ECB, nor any NCB, nor any member of their decision-making bodies shall seek or take instructions from Community institutions, member state governments or any other body. The statute obliges Community institutions and governments to respect this principle. The statute also states that the primary objective of the ESCB in the conduct of monetary policy must be the maintenance of price stability. Without prejudice to that objective it must also support the general economic policies of the Community.

MONETARY UNION: GETTING THERE

There are two problems here: one relates to political will and the other is concerned with the technicalities of achieving convergence. In the first place we have to note that in the final negotiation the UK secured an opt-out arrangement. Under the relevant protocol, the UK is not committed to moving on to the third stage of EMU. This does not prevent it from entering the third stage but such a move would require a separate decision to that effect by the UK government and parliament. The UK is required to notify its intentions to the Council of Ministers before the convergence assessment is carried out. Denmark too signalled that its constitution might imply a need for a referendum before it could enter the third stage. It too is required to indicate its position prior to the convergence exercise and by protocol was granted the right to an exemption. The adverse result in the Danish referendum in June 1992 highlighted the likelihood that a favourable result was not likely to be extracted from the Danish people in a second referendum, unless some accommodations or clarifications could be extracted from the Community. The European Council at Edinburgh in December 1992 endeavoured to provide such assistance by adopting a conciliatory response to the Danish government's statement of concerns. Included in this response was an acceptance of the Danish decision not to participate in the single currency and to retain its existing powers in the field of monetary policy. Denmark, however, is not constrained to this position. Thus in the final analysis both the UK and Denmark could choose to join.

But the problem of political will, or rather the lack of it, is not exhausted by merely reviewing the formal stance of the UK and Denmark. The lack of political will could torpedo the whole exercise. This can be illustrated by reference to Germany, whose government in the run-up to Maastricht came to be one of the most enthusiastic supporters of EMU. It is by no means certain that the German people and their representatives in the Bundestag will meekly accept an *automatic* progression to EMU.

One of the key features of the process of closer European union in the period since 1950 has been the relatively elitist nature of that development. It was based on an essentially 'top-down' process in which the political (and business) elite, with good intentions, made the running. The process was accomplished in an incremental fashion. The steps were always in one direction (closer union) and usually were not sufficiently dramatic to create any great disturbance in the minds of the citizenry. However there is some reason to believe that at Maastricht the elite got rather too far ahead of their electorates. The proposed move towards EMU is far from incremental in the mathematical sense of a small change. It embodies a large step. For Germany, the ditching of the Deutsche Mark is a major undertaking which touches every citizen, his or her pocket and accumulated wealth intimately. Public opinion is not enthusiastic. It has also been argued that the German public was distracted by the issue of German reunification. This tended to draw attention away from the implications of what was being agreed at Maastricht. Only later were the consequences brought home to the voters.

Reviewing the German position, it can be argued that Germany too has an opt-out and that there is no guarantee of an automatic progression. When the Maastricht Treaty was approved through the Zustimmungsgesetz (Act of Parliament implementing the treaty), the Bundestag declared that the future European currency had to be, and had to remain, as stable as the Mark. Most significantly it also claimed for itself the right to vote on entry to the third stage of EMU and said that without its consent entry would not be possible. The government, however, said that it would take any vote into account but that the Bundestag's declaration was not binding. Apparently the opposition maintained that it was binding and was a condition of ratification. Interestingly the German Constitutional Court (the Bundesverfassungsgericht) was at a late stage involved in a challenge to ratification. Its decision of October 1993 fell short of saying that a Bundestag vote would be a constitutional requirement but commentators have concluded that the government of the day will follow that procedure.[5]

The Maastricht Treaty provides for an exercise of political will in 1996, since the move to EMU depends not only on having a majority of converged states *but also on there being a willingness to take the final step*. But in 1998/9, the process seems to imply an automatic step for those who have converged. This is plainly unrealistic and we cannot rule out the possibility that this aspect of the Treaty will be reformed in 1996. In any case the views of any new members will have to be taken into account. However, before members can contemplate moving to the third stage and setting a date, they have to have converged in terms of economic performance. How likely is it that they will?

In 1991, *The Economist* carried out an exercise in which it asked the question, if the test had been carried out at that time, how many states would have satisfied the five criteria. In 1994, the *Financial Times* did a somewhat similar exercise in respect of 1993. The results of both exercises are shown in Table 7.2. The figures, and criteria satisfied without parentheses, relate to 1991, while the criteria satisfied within brackets refer to 1993. In 1991, two states had scored 0 out of 5 and two others had scored 1 out of 5. Only two states qualified – France and Luxembourg. Clearly there was a long way to go! The 1993 data provided by the *Financial Times* only related to the inflation, interest rate, debt and deficit criteria. These have been supplemented by the currency criteria in which (see below) the effects of the turmoil in the ERM have been added. In this connection it has been assumed that, since only Germany and the Netherlands stuck to the old $\pm 2^{1}/_{4}$ per cent band, the rest either left the ERM, devalued or adopted ± 15 per cent band, only Germany and the Netherlands satisfied the currency criteria.

On the above basis, and considering all five criteria, the situation had deteriorated. In 1991, the Twelve scored 31 out of a possible maximum of 60. In 1993, this had fallen to 24. If we focus on four criteria (excluding the currency criterion) then the position had not improved from 1991 to 1993. In fact it had deteriorated slightly, falling from 24 out of a possible 48 to 23. More progress might have been made had it not been for the recession which tended to inflate budget deficits, which had increased in eight out of the 12 states.

As we have seen, the major problem area was in the currency field – exchange rates. As we have noted, the Maastricht criteria require that to qualify a member state currency must for two years have been within the normal band of the ERM of the EMS and not have been devalued. From an exchange rate point of view, the signing of the Maastricht Treaty in February 1992 marked the high point on the road to EMU. From that relatively euphoric point onwards expectations quite quickly began to go downhill. A series of events took place which sent shock waves through the European currency markets. The Danish 'no' vote on 2 June 1992 was probably a critical event in undermining confidence in a smooth monetary transition. Not only did it reinforce the view that the Danes would require special treatment, but it launched an anti-monetary union atmosphere across Europe. In Germany an opinion poll revealed that a majority of Germans were not favourably disposed towards giving up the stable Deutsche Mark in favour of an untried ECU. The 'yes' vote in the French referendum in September 1992 did something to restore confidence in the likelihood that EMU would transpire, but the closeness of the vote gave rise to concern.

Table 7.2   EMU convergence: performance in 1991 and 1993

	Convergence indicators				Criteria satisfied?					Score out of 5		Score out of 4 (excluding currency)	
	Inflation rate	long-term govt bonds	Budget deficit	Public debt	Inflation rate	Long-term govt bonds	Budget deficit	Public debt	Currency				
	latest %		1991 estimate	% of GDP						1991	1993	1991	1993
France	2.5	8.8	−1.5	47	yes (yes)	yes (yes)	yes (no)	yes (yes)	yes (no)	5	3	4	3
Luxembourg	2.4	8.1	+2.0	7	yes (no)	yes (yes)	yes (yes)	yes (yes)	yes (no)	5	3	4	3
Denmark	1.8	8.8	−1.7	67	yes (yes)	yes (yes)	yes (no)	no (no)	yes (no)	4	2	3	2
Britain	3.7	9.7	−1.9	44	yes (yes)	yes (yes)	yes (no)	yes (yes)	no (no)	4	3	4	3
Germany	4.1	8.1	−3.6	46	no (no)	yes (yes)	no (no)	yes (yes)	yes (yes)	3	3	2	2
Belgium	2.8	8.9	−6.4	129	yes (yes)	yes (yes)	no (yes)	no (no)	yes (no)	3	3	2	2
Ireland	3.5	9.3	−4.1	103	yes (yes)	yes (yes)	no (yes)	no (no)	yes (no)	3	3	2	3
Holland	4.8	8.6	−4.4	78	no (yes)	yes (yes)	no (no)	no (no)	yes (yes)	2	4	1	3
Italy	6.2	12.6	−9.9	101	no (no)	no (no)	no (no)	no (no)	yes (no)	1	0	0	0
Spain	5.5	11.7	−3.9	46	no (no)	no (no)	no (no)	yes (yes)	no (no)	1	1	1	1
Greece	17.6	20.8	−17.9	96	no (no)	no (no)	no (no)	no (no)	no (no)	0	0	0	0
Portugal	9.8	14.1	−5.4	65	no (no)	no (no)	no (no)	no (no)	no (no)	0	0	0	0

Notes: The figures in the left-hand section are for 1991. The inflation rate and bond interest rate were the latest percentage rates then available. Deficits and debts were estimates for 1991 expressed as a percentage of GDP. In the centre section the criteria satisfied not shown in parentheses refer to 1991. Those in parentheses relate to 1993.

Source: *The Economist*, 14 December 1991, p. 56; *Financial Times*, 12 May 1994, p. 2.

The speculative pressures and episodes experienced by the ERM will not be discussed in any great detail. Suffice it to say that currency after currency was tested. The lira was devalued in September 1992. Subsequently sterling came under intense pressure and on 16 September (referred to as 'Black Wednesday') massive intervention by the Bank of England failed to prevent the pound from breaching its lower limit against the Deutsche Mark. The lira too came under renewed pressure and both currencies were floated out of the ERM, while the peseta was also devalued. Both Spain and Ireland reimposed exchange controls in order to protect their currencies. In November 1992, further speculative attacks focused on the peseta and escudo and led to a third round of devaluations; in January 1993, the punt went the same way. In May the escudo and peseta were devalued yet again. These references to the pound, peseta, escudo, lira and punt should not disguise the fact that at various times other currencies were in difficulties, plummeting to the bottom of their ERM bands. Notable among these were the French franc, the Belgian franc and the Danish krone. The French policy of refusing to devalue (the *franc fort* policy) inevitably implied high domestic interest rates which ran counter to the needs of its domestic economy, which was moving sharply into recession. Friday 30 July 1993 ('Black Friday') was the most frenetic in the history of the ERM. On Monday 2 August the world woke up to the news that the finance ministers had reformed the ERM. The fluctuation bands had been widened to ±15 per cent for all currencies except the Deutsche Mark and the Dutch guilder.

This year of turmoil highlighted three potential causes of ERM instability. The first was that the single market programme itself, reinforced by the commitment contained in the Maastricht Treaty, had required the removal of controls on capital movements. Vast amounts of footloose money were sitting in the various financial centres of the Community and were consequently absolutely free to move. Moreover the quantity was dauntingly large, sufficient indeed to overwhelm even the most determined central bank. Added to that was the fact that the ERM constituted what might be termed a speculator's charter. Under a floating rate system, speculative movements out of a currency would cause the rate to weaken, thus undermining the expected profit to be made on repurchase of the currency. Under the ERM, member states were obliged to support the rate, certainly not letting it drop below the lower band level. Speculators were therefore supported on their way out and thus could make a healthy profit, if the currency was devalued, when they

repurchased. The third problem was associated with the possible consequences of asymmetric shocks – economic shocks which affect only
one member state and dictate a policy response on its behalf which is
not appropriate to other member states who are not directly affected by
the shock. The asymmetric shock which undermined the system was
German reunification. Its inflationary effects dictated a need for relatively high German interest rates. In the interests of supporting their
exchange rates, other member states were forced to follow the German
interest rate policy although their domestic recessionary conditions
demanded lower rates. Attempts to persuade Germany to cut its interest
rate, as in June 1993, when the French economics minister openly
criticized the restrictive German policy and pressured the Bundesbank
to ease its rates, fell on deaf ears. The Bundesbank's first, and really
only, obligation was to preserve the stability of its own currency and
not to solve Europe's unemployment problem. Inevitably some countries, the UK being an early example, decided to break ranks. Devalu-
ing or leaving the system enabled domestic interest rates to be lowered.

The conclusion drawn by commentators on the ERM was that a
policy of staying put was unsustainable. There had to be a movement
either backwards or forwards. One possible backward movement was
to generally reinstate exchange controls. It will be recollected that
Spain and Ireland had introduced temporary controls in 1992 but this
was by virtue of a special transitional arrangement allowed in the
capital movements directive. The possibility of a general reimposition
was reported to have been advocated by Commission President Jacques
Delors in an address to the European Parliament in September 1993,
but the commission quickly mounted a damage limitation exercise,
claiming that the president had been misinterpreted. An alternative
idea, essentially a backward movement, was canvassed by Eichengreen
and Wyplosz (1993). This involved the imposition of a tax on speculators by, for example, requiring institutions who took an open position
in currencies to make a non-interest-bearing deposit with their central
bank. They argued that, for long-term capital movements of beyond a
year, the cost would be negligible but for short-term round-trips, which
were characteristic of pure speculation, the costs would be high. However Foley pointed out that such a tax would only be effective if
applied in all countries where ERM currencies were traded. Much of
the speculative pressure emanated from outside the EC and it was
unlikely that the authorities in Japan or the USA would cooperate in
such a scheme (Foley, 1993, p. 2). Wyplosz also argued that the most

effective approach would be in fact to move to a quick monetary union (Wyplosz, 1994, p. 4). In short, he appeared to be arguing in favour of the old monetarist approach: to fix the exchange rates irrevocably and force members to converge. However he regretted that this was not an available option, being ruled out by the Bundesbank. Here he was obviously referring to the German preference for convergence first and the single currency second – the old economist stance.

In the event, and as we have seen, the solution chosen was to move backwards by widening the ERM bands for most but not all states. Some commentators felt that this threatened to undermine the process of achieving greater convergence since national rates of inflation could differ significantly before exchange rates fell or rose to the floor or ceiling. On the other hand the wider band was a deterrent to the speculator. Wyplosz argued that the wider bands ought to be declared normal since the defence of realistic parities was less hopeless than was the case with narrow bands. Goodhart was of the view that the perceived benefit of the ERM in forcing convergence had obviously taken a knock. Instead he favoured relatively wider bands or bands with soft edges. In parallel, domestic economic policies should be directed towards the achievement of convergence. In tandem with this, political developments should focus on underpinning the mandate of federal institutions. When convergence had been achieved there should be a quick move to full EMU, thus avoiding a potentially unstable period of pegged exchange rates (Goodhart, 1993).

One thing was clear: if the 1996 convergence assessment was still on the cards then in 1994 the Council of Ministers had to decide what was the 'normal' as opposed to the 'temporary' band since, as we have seen, to qualify in 1996 for the final stage, member states had to have remained within the normal band for two years.

MONETARY UNION: THE FINAL STAGE CONSIDERED

One of the features which has attracted considerable attention is the independence required of the ESCB. The relative merits of dependence versus independence have been subjected to close scrutiny. It is argued that there are significant potential disadvantages for macroeconomic management in having an independent central bank. The first is that it gives rise to a non-optimal policy goal. This is based on the assumption that there is a trade-off between unemployment and inflation. If the independent central bank decides to pursue the goal of price stability, this may be purchased at too high a cost. In other words, a stable price level may entail an unacceptably high level of unemployment. Independence can also give rise to a non-optimal policy mix. Thus a government which enjoyed complete freedom of action could choose what it felt was the appropriate combination of monetary and fiscal policy, but with independence it would lose the ability to dictate the monetary condition and would only be able to manipulate the fiscal condition. Even the room for fiscal manoeuvre would be constrained. For example, if the government sought to provide a fiscal stimulus to the economy by increased spending, financed by borrowing, the effectiveness of the fiscal stimulus would depend on the attitude of the bank. If the bank was not accommodating and allowed monetary conditions to tighten, interest rates would rise and the effectiveness of the fiscal stimulus would be undermined. Finally it can be argued that independence is undemocratic. If the voters do not like the monetary policy of a government they can in due course boot them out of office but an independent central bank is a law unto itself.

On the other side, the advocates of independence point to the possibility that a government may be tempted to misuse its monetary powers. The concept of seigniorage emphasizes the idea that governments may acquire control over real resources by, in effect, printing money rather than by the electorally unpopular method of raising taxes. Also a government's command over real resources can be increased by adopting a lax monetary policy which allows prices to rise, thus eroding the real value of its debt. Finally governments may manipulate the economy for electoral advantage. In other words, they may be tempted to inflate the economy prior to an election in order to make voters 'feel good' and vote appropriately (see, on all this, Masciandaro, 1991, p. 11). All this points to the hypothesis that in the context of a dependent central bank macroeconomic policy will tend to be relatively inflationary, whilst an independent central bank will be associated with relative price stability.

Clearly, to the extent that the differing degrees of central bank independence can be measured (see, on this, Bade and Parkin, 1982, Alesina, 1988) it is tempting to speculate as to what kind of relationship exists between central bank autonomy and inflation. Not surprisingly this has attracted a good deal of academic attention. In Figure 7.1 we present the conclusions drawn by Alesina and Summers on this and other relationships (Alesina and Summers, 1993). The evidence seems to point quite clearly to an inverse relationship: the higher the independence the lower the rate of inflation and the less variable the rate of inflation. However the Alesina and Summers evidence does not suggest that greater bank autonomy will lead to a faster rate of growth of gross national product (GNP) per capita. Enthusiastic advocates of central bank independence therefore seize upon the point that such autonomy leads to lower inflation and at least gives rise to no greater costs in terms of real macroeconomic performance. In a subsequent study, and rather tentatively, De Long and Summers suggest that, after controlling for differences in the initial GDP per worker, there was some evidence that greater autonomy could lead to a better real performance (De Long and Summers, 1992, p. 17).

While independence versus dependence is a relevant subject for debate in respect of the monetary system of a single state, it can be argued that there is really no choice in the context of a monetary union embracing 12, 16 or even more member states. Giving every country a voice in the day-to-day conduct of Union monetary policy, whether via their central bank governors on the board of the Union central bank or through the Council of Ministers, sounds like a recipe for chaos.

Some concern has been expressed about the ability of the ESCB to deliver the goods in terms of price stability. Vaubel has argued that Germany's good inflation performance has owed much to the effect of German public opinion, which is still painfully aware of the disastrous effects of inflation, even though the main episode harks back to the 1920s. The ESCB will be subjected to European public opinion whose preferences are different. He has therefore proposed that the ESCB needs to be under threat of dismissal if it fails to deliver the goods (Vaubel, 1990). Others (see Burdekin *et al.* 1992, p. 241) have suggested that the salaries of the governing council should be tied to the ESCB's inflation performance.

One thing is clear. In the final state, as envisaged in Maastricht, substantial economic sovereignty is given up. This can be most dramatically illustrated by considering the case of a country such as the UK, which originally stands outside the ERM and in which the central bank is still dependent. The chancellor of the exchequer would cease to control the supply of money, interest rates (we are assuming that, being outside the ERM, he enjoyed some discretion in this matter) and the exchange rate; in other words, no more devaluations (or revaluations). He would, it is true, have a say over the exchange rate policy in respect

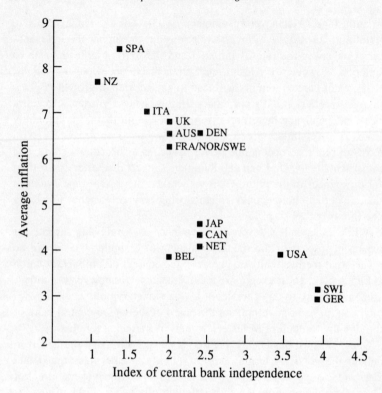

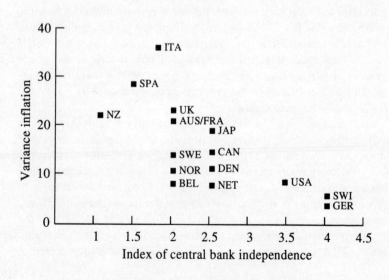

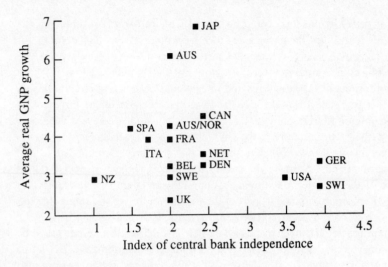

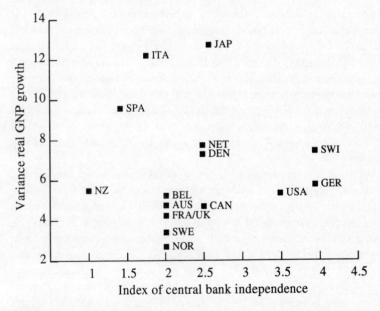

Source: Alesina, A. and Summers, L.H. (1993), 'Central Bank Independence and Macroeconomic Performance: Some Comparative Evidence', *Journal of Money, Credit and Banking*, **25**, (2) (May), pp. 155–6.

Figure 7.1   Central bank autonomy and macroeconomic performance

of the ECU but this would be shared with 11 (or more) other finance ministers. On the fiscal side, too, he would have reduced room for manoeuvre since, as we have seen, budget and debt levels would be subject to Community scrutiny. Not only that, but his freedom of action in respect of tax structures and rates would be severely circumscribed. It is true that he would levy the taxes but, because of the influence of Common Market obligations, his discretion would be severely circumscribed. The structure of the key indirect tax is a *fait accompli*: it has to be the VAT *à la* EC. Ultimately rates will be approximated, if not harmonized. Likewise the range of products subject to excise duties will also be determined by the Community and their structure and rates will be approximated as part of the final unfolding of the single market. The possibility that corporation tax structures and rates will also be harmonized has been discussed earlier. That leaves the income tax to be considered. No proposal has yet been made to harmonize it. But let us not forget that, from 1 November 1993, citizens of the Twelve also became citizens of the Union. In the longer term, states may feel it prudent to keep their tax systems in line with their partners if they are to avoid a drain of talent and revenue. In all this it should be remembered that market forces as well as directives will be exercising a harmonizing influence. The general conclusion which can be drawn is that the chancellor of the exchequer will enjoy a declining significance, while that of the governor of the Bank of England will rise and rise. He will preside independently over the Bank of England and with his fellow governors will independently call the monetary shots in the Union.

It must be conceded that this is an extreme and partial assessment. Since we have focused on a particular minister we have to recognize that, while the UK chancellor may have played a key monetary role, his German equivalent ceded it long ago to the Bundesbank. If, however, we focus on state sovereignty then it is true that both countries have to hand over the monetary role to the ESCB. The degree of monetary policy discretion enjoyed by so-called 'independent states' can of course be exaggerated. The idea that they can choose between different objectives – that is, trade off different rates of inflation against different rates of unemployment – is countered by the proposition that the long-run Phillips curve is vertical. David Llewellyn concludes:

> then the menu of choice disappears and all that an independent monetary policy allows is the ability to choose the actual rate of inflation and not a

choice between unemployment and inflation. In this event, as there is no power to determine real magnitudes in the economy, governments might as well simply choose to agree on a common low level of inflation. Nothing of substance is surrendered by collectivizing monetary policy in this case. (Allen *et al.*, 1992, p. 257)

There is also doubt as to the extent to which countries really lose sovereignty when they cease to be able to devalue or revalue. Llewellyn notes that

> there is considerable doubt as to whether nominal exchange rate adjustments do in practice (in anything other than the short term) have permanent affects on real exchange rates, the balance of payments, or the level of unemployment and output. Because of the growing openness of EC economies, and the erosion of money illusion, there is little evidence that the exchange rate is in fact a powerful instrument to affect long-run competitiveness, as any short-term change in real wages tends to be offset by changes in money wage levels. In this case little is surrendered by eschewing exchange rate adjustments. (Ibid.)

Llewellyn goes on to argue that the argument about loss of sovereignty is about governments' perceptions about their power: in practice, they tend to be reluctant to give it up and to overstate their real influence. To that extent the case against monetary union tends to be exaggerated. Some weight must also be attached to the point that, even if there is a real loss of individual state power, it is likely to be counterbalanced in some degree by the emergence of a collective power from which they can benefit.

Three other features of the final state are worthy of comment. First, the Maastricht Treaty does not place the ESCB in full control of foreign exchange policy. It is charged with the conduct of day-to-day operations, but Article 109 allows the Council of Ministers to determine exchange rate policy. This has attracted some criticism, since governments have been known to prefer undervalued exchange rates and in Germany this tended to undermine the anti-inflationary stance adopted by the Bundesbank (see Burdekin *et al.* 1992, p. 244, citing former Bundesbank President K.O. Pohl). Another notable feature of the Maastricht model is the absence of any provision for a substantial central budget which can transfer resources to member states who experience difficulties in adjusting to the monetary union. As we shall see in the next chapter, in the period up to 1999 the member states have resisted anything more that just a very modest increase in the resources devoted to the Community budget. The third relates to the asymmetry of the budget deficit rule. This, it has been alleged, will give a deflationary bias to the system. Thus if an individual economy in the monetary union suffers a negative demand shock, its level of economic activity and therefore income will fall. This in turn will cause tax receipts to fall and expenditure on unemployment benefit would be likely to rise. If the economy in question was close to its budget deficit ceiling (under union rules) then these two effects would cause it to overshoot its ceiling. In which case the government concerned would have to take preventative action by, for example, raising taxes. But the deflationary effect imposed upon it would not necessarily be offset by any automatic compensatory action elsewhere in the monetary union.

MONETARY UNION: WILL IT EVER HAPPEN?

The only prudent answer which can be given to the above question is that, if it happens at all, it will be later rather than sooner. At the first meeting of the EMI in January 1994, the president, Alexandre Lamfalussy, declared that 'the single currency from 1997 seems an unrealistic perspective for the moment' (De Saint-Chéron, 1994, p. 3). Thus 1999 seems the earliest feasible date for entry to the third stage. No doubt it could happen earlier if the Community was prepared to bend the convergence rules. In April 1984, French European Affairs Minister Alain Lamassoure was reported as saying that the decision as to which countries were fit for the single currency was essentially a political one. Moreover he was of the view that it was inconceivable that Belgium (whose debt level, it should be noted, was far in excess of the Maastricht guideline) would not be a founder member. The governor of the Bank of France, Jean-Claude Trichet, added that the Maastricht debt criterion 'could perhaps be looked at more closely' (*Financial Times*, 1994, p. 3). However these observations seem wide of the mark. The view of the Bundesbank has always been that the convergence criteria are not be tampered with. Of crucial importance is the judgement of the German Constitutional Court to the effect that it is not within the Council of Ministers' discretion to diverge from the criteria laid down in Article 109(j)(1) and in the related Protocol. These criteria cannot be changed without German agreement and the cooperation of the Bundestag.

Even if the final stage is eventually achieved, the question of its durability must also be considered. According to the German court, dissolution of the third stage is a possibility as a last resort if stability is not achieved. The possibility of *unilateral* withdrawals was not discussed by the judges.

NOTES

1. The European Monetary Cooperation Fund (EMCF) came into existence in the 1970s in connection with the original plan to create an EMU by 1980. It was responsible for running the exchange rate arrangement referred to as the 'snake in the tunnel' and in addition was responsible for running the associated very short-term credit facility and the short-term monetary support scheme. Under the EMS the EMCF was empowered to receive monetary reserves from the appropriate authorities of the member states and to issue ECUs in exchange. The latter could be used to settle debts between member states and in transactions with the EMCF.
2. It does not follow that EMU cannot start any later than 1 January 1999. Peter Coffey has pointed out (see *Financial Times*, 28 July 1992) that the final start date of 1 January 1999 only applies *if no start date has been agreed by the end of 1997*. The Community might agree in 1996 to start, for example, on 1 January 2003. Strictly interpreted, the treaty could be read that way, but in practice there would be little logic in assessing in 1996 that the economies had converged, only to leave the actual commencement to, say, 2003, since by the latter date they could have diverged. A decision to enter the third stage taken in 1996 would suggest that the actual third stage would be likely to commence fairly quickly thereafter.
3. The possibility that there will be some jockeying for position cannot be ruled out since a massaging of exchange rates could affect the final conversion rate and produce sizeable once-for-all gains for individual countries.
4. The decision-making bodies are specifically the governing council and the executive board.
5. I am extremely grateful to Philip Hall for help on these legal points.

REFERENCES

Alesina, A. (1988), 'Macroeconomics and Politics', in S. Fischer (ed.), *NBER Macroeconomics Annual* (Cambridge, Mass.: MIT Press).

Alesina, A., and L.H. Summers (1993), 'Central Bank Independence and Macroeconomic Performance: Some Comparative Evidence', *Journal of Money Credit and Banking*, **25** (2) (May).

Allen, D., D.T. Llewellyn and D. Swann (1992), 'A Forward View', in D. Swann (ed.), *The Single European Market and Beyond* (London: Routledge).

Bade, R. and M. Parkin (1982), 'Central Bank Laws and Monetary Policy', unpublished.

Burdekin, R.C.K., C. Wihlborg and T.D. Willett (1992), 'A Monetary Constitution Case for an Independent European Central Bank', *World Economy*, **15**.

De Long, J.B. and L.H. Summers (1992), 'Macroeconomic Policy and Long-Run Growth', unpublished paper (August).

De Saint-Chéron, M. (1994), 'Institute President Lamfalussy unveils his intentions for EMI', *The ECU for European Business*, no. 15 (February).

Eichengreen, B. and C. Wyplosz (1993), *The Unstable EMS*, Centre for Economic Policy Research Discussion Paper, no. 817 (May).

Financial Times (1994), 16/17 April.

Foley, P. (1993), 'Reforming the ERM', *Lloyds Bank Economic Bulletin*, no. 174 (June).

Goodhart, C. (1993), 'ERM and EMU', *LSE Financial Markets Group Special Paper*, no. 58 (November).

Masciandaro, D. (1991), *Central Bank Independence, Macroeconomic Models and Monetary Regimes*, Centre for Monetary and Financial Economics, Università Commerciale Luigi Bocconi, Milan (February).

Vaubel, R. (1990), 'Currency Competition and European Monetary Integration', *Economic Journal*, **100**.

Wyplosz, C. (1994), 'The EMS Crisis: Please Save the Maastricht Treaty!', *The ECU for European Business*, no. 15 (February).

8.　The budget and agriculture in the 1990s

INTRODUCTION

Both the SEA and the Maastricht Treaty on European Union had significant implications for the Community budget. This will be explained later. First, however, we need to consider the budget's origins and nature. The Community budget is the main financial instrument of what, following the Maastricht Treaty, has come to be called the European Union: the three Communities plus the other forms of cooperation covered by the Treaty. It is not of course the sole financial instrument of the Union. Later reference will be made to the EDF, which is financed separately from the budget. In addition, as we noted earlier, the Union possesses several *borrowing* facilities, notably the EIB and the Ortoli facility or New Community Instrument. The budget, however, is effectively a 'taxation' rather than borrowing instrument and the proceeds of that 'taxation' finance the various policies, in the main by feeding monies into certain funds which serve particular policies, such as the CAP.

SIZE AND NATURE

The Community budget, at least in relative terms, is a modest affair. Currently budget spending represents approximately 1 per cent of the combined GNPs of the member states. Budget spending can also be expressed as a proportion of the combined public spending of the member states, in which case the figure rises to somewhere around 3–4 per cent. However, while it is proportionately small, in absolute terms budget spending is nevertheless substantial and member states have been known to get extremely excited about its impact upon them. By 1999, total budget spending will, at 1992 prices, be approximately 80 000 million ECUs. If we allow for the kind of inflation rate incorporated in the 1992 budget calculations then, at *current* prices, the 1999 figure would be of the order of 107 000 million ECUs. With the admission of new members it would be still greater – three new members from EFTA would suggest a (current price) figure of around 116 000 million ECUs.

The budget, at least at its inception, was extremely limited in scope, although later we will see that this has tended to change. In the first place national budgets tend to perform a built-in stabilizer function. That is to say, when the economy expands tax revenues rise, thus removing purchasing power from the system, and expenditure on unemployment pay tends to fall, again holding demand in check. This takes the top off the boom and helps to prevent inflation. In a recession the reverse is the case. Tax revenues fall and unemployment pay rises, both of which help to boost demand and reduce unemployment. Indeed, following the Keynesian revolution, governments came to accept that it was legitimate to use the budget as an instrument of macroeconomic control in which budget deficits were seen as appropriate reflationary devices and budget surpluses were seen as methods of reining in inflationary tendencies. However the built-in stabilizer function and the discretionary budgetary approach are not relevant in the case of the Community budget since its revenue and expenditure structure is not geared appropriately and, most important of all, Rome Treaty Article 199 declares that the budget must balance.

Originally the character of the budget was also limited in another way. Federal systems tend to embody a mechanism of resource transfer in which tax revenues are shifted from the relatively prosperous states, provinces or *Länder* to the poorer states, provinces or *Länder* of a union. Indeed it can be argued that such resource transfers make membership of a federal monetary arrangement tolerable. Since states and so on have in effect surrendered their economic sovereignty by being members of a single currency union, they are, for example, unable to combat a lack of competitiveness and unemployment with acts of currency devaluation. However the possibility of compensating resource transfers renders that prospect less inhibiting. We may describe such resource transfers as the 'Robin Hood function' since, as we recollect, that mythical figure is usually credited with the role of taking from the rich and giving to the poor. However, as we noted earlier, whilst the *preamble* to the Rome Treaty referred to the desirability of reducing disparities between the living standards of the various regions, the Treaty provided no significant grant-giving power to accomplish that end and the original budget did not embody such a provision. What we may term 'Robin Hoodery' was markedly absent, although the loan activities of the EIB did focus on the poorer regions.

The original budget was quite simply a functional budget, in that it was designed to raise revenues to finance whatever policies the Community chose to introduce. Two further points need to be borne in mind. First, we are not asserting that the budget did not redistribute – in fact it did – but the effects could be haphazard and not necessarily egalitarian in character. Second, this lack of a Robin Hood element changed in due course, the key developments being the entry into operation of the ERDF in 1975, the Single Act and the budget reform of 1988 and the Maastricht Treaty and the budget reform of 1992.

POLICY DEVELOPMENTS AND EXPENDITURE IMPLICATIONS

Had the Rome Treaty envisaged nothing more than the creation of a Common Market, then the Community budget would have been of little interest. All that the Community budget would have needed to do would have been to raise sufficient revenues to cover the salaries, expenses, pensions and running costs of the administration – currently the European Commission, Council of Ministers, Court of Justice, European Parliament, Economic and Social Committee, Court of Auditors and so on. In 1999, these will account for just under 5 per cent of budget commitment appropriations.

In fact the Community went well beyond merely setting up a Common Market. Article 3(i) of the original Rome Treaty[1] provided explicitly for the creation of a ESF. Thus, while the vehicle of economic integration was to be competitive trade interpenetration – a feature underlined by Article 3(f)[2] which called for the creation of conditions of undistorted competition – it was obviously possible that there would be losers as well as winners. In short, some firms might shrink or go under, with consequent unemployment for their workers. There was therefore a need to provide funds for the conversion of enterprises to new lines of production and to provide for the retraining and geographical mobility of displaced workers. Here the Community would play a role and its financing would in part proceed from the ESF.

The Rome Treaty also envisaged the creation of a CAP (Article 3(d)[3]). This was to prove exceedingly costly and indeed it is impossible to decouple the story of the evolution of the budget from that of the CAP, since the latter came to dominate the former. To the founding fathers, the idea of creating a European Community which excluded agriculture was quite impossible to contemplate. Europe had suffered from shortages of food and was still significantly import-dependent. The need to guarantee an adequate domestic supply was regarded as absolute. Agriculture was also a substantial employer: farming in the Six in 1958 occupied some 15 million people, or 20 per cent of the working population. It was an important way of life, which demanded protection. The response, in the form of the CAP, is best regarded as a social policy designed to protect and indeed improve the standard of living of those engaged in that way of life. Moreover the European idea was sold to the farmers on the basis that the CAP would provide a better deal than that which they had previously received at the hands of the member state governments. Politicians were of course acutely aware that farmers had votes!

The basic problem was that, if the Community market was open to free importation, many farmers would go to the wall since world market prices were low and the price required by most of the farmers of the Six (many of whom were relatively inefficient small-scale producers) was high. The solutions devised to deal with this problem varied from product to product, but typically for northern temperate products (such as cereals) the general thrust of the price (and thus income) support mechanism was as portrayed in Figure 8.1. SS is the supply curve of EC producers and DD is the demand curve of EC consumers. P_1W is the supply curve of imports from the world market. If free importation had been allowed, the internal price would have ridden down to the world market price level P_1 with equilibrium between supply and demand occurring at J. Only the most efficient EC farmers would have survived: that is, those on the supply curve below C. In order to protect the less efficient farmers, a levy was introduced which raised the price of the imported product: that is, it caused a parallel upward shift of P_1W. A levy of P_1P_2 per unit would in fact lead to equilibrium at F.

More EC farmers would now be protected: those below E on the supply curve. Imports would fall from CJ to EF. However the Community would not be self-sufficient. But we now have to introduce a further factor, namely technological change. Better breeds of animal, improved strains of crop, more fertilizers, more pesticides and so on tended to lead to greater yields per cow, per acre and so on. This tended to cause the supply curve to shift to the right, for example, to S_1S_1. The

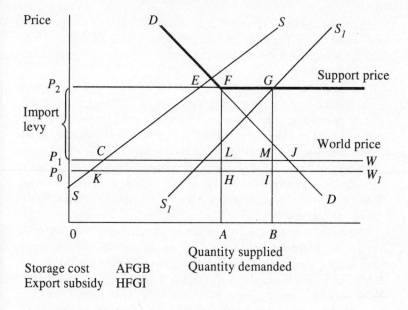

Figure 8.1 Price support under the CAP

combined effect of increased prices and increasing yields was the emergence of surpluses: at price P_2 the surplus is FG. It should be noted that, while supply increased (shifted to the right), the low income elasticity of demand for food meant that demand did not shift commensurately to the right, hence the emergence of the surplus gap such as FG. Here the second aspect of the price support system came to the rescue. If the price was to be held at the support level P_2, the excess FG had to be taken out of the market. One approach was for the appropriate intervention authority to purchase and store FG. In short, the demand curve would become perfectly elastic at the support level P_2. The cost of purchasing the surplus was $AFGB$. Alternatively farmers could be offered an export subsidy of P_1P_2 per unit to enable them to dispose of the surplus on the world market at a loss. The total cost of the export subsidy would be $LFGM$. However if the dumping forced the world price down to P_0 then the subsidy would have to be greater – $HFGI$.

In order to finance these kinds of operation, the Community established the EAGGF, which was fed from the budget. Guarantee money was devoted to price support operations. Guidance money (a very small proportion of total farm spending) was for structural improvements in the farming industry. The Community introduced *common price support mechanisms* for all the major agricultural products. Internal trade barriers were also removed with the aim of leading to common prices for those products.

The expenditure problems of the CAP were exacerbated by the open-ended nature of the support mechanism depicted in Figure 8.1. That is to say, in order to support prices, whatever surplus farmers produced had to be taken out of the market. Because of the tendency for the increase of supply to outstrip the increase of demand (the effect of the low income elasticity of demand) the size of the gap *FG* tended to become greater and greater over time. Unless support prices fell and/or world prices rose, this implied a growing guarantee spending burden which inevitably fell upon the Community budget.

The decision of the UK to seek membership of the Community also contributed to the introduction of a third fund, the ERDF. In the accession negotiations the UK became increasingly aware that the budget might not have a favourable impact upon it. In short, it might find itself paying more in than it got out – it would be a net contributor. This suggested that it would be desirable if budget spending could be structured in a way which benefited the UK. One obvious possibility was the introduction of a regional grant-giving operation since British living standards and the existence of regional unemployment problems held out the prospect that the UK would be relatively well placed to receive regional aid. There was, however, another factor at work. As we noted earlier, by the time of the final UK accession negotiations, the Community had already embarked on the 'EMU by 1980' programme. The Werner Committee reports, which had mapped out the EMU strategy, identified the need for a system of regional transfers as an integral part of a monetary union exercise. The ERDF, again fed from the budget, formally came into operation in 1975.

As we noted earlier, the EEC of the early 1970s was in a bullish mood and at the Paris summit a series of new initiatives were given the blessing of the heads of state and government. These included a policy on R&TD which came to involve the Community in injecting financial contributions into key research programmes in areas of vital technology. This, alongside other internal spending activities, is categorized in Figure 8.2 as 'Other, e.g. R&TD'.

Finally the Community decided to devote some of its budget resources to overseas aid – areas suffering from famine, natural disasters and so on. This aid expenditure must be distinguished from that granted

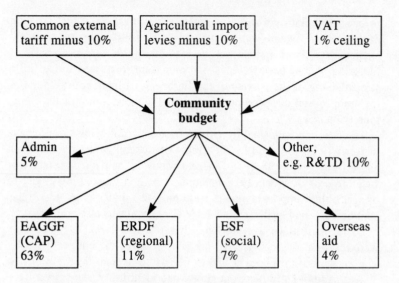

EDF (European Development Fund) financed separately

Figure 8.2   Community budget: original revenue sources, expenditure pattern 1991

to the ex-colonial dependencies under the Rome Treaty Part Four Association provisions, which later gave rise to the Lomé Conventions. This aid, via the EDF, was financed by the member states separately from the Community budget. The relative proportions of these main categories of spending in 1991 are shown in Figure 8.2. It should be emphasized that, on occasions in the 1970s, the EAGGF expenditure percentage could rise to the high seventies. By 1991, it had fallen somewhat and by 1999 it may be down to around 45 per cent.

FINANCING AND CONTROL

At the Hague summit in 1969, the heads of state and government gave consideration to the question of how the spending of the Community should be financed. Previously (here and later we are focusing on the EC) it had been supported by national contributions. However the Rome Treaty provided a clue since it referred to the fact that the Community possessed its 'own resources'. Indeed Article 201 referred to one particular own resource, namely the proceeds of the common external tariff which were actually being pocketed by the national exchequers. It was agreed that the idea of an own resources basis of financing should be developed and alongside this there should be a strengthening of the powers of the European Parliament in relation to the composition of spending and the final legal adoption of the Community budget.

This was accomplished by virtue of a Council of Ministers decision in April 1970, followed by the Treaty of Luxembourg later that year and a further treaty in 1975. These agreements embodied a stage-by-stage process in which the Community was first granted the proceeds of agricultural import levies (in addition to the duties imposed via the common external tariff) and later a VAT element was also added.

Levies and duties were to be collected by the member states who were allowed to keep back 10 per cent to cover the collection costs. The balance of 90 per cent had to be passed over to the Community budget. Additionally the Community had identified a *common* collection of goods which were to be subject to the Community's main form of turnover tax, the VAT. The proceeds of up to a *ceiling* rate of 1 per cent on this collection of goods were also payable into the budget. VAT was paid over not only in respect of those goods which were actually subject to VAT but also of those that were zero rated. These three basic budget resources are depicted in Figure 8.2.

Alongside this arrangement were the procedures in relation to the adoption of the budget. Basically the preliminary draft budget for the coming year emerges from the Commission and is then considered by the Council of Ministers.[4] It in turn adopts a draft budget which it then forwards to the European Parliament. The dialogue which then ensues between these two latter bodies centres on a distinction between compulsory and non-compulsory expenditure. The nature of that distinction, as it existed in 1989, is shown in Table 8.1. It will be apparent that *at that time* compulsory expenditure amounted to about three-quarters of the total and non-compulsory to about a quarter. The dialogue is such that, in the final analysis, the Council of Ministers has the final say over the compulsory expenditure and the parliament has the final say over the non-compulsory element. Having said that, we need to take account of the fact that the parliament's room for manoeuvre is limited by the imposition of a maximum rate on non-compulsory expenditure. The maximum rate is a maximum percentage rate of increase. This is calculated by taking account of developments two years back in (a)

Table 8.1 *The Community budget, compulsory and non-compulsory expenditure: commission's appropriations for payments in 1989**

Section	Non-compulsory expenditure(%)	Compulsory expenditure(%)
Staff and Administration	86.79	13.21
EAGGF Guarantee Section	—	100.00
EAGGF Guidance Section	70.87	29.13
Fisheries	38.96	61.04
Regional Development and Transport	100.00	—
Social Policy	100.00	—
Research, Energy and Technology	99.99	0.01
Development Cooperation	74.68	25.32
Other	—	100.00
% of total appropriations	27.91	72.09

Note: *These arrangements were part of the 1988 Inter-Institution Agreement. Details were changed in the renewed agreement of 1993 which is itself due for reconsideration at the 1996 IGC.

Source: Commission of the European Communities (1989), *The Community Budget: The Facts in Figures*, p. 67.

GNP in the Union in volume terms, (b) variations in national budgets in value terms and (c) the trend in the cost of living in the Union.

It is important to recognize that the percentages of compulsory and non-compulsory expenditure were not set for all time. Indeed we will see later that *relatively major* items in the non-compulsory list are destined to rise during the 1990s, while at least one major item of compulsory spending is set to fall. Thus the budgetary influence of the parliament is bound to rise.

Finally we need to take account of a number of other points. At the end of the process the Community budget only becomes law when the parliament votes to adopt it. The parliament may reject the budget, which requires that two-thirds of the votes be cast for rejection, they representing the views of a majority of its members. In the absence of a budget, the Community can continue to spend but is constrained not to disburse each month more than one-twelfth of what is spent in the previous year. We also need to take account of the Court of Auditors, which came into existence by virtue of the 1975 treaty and which was raised by the Maastricht Treaty to an equal status with the other major institutions. This court is empowered to determine whether all revenue has been received and expenditure has been incurred in a lawful manner and also whether financial management has been sound. Apart from vetting the budget, the Court of Auditors also carries out more detailed value-for-money investigations, somewhat on the lines of the UK Audit Commission. The court does not, however, finally declare budget spending to be proper. Rather there is a complicated process in which the court reports to the Council of Ministers Budget Committee, after which the matter goes to Coreper and then to the Council of Economics and Finance Ministers. But it is the European Parliament which finally has the powers to grant a discharge: that is, to declare budget spending to be proper (House of Lords, 1987, p. 10).

REFORM: STAGE ONE

The own resources method of financing Community expenditure depicted in Figure 8.2 was phased in progressively and did not come into full operation until 1980. When it did so the worst fears of the UK government were realized. The UK emerged as a net contributor, although it was not alone in this respect. To the then British prime minister, Margaret Thatcher, this was an ironic situation when it was set against the fact that, in terms of income per capita, the UK was some way down the list (see Table 8.2). Nor was this a situation which would have commended itself to Robin Hood! It was a product of two factors. UK trade was still significantly oriented towards the rest of the world and this gave rise to significant payments into the budget alongside the VAT element. Additionally the agricultural sector in the UK was relatively small and thus the generation of surpluses, which attract budget spending, was not a major compensating factor in its case.

The result was, as we noted earlier, a demand by the British prime minister for 'her money back'. This in turn led to a series of annual haggles, at the end of which an *ad hoc* rebate was agreed. However the UK sought, if not a permanent rebate, at least an arrangement which would stand for a term of years. This was not the only problem which plagued the Community in a period which we earlier described as being one of Eurosclerosis. It was also increasingly evident that the CAP was running out of control. With it went an increasing agricultural spending burden which forced the Community progressively to in-

Table 8.2   *The Community budget: estimated net budget receipts, 1980 and per capita national income, 1979*

	Estimated net budget receipts for 1980 (£m)	Per capita GDP, 1979, relative to average	
		(a)	(b)
Belgium	+557	124	108
Luxembourg		125	111
Denmark	+188	138	116
France	−248	116	112
Germany	−724	135	118
Ireland	+289	49	61
Italy	+491	62	77
Netherlands	+193	117	105
UK	−1 203	76	91
Community		100	100

Note: GDP (a) is based on a straight exchange rate conversion; GDP (b) is based on 1979 purchasing power parities.

Source: Budget: W. Godley, 'The United Kingdom and the Community Budget', in W. Wallace (ed.), *Britain in Europe* (Heinemann, 1980, p. 73); per capita GDP (b): ibid.; per capita GDP (a): D. Strasser, *The Finances of Europe* (OPEC, 1981, p. 346).

crease the VAT call rate, until it eventually reached the crisis point of the 1 per cent ceiling.

The financial problem facing the budget was addressed at the Fontainebleau summit of 1984. The need for extra revenue was countered by British demands for reform of the CAP and a more durable arrangement in relation to the UK rebate. Solutions were found to all three problems. The Community duly embarked on a serious attempt to reform the CAP by agreeing to the institution of milk quotas. This marked the beginning of the end of the open-ended commitment system. The Community would only support a limited quantity of milk production: with reference to Figure 8.1, if the Community was to aim for absolutely no surplus then it would support P_2F and not P_2G. The UK also secured a more durable rebate arrangement in which it received back two-thirds of the excess of its VAT payments into the budget over its receipts from the budget. In the light of these two achievements, the member states including the UK were agreeable to the raising of the VAT ceiling rate to 1.4 per cent. The new financing basis therefore appeared as in Figure 8.3.

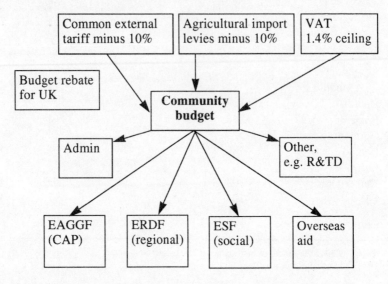

Figure 8.3   Community budget revenue: the reform of 1984

REFORM: STAGE TWO AND THE IMPACT OF THE SINGLE ACT

Although the Community had been invested with additional revenue-raising capacity, by 1986 the message which was coming out of Brussels was that the Community was once more in danger of running into financial difficulties. By 1987, it was forecast that a budget shortfall of some 6 billion ECUs was on the cards, agricultural spending being a major culprit. An agricultural guideline had been associated with the 1984 settlement and this was supposed to hold the line on agricultural spending. However, according to a briefing given by the British foreign secretary in 1988, it had in practice been ineffective, for three reasons. First, it was not legal. Second, it was full of exceptions which allowed spending limits to be breached. Third, the support mechanisms themselves had for the most part not been adjusted so as to enable effective curbs on over-supply to be imposed.

Early in 1987, President of the European Commission Jacques Delors put forward a new plan for the financing of the Community budget. It suggested an own resource ceiling up to 1992 of 1.4 per cent of Community GNP. The funds raised within this limit would be derived from four sources. The first would be agricultural levies *but with no deduction for collection costs.* The second would be the proceeds of the common external tariff, *again with no deduction for the costs of collection.* The third would be the proceeds of a 1 per cent levy on the VAT base, *including goods which were zero-rated.* The fourth would be a levy on what was to be called the additional base, that is the difference between the collection of goods which make up the VAT base and GNP. The additional base levy would, for example, apply to items such as investment which are not included in the VAT base. The total GNP of each member state would therefore serve as a basis for financing the budget, although the rates of the VAT base and of the additional base would differ.

The Delors Plan was considered by the heads of state and of government at the Brussels summit in July 1987. Unfortunately no agreement was forthcoming on the provision of additional long-term financing for the budget. Despite reference in the plan to the need for control of expenditure, as well as the need for greater revenues, the UK prime minister, Margaret Thatcher, rejected the package on the grounds that the provisions on controlling spending, particularly on agriculture, were inadequate. Work continued on the package and it was hoped that sufficient progress would be made for agreement to be reached at the Copenhagen summit in December 1987, but this did not happen. The immediate problem of the budgetary shortfall in 1987 was dealt with by switching to paying farmers in arrears and by other savings.

Matters came to a head at the Brussels summit in February 1988. Extremely tough negotiations ensued in which the UK and the Netherlands demanded strong curbs on agricultural overproduction. A last-minute compromise was finally worked out on the issue of agricultural curbs, the details of which are dealt with below. The new budget accord of 1988, often referred to as Delors I, brought into existence a broad pattern of budgetary income, expenditure and control which in modified form will, as we shall see, continue into the late 1990s. The Budget agreement (European Communities Commission, 1988) first of all incorporated a ceiling on budgetary expenditure. The latter should not, on a payments basis,[5] exceed 1.2 per cent of the combined GNPs of the member states. It also incorporated a financial perspective mapping out

Table 8.3   The Community budget: Delors I financial perspective, 1988–92 (appropriations for commitments)

| | Amounts in million ECU at 1988 prices | | | | |
	1988	1989	1990	1991	1992
1. EAGGF guarantee	27 500	27 700	28 400	29 000	29 600
2. Structural operations	7 790	9 200	10 600	12 100	13 450
3. Policies with multiannual allocations (IMPS, research)	1 210	1 650	1 900	2 150	2 400
4. Other policies	2 103	2 385	2 500	2 700	2 800
of which: non-compulsory	1 646	1 801	1 860	1 910	1 970
5. Repayments and administration	5 700	4 950	4 500	4 000	3 550
of which: stock disposal	1 240	1 400	1 400	1 400	1 400
6. Monetary reserve	1 000	1 000	1 000	1 000	1 000
Total	45 303	46 885	48 900	50 950	52 800
of which: compulsory	33 698	32 607	32 810	32 980	33 400
of which: non-compulsory	11 605	14 278	16 090	17 970	19 400
Appropriations for payments required	43 779	45 300	46 900	48 600	50 100
of which: compulsory	33 640	32 604	32 740	32 910	33 110
of which: non-compulsory	10 139	12 296	14 160	15 690	16 990
Appropriations for payments as % of GDP	1.12	1.14	1.15	1.16	1.17
Margin for unforeseen expenditure	0.03	0.03	0.03	0.03	0.03
Own resources required as % of GDP	1.15	1.17	1.18	1.19	1.20

Source: EC Commission, *Twenty-second General Report on the Activities of the Communities*, Brussels, 1988.

expenditure under broad heads, together with own resource requirements, for the five-year period 1988–92. This is shown in Table 8.3.

It was also agreed that the growth of agricultural spending – specifically guarantee spending – should be held down below the growth of
the Community economy. A figure of 74 per cent of economic growth
was adopted. This agricultural guideline, unlike its predecessor, was
regarded as a legal limit. It was also concluded that the common assessment base upon which VAT was levied should be capped down to 55
per cent of national GNP. No country would pay VAT into the budget
on more than 55 per cent of its GNP. The problem here was one of
budgetary unfairness, in that the value of the goods and services subject
to VAT in the various member states, expressed as a proportion of GNP,
varied considerably. This created a differential burden. Since consump-
tion as a proportion of national income is highest in poorer countries,
the VAT element was actually regressive. This point had been made by
Daniel Strasser, a former director-general for budgets in the Commission, as far back as 1981 (Strasser, 1981, p. 121). This problem arose
again in 1992, when it was pointed out that the average capped VAT
base was 49.3 per cent at a time when some states were capped down to
55 per cent (European Communities Commission, 1992, p. 8). This
suggested that in the case of some states their uncapped VAT base was
more than 55 per cent and might be in the region of 60 per cent, while
others were below 49 per cent and might be as little as 45 per cent.
Considerable unfairness was therefore possible if bases were not capped
down so as to bring the *effective* bases closer together. The heads of
state and government also decided to introduce a new fourth revenue
resource. Each member state would in future pay a uniform percentage
of its GNP into the budget. In addition the UK rebate was continued,
but this time the two-thirds rebate related to the excess of UK VAT and
GNP payments into, over receipts from, the budget. These new arrangements are depicted in Figure 8.4.

On this occasion the budget settlement was also influenced by the
SEA. The reader will recall that the Act incorporated provisions concerned with economic and social cohesion. These had been inserted
with the new members, Spain and Portugal, particularly in mind. Their
ability to cope with the intensified competition which would be unleashed by the single market would be facilitated by a transfer of
resources. This demand was responded to in the budget settlement. It
was agreed that appropriations for the structural funds (ESF, ERDF and
guidance expenditure under the farm fund) should be doubled in real

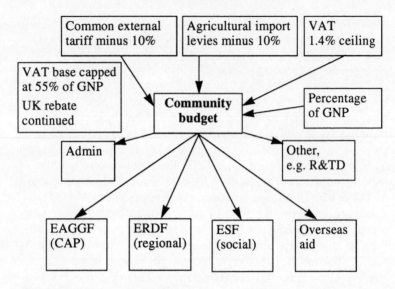

Figure 8.4   Community budget resources: the reform of 1988

terms by 1993 as compared with the 1987 level. In addition it was agreed that the contribution of the structural funds to Objective 1 regions (regions where the per capita income was less than 75 per cent of the Community average) should be doubled. Moreover in this latter context a special effort would be made to help the least prosperous regions. Here we see a definite attempt to inject what we earlier described as a 'Robin Hood' element. The rapid escalation of structural spending is apparent in the second row of Table 8.3. A special programme was also approved for the modernization of Portuguese industry.

As in 1984, so in 1988, budget reform was coupled with CAP reform. Reform had two elements. Set-aside measures would be assisted by grants from the EAGGF. Also budget stabilizers were to be introduced. Under these arrangements a production ceiling would be announced for certain products, such as cereals. If production exceeded these limits, price cuts would be introduced in the subsequent marketing year and such cuts would cumulate if output persistently exceeded the stipulated limit. This is illustrated in Figure 8.5, where the output limit is $0A$. If the support price was initially $0P_1$, output would be likely to exceed the limit by MN. It was assumed that, if a price cut of P_1P_2 was imposed the following season, the surplus would decline to QR

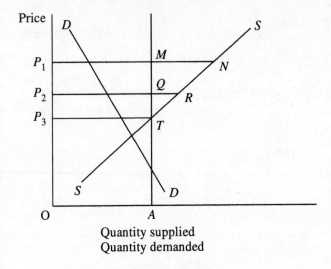

Quantity supplied
Quantity demanded

Figure 8.5   Budget stabilizers

and that, if a further cut of P_2P_3 was imposed the following year, the output level would finally shrink to the stipulated ceiling at T.

REFORM: STAGE THREE AND THE MAASTRICHT TREATY

This is an appropriate point to pause and ask the question, was the Community's budgetary system of the 1988–92 period a fair one? An interesting study by Bowles and Jones of the impact of the budget in the 1985–9 period throws some light on this (Bowles and Jones, 1992, p. 100). Some of their findings in respect of 1989 are shown in Figure 8.6. Here per capita income in the 12 member states is measured on the horizontal axis and national net contributions per head are shown on the vertical axes. Those greater than zero are net contribution levels per capita and those less than zero are net benefits per capita. The general thrust of the relationship is from bottom left to top right, but there were some curious anomalies. The richest member state in per capita income terms (Denmark) was actually a net beneficiary per capita to almost the same extent as the poorest state (Portugal). Spain, only half as well off in per capita terms as Denmark, ended up in balance. Indeed participa-

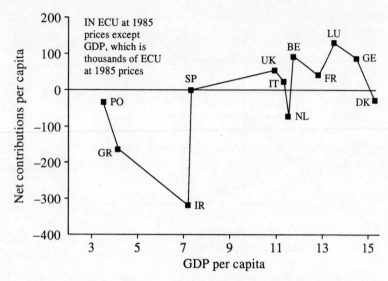

Source: Bowles, R. and P. Jones (1992),' Equity and the EC Budget: A Pooled Cross-Section Time Series Analysis', *Journal of European Social Policy*, **2**, (2).

Figure 8.6   Community budget: net contributions and GDP, 1989

tion in the budget appeared to qualify as one of the biggest non-events in Spanish history! The Irish Republic, however, did extremely well and the varying experiences of these two countries (with relatively similar per capita income levels) were mainly due to the differential impact of Community budget agricultural expenditures.

In Chapter 5 we noted that, in the lead-up to the two IGCs, Spanish demands centred on the need for further transfers of resources. The budget experience of 1989 of course helps to explain that reaction. Interestingly the Spanish were joined by the Irish although, as we have just noted, the latter were at that time in a much more favourable position. Spain couched its demand under three heads: (a) contributions to the budget should be progressive, that is related to the ability to pay; (b) the budget should have an equalizing aim, that is it should provide funds for investment in physical and human capital in countries where the GDP per capita was less than 90 per cent of the Community average; (c) where member states had to contribute towards Community-financed projects, allowance should be made for the ability of the state to contribute (Gardener, 1991). This condition would be met if, for example, in the case of a grant to Denmark, the Danes had to find three-quarters of the cost of the project and the Community but a quarter, while in the case of a grant to Portugal the proportions would be reversed.

The result of Spanish-led pressure was in fact the incorporation in the Maastricht Treaty of a protocol which involved a commitment to establish a Cohesion Fund before 31 December 1993. This would provide budget-financed contributions for projects in the fields of the environment and trans-European networks in those member states whose per capita incomes were less than 90 per cent of the Community average. The obvious beneficiaries were Spain, Portugal, Ireland and Greece. No actual figure was mentioned. That was left to be settled in the negotiations leading to the new budget agreement which would operate from 1993 onwards.

During 1992, the opening shots were fired in the run-up to the new budget agreement. Commission President Jacques Delors put forward the commission's proposal on future spending (this is generally referred to as Delors II). The March 1992 version sought to persuade the heads of state and government to endorse a raising of the spending ceiling from the 1988 level of 1.20 per cent to 1.37 per cent. This encountered stiff opposition from Germany, faced with the burden of reunification, and the UK, itself in favour of tight controls on public expenditure. There were also some rumblings about the continuance of the British rebate.

The final shape of the budget spending and revenue programme was agreed at the Edinburgh summit in December 1992, when the UK was occupying the presidency (see Table 8.4).[6] It was decided that the own resources ceiling should rise to only 1.27 per cent and not to the 1.37 per cent desired by the commission. The need to keep spending down also revealed itself in a lengthened financial perspective, seven years rather than five, and in the delaying of most of the increase of the ceiling until towards the end of the decade. Respecting the need for more budgetary fairness, the heads of state and government agreed to further cap down the VAT base to 50 per cent of GNP. This change was to occur in 1995 in the case of the poorer countries but in four equal stages from 1995 to 1999 in respect of the richer ones. The VAT rate was to be lowered from 1.4 per cent to 1.0 per cent in four equal stages from 1995; this applied to all member states.

Changes on the spending side were particularly significant and represented a further move towards a budget which transfers resources to the poorer members. First, the Cohesion Fund was formally established,

Table 8.4 The Community budget: Delors II European Council Agreement, December 1992. *Financial perspective table*

	Appropriations for commitments (ECU million 1992 prices)						
	1993	1994	1995	1996	1997	1998	1999
Agricultural guideline	35 230	35 095	35 722	36 364	37 023	37 697	38 389
Structural actions	21 277	21 885	23 480	24 990	26 526	28 240	30 000
(a) Cohesion Fund	1 500	1 750	2 000	2 250	2 500	2 550	2 600
(b) Structural Funds & other operations	19 777	20 135	21 480	22 740	24 026	25 690	27 400
of which: Objective 1 regions*	12 328	13 220	14 300	15 330	16 396	17 820	19 280
Internal policies	3 940	4 084	4 323	4 520	4 710	4 910	5 100
External action	3 950	4 000	4 280	4 560	4 830	5 180	5 600
Administrative expenditure	3 280	3 380	3 580	3 690	3 800	3 850	3 900
Reserves	1 500	1 500	1 100	1 100	1 100	1 100	1 100
(a) Monetary reserve	1 000	1 000	500	500	500	500	500
(b) External action							
emergency aid	200	200	300	300	300	300	300
loan guarantees	300	300	300	300	300	300	300
Total commitment Appropriations	69 177	69 944	72 485	75 224	77 989	80 977	84 089
Appropriations for payments required	65 908	67 036	69 150	71 290	74 491	77 249	80 114
Payment approps as % of GNP	1.20	1.19	1.20	1.21	1.23	1.25	1.26
Margin for unforeseen expenditure (% GNP)	0.01	0.01	0.01	0.01	0.01	0.01	0.01
Own resources (% GNP)	1.20	1.20	1.21	1.22	1.24	1.26	1.27
Total external expenditure	4 450	4 500	4 880	5 160	5 430	5 780	6 200

Notes:
The inflation rate applicable for the budget is 4.3 per cent.
*Lagging behind.

Source: European Council, *Conclusions of the Presidency* (Edinburgh, 11–12 December 1992).

162

with a rising financial allocation in real terms. Second, structural spending was to rise significantly in real terms: the 1999 level would be 41 per cent above that of 1993. Most significant of all, the bulk of such spending was to be devoted to Objective 1 regions – regions lagging behind with income levels less than 75 per cent of the Community average. This expenditure runs from 12 328 million Ecus in 1993 to 19 280 million Ecus in 1999.

The combination of the Cohesion Fund and the biasing of structural spending to the poorest regions meant that countries such as Spain obtained a very good deal at Edinburgh. By 1993, Spain had become a substantial net beneficiary. It should be added that the UK rebate was allowed to continue.

FEATURES OF THE 1993–9 BUDGET

Overall budget spending is set to rise. In real terms the budget spending of the Twelve in 1999 would be 27 per cent greater than that of 1992. Current price spending would obviously rise even faster and the adhesion of three ex-EFTA states would also help to boost the total. Indeed, as we noted earlier, by 1999 these two latter factors could mean that, on a current price basis, the 1999 spending level would be 83 per cent up on the 1993 level.

Of particular interest is the relative future levels of agricultural and structural spending. As we have seen, the Community had already been through two phases of agricultural reform, in 1984 and 1988. Unfortunately the 1988 budget stabilizer experiment appears not to have been a great success. The growth of Community production was checked but not stopped permanently by the introduction of stabilizers. After an initial decline, both production and intervention stocks contained their upward trends. The problem appeared to be that price cuts do not lead to a reduction in output. Rather, if farmers receive less per unit of production, they tend to compensate by increasing output, for example by securing greater yields per acre and so on. What was needed was a system which would break the linkage between the reward to farmers and their production. This is precisely what the third phase of agricultural reform, the McSharry proposals, aimed to do. In June 1992, the Council of Ministers adopted a set of proposals[7] which embodied what was claimed to be a fundamental reform of the CAP (OJ, 1992). They sought to decouple production and reward.

Rather than reviewing every sector of the new policy, we will concentrate on cereals (including oilseeds and pulses) and livestock since the approach to them exhibits the core of the new philosophy. Over three years, starting in 1993/4, the price of cereals would be reduced by 29 per cent, bringing them close to world levels. Larger arable farmers would be required to take 15 per cent of their land out of production if they were to receive compensation for the price cut. This set-aside will itself help to reduce production. In addition the compensation for the price cuts will relate to *historic* yields per acre. Thus, to that extent, if a farmer increases his yield per acre he will receive no more per acre since compensation will be based on *what he used to produce per acre.* This, together with the price cut, will reduce the incentive to increase output. It is hoped that the balance of farm renumeration expenditure will tend to shift from export subsidies[8] to direct income compensation. Lower cereal prices will feed through as lower input costs (and therefore output prices) for those using cereals in cattle, pig and poultry rearing. A less intensive, more environmentally friendly farming system will emerge. In the case of livestock, a similar approach has been adopted. Farmers are being encouraged to reduce their stocking levels – the number of cattle per acre. Again they will be directly compensated for adopting this less intensive and more environmentally friendly method of production.

In all this it is apparent that environmental considerations are becoming a more important aspect of the CAP. This is in line with more recent environmental action programmes, notably the fifth, and with new Article 130 inserted by virtue of the Maastricht Treaty. They have emphasized the importance of integration – that environmental considerations must not just be peripheral but must be a central consideration in the formulation of all policies.

Despite the reform of the agricultural support system it is instructive to note that, in real terms, CAP spending will continue to rise right up to 1999. However, as Table 8.5 indicates, as a proportion of budget spending it will fall while, not surprisingly, structural spending will rise proportionately. The structural fund spending of the Community was itself reformed in 1993 (OJ, 1993). Of particular note were the changes in the areas designated as Objective 1 regions. East Berlin and the East German *Länder* were now included. In the case of the UK, the Highlands and Islands of Scotland and Merseyside were added to Northern Ireland (already on the list) as areas entitled to assistance. The full list of eligible regions is shown in Table 8.6.

Table 8.5   Allocation of commitment appropriations, 1992 and 1999

	1992	1999
CAP	53.1	45.7
Structural	27.9	35.7
Internal (e.g. RT&D)	6.0	6.0
External action (i.e. aid)	5.5	6.7
Administration	6.0	4.6
Reserve	1.5	1.3
	100.0	100.0

Table 8.6   Objective 1 regions

Belgium	Hainaut
Germany	Brandenburg, Mecklenburg–Western Pomerania, East Berlin, Saxony, Saxony–Anhalt, Thuringia
Greece	Entire country
Spain	Andalucía, Asturias, Cantabria, Castilla y León, Castilla–La Mancha, Ceuta y Melilla, Comunidad Valenciana, Extremadura, Galicia, Canary Islands, Murcia
France	French overseas departments, Corsica, the 'arrondissements' of Avesnes, Douai and Valenciennes
Ireland	Entire country
Italy	Abruzzi (1994–6), Basilicata, Calabria, Campania, Molise, Apulia, Sardinia, Sicily
Netherlands	Flevoland
Portugal	Entire country
United Kingdom	Highlands and Islands Enterprise area, Merseyside, Northern Ireland

Source: *Official Journal of the European Communities*, L193, 31 July 1993.

In the period to 1999 the contributions of the VAT source will change. During the 1980s it tended to increase as a proportion of budget revenue – both levies and import duties fell proportionately over the same period. By 1991, VAT was providing about 54 per cent of budget revenue. This will now change as the VAT base is further capped down and the VAT rate is reduced. Increasingly the Community will have to rely on the GNP-related element.[9] The budget will be increasingly financed on a proportionate, but not a progressive, tax basis. The idea of a fifth resource was examined in the lead-up to the 1992 budget agreement, but no progress has yet been made on that issue.

The whole of the 1993–9 financial perspective will of course alter as a result of the membership of ex-EFTA members. They are expected to be net contributors. During the accession negotiations they obtained various forms of transitional relief, the details of which will be discussed in Chapter 9. In relation to Community GDP, the budget will continue to be small. It has a long way to go before it can emulate the redistributive capacity of current federal systems and as yet hardly provides a credible safety net for those who approach EMU with trepidation.

NOTES

1. As did Article 3(i) of the revamped Rome Treaty following the Maastricht Treaty-based amendments.
2. Now Article 3(g) of the revamped Rome Treaty following the Maastricht Treaty-based amendments.
3. Now Article 3(e) of the revamped Rome Treaty following the Maastricht Treaty-based amendments.
4. This is a somewhat simplified view of the proceedings since the budget committee of the council and Coreper itself are also involved.
5. Payment appropriations define actual expenditure to be incurred in the financial year. Part of the payments may be in settlement of commitments made in a previous year. Commitment appropriations refer to pledges made this year but perhaps falling due for actual payment in a subsequent year.
6. The assumption behind these figures was that GDP would increase by 2.5 per cent per annum.
7. The McSharry reforms also included an agri-environmental scheme designed to foster a more environmentally friendly agriculture, an early retirement package and an afforestation programme: see Regulations 2078/92, 2079/92 and 2080/92 which are commented on in House of Lords, *Fourteenth Report from the European Communities Committee*, Session 1992–3.
8. In 1992 the Community and the US concluded the Blair House Accord – part of which required cuts in export subsidies.
9. A rough calculation suggests that by 1999 the VAT proportion could be as low as 35 per cent and the GNP figure could rise to 51 per cent. In 1991, the VAT proportion was 54 per cent.

REFERENCES

Bowles, R. and P. Jones (1992), 'Equity and the EC Budget: A Pooled Cross-Section Time Series Analysis', *Journal of European Social Policy*, **2**.

European Communities Commission (1988), *Bulletin of the European Communities*, no. 2 (Brussels).

European Communities Commission (1992), *The Community's Finances Between Now and 1997*, COM(92) 2001 final (Brussels).

Gardener, D. (1991), 'Southern discomfort', *Financial Times*, 18 June.

House of Lords Select Committee on the European Communities (1987), *Court of Auditors*, 6th Report, Session 1986–7.

OJ (1992), *Official Journal of the European Communities*, L181, 1 July 1992.

OJ (1993), *Official Journal of the European Communities*, L193, 31 July 1993.

Strasser, D. (1981), *The Finances of Europe* (Luxembourg: Office for Official Publications of the European Communities).

9.   The magnetism of the European Union

INTRODUCTION

Various groups of countries have been, or are over various time scales, anxious to become part of the European Union, hence the title of this chapter. The broad picture is as follows. EFTA, which came into existence in 1960 as a rival block to the EC, began to dissolve very quickly as, within a year of signing the founding Stockholm Convention, the UK had indicated its desire to join the Community. However that aim was frustrated until 1973. When the UK and Denmark finally deserted EFTA, the rump of EFTA states each signed reciprocal free trade area agreements with the EC. These abolished tariffs and quotas on trade in industrial goods and on a limited range of processed agricultural products. That arrangement in turn, as we shall see below, was succeeded by the European Economic Area (EEA) agreement which in practice was, for some, merely a temporary waiting room. Subsequently four key members of the EFTA rump, Austria, Finland, Norway and Sweden, applied for full European Union membership, and all except Norway successfully negotiated accession terms, ratified the agreements and became members on 1 January 1995. Switzerland had held a referendum on EEA membership and it had been rejected. Although the Swiss did apply for full Union membership, this would now appear, in the light of the EEA referendum, to be in cold storage. The other countries which signed up to the EEA agreement were Iceland and Liechtenstein.

The second group of countries with membership aspirations are located in the Mediterranean.[1] The oldest aspirant is Turkey. Turkey and Greece were the first outsiders to take advantage of the Article 238 provision. Both the Greek association agreement, which entered into operation in 1962, and the Turkish arrangement, which commenced in 1964, involved substantial transition periods but specifically envisaged full membership at the end of the process. Both were thrown off course by lapses from democracy, but Greece, following the restoration of a democratic system, was admitted in 1981. By contrast, Turkey's membership application, which was formally lodged in 1987, has been delayed by three factors. The first is its relative economic backwardness. Other backward economies have been admitted, but in the case of Turkey the problem is compounded by its size: it has a population of about 50 million, whereas that of Greece is only 10 million. The second problem derives from its record in the fields of fundamental rights, the rule of law and representative government. The European Parliament has been highly critical and it is a general principle that Community membership requires a clean bill of health on these issues. Moreover, as we saw earlier, the parliament now has the final say on the admission of new members and it is safe to say that it will insist on being satisfied in respect of Turkey's record on fundamental rights and legal and political processes. The third problem arises in connection with Cyprus. Greece, like every other member, has a veto on new members and will not be disposed to accede to Turkish membership until the Cyprus issue is satisfactorily resolved.

On the other hand, as John Pinder has pointed out (Pinder, 1991, p. 57), there is a case for encouraging the fragile Turkish democracy and there are strategic reasons for consolidating Turkey's relationship with Western Europe. The commission's opinion on Turkey's application was that its economic and political system had some way to go before it could satisfy Community requirements. Apparently this was endorsed by the European Council. The Turks have been told that they cannot join until after the year 2000, if then (*The Economist*, 1994, p. 40).

Both Malta and Cyprus, each of which has an association agreement with the Union, lodged applications in 1990. The commission indicated that it saw no insuperable obstacle to Malta's adoption of the *acquis communautaire*. In connection with its constitutional neutrality, the Maltese government indicated that it saw no obstacle to its participation in the CFSP, including any future defence aspects. The commission did see the need for significant restructuring of the shipyard, pointed out that there would need to be a root and branch reform of the regulatory and operational framework of the Maltese economy and doubted whether Malta had the expertise to play a full role in the Community institutions, most notably the presidency. In respect of the Cyprus application the commission also saw no difficulty in its adoption of the *acquis*; the unresolved dispute over the partition of the island was the major stumbling block.

Both of these economies are very small – the population of Malta is only about 360 000 and that of Cyprus is 700 000. Their smallness poses the major problem of how to fit them into the Community's institutional structure. There is also obviously bound to be some concern among the larger countries about their continued ability to block measures which they fundamentally disapprove of, an issue which reared its ugly head at the end of the EFTA membership negotiations. It therefore seems likely that nothing will happen until after 1996 when, it is hoped, the conference to review Maastricht will have had an opportunity to consider such matters. At the Corfu summit in June 1994, the European Council stated that the next phase of enlargement would involve Cyprus and Malta, but was subject to the resolution of the Cyprus conflict.

The third group of aspirants are located in Central and Eastern Europe. Following the collapse of the Communist system in Central and Eastern Europe, the demise of the Council for Mutual Economic Assistance (CMEA) in 1991 and the liberalization of economic and political systems, most of these economies quite quickly expressed keenness to become full members of the European Union. In the vanguard are the Visegrad Four (Poland, Hungary, the Czech Republic and Slovakia)[2] who signed European association agreements with the European Union. At the Copenhagen summit in June 1993, the heads of state and government declared that those Central and East European Countries (CEECs) who so desire shall become full members. A major obstacle is their need to satisfy the necessary economic and political conditions, although the European Council did ominously draw attention to another possible stumbling block, namely the ability of the Union to absorb extra members (see below). Not surprisingly the Visegrad Four want early membership (particularly Hungary and Poland, who have thrown their membership hats in the ring) and hope it will occur by the year 2000. A further group consisting of Bulgaria, Romania,[3] Slovenia, Albania and the Baltic Three (Estonia, Latvia and Lithuania) declare that membership is a medium-term goal. The European Union has however set its eastward boundary so as to exclude Russia and the other ex-Soviet republics (with the exception of the three Baltic states). Russia and the ex-Soviet states have been offered partnership and co-operation deals; Russia and the Ukraine led the way in 1994.

THE EFTA GROUP

While it is true to say that the EFTA countries enjoyed a comparatively privileged status *vis-à-vis* the Community, in that they were involved in reciprocal bilateral free trade arrangements from 1973 onwards, they were not entirely satisfied with the relationship. They began to press for closer ties. This process began in 1984 as a result of a joint meeting between EFTA and the EC in Luxembourg. This gave rise to the Luxembourg Declaration and the so-called 'Luxembourg Process.' Twenty-five working groups were established, and charged with the task of injecting into the EFTA–EC relationship three basic principles: multilateralism (without new institutions), a political commitment to the special nature of the relationship and the introduction of elements of Common Market integration into the free trade system – to create a European Economic Space (EES) (Weiss, 1989, pp. 331–65).

Some progress was made but it seemed insufficient when compared with the dynamic process initiated in the EC following the Single Act of 1986. Moreover, in 1989, Commission President Jacques Delors, when addressing the European Parliament, expressed some doubts as to whether the existing framework was adequate and the EFTA heads of state expressed similar sentiments in the subsequent Oslo Declaration of 15 March 1989. This in turn led to exploratory negotiations and to the signing on 2 May 1992 in Oporto of an agreement creating the EEA (Laredo, 1992, p. 1200; see also Pederson, 1991). The main features of the agreement were as follows. First, the four freedoms of the single market were to apply throughout the EEA. This implied free movement of goods, services, capital and people. Second, an EEA competition regime, based on the existing EC competition rules, would aim to ensure competition throughout the EEA. Third, there would be closer cooperation between the EC and EFTA in a number of important areas, including R&D, education and the environment. Fourth, EFTA would set up a new fund to assist some of the poorer regions of the EC. Fifth, new institutions would be set up to administer the agreement and ensure that both sides complied with the rules. Finally, the EEA would be based on a dynamic agreement, in that EFTA would take on new single market measures as they were adopted and would have an opportunity to influence new proposals (Department of Trade and Industry, 1992, pp. 4–5).

The free movement of goods involved the removal of NTBs, further tariff reductions and a simplification of trading procedures. The NTB

aspect required the EFTA countries to adopt most EC legislation concerned with technical and safety regulations. However this did not
mean that standards would be the same for all states. Thus the EFTA
countries could specify higher standards for their own manufacturers
but would not be able to exclude products from other EEA states. The
NTB aspect also involved a ban on discriminatory taxation and an open
public purchasing policy. State monopolies would no longer be able to
pursue marketing and purchasing policies which discriminated against
products emanating from other EEA states. The tariff reductions involved the abolition of protection (including quotas) on a range of
manufactured food and drink products not included in the old bilateral
free trade agreements. Tariffs on imports of fish and fish products were
also to be abolished or gradually phased out. The CAP of course
remained inviolate!

The free movement of services meant that the provisions of the
Second Banking Directive (see Chapter 4) would apply throughout the
EEA. Professional, commercial, telecommunication and transport services would also be liberalized. A Common Market element would be
introduced in that the EEA agreement introduced a right of establishment for EEA nationals throughout the area. Free movement of people
was also provided for – EC and EFTA nationals had the right to work
throughout the EEA. They would be free to accept offers of employment in any EEA country, could stay in that country to work and,
subject to status, could remain there afterwards. The EEA agreement
also removed restrictions on the movement of capital belonging to
EEA companies and individuals.

The agreement aimed to achieve a common approach to competition
by extending the EC competition rules to the whole of the EEA. This
covered cartels, abuses of dominant positions, mergers and state aids.
Parallel to the European Commission and European Court of Justice,
an EFTA Surveillance Authority (ESA) was to be established in order
to guarantee that the rules were enforced in the EFTA. A division of
labour was prescribed which decided which authorities dealt with cartels, dominant firms and state aids, but all merger cases fell to the
European Commission.

Fisheries were bound to be a difficult problem, largely because of
Norway's interest in the matter. In the final agreement EFTA undertook
to give the EC greater access to its fishing opportunities. The EC share
of the total allowable catch of North Norway cod was to increase from
2.14 per cent to 2.9 per cent. This in turn was allocated to various EC

states. On top of this some additional Norwegian cod was to be made available to the poorer countries in the EC, specifically Spain, Portugal and Ireland.

An EEA financial mechanism was established which provided funds for the less favoured regions of the EC. Over five years, EFTA was required to provide 500 million ECUs by way of grants and an interest rate subsidy of 3 per cent on 1.5 billion ECUs of loans. Northern Ireland was a potential beneficiary.

Apart from the competition institution already referred to, the agreement also set up an EEA Council where ministers from the member states of the EC and EFTA could meet in order to give political direction, whilst day-to-day matters would be under the direction of an EEA Joint Committee. Originally it had been decided to create a joint EEA panel of judges to resolve disputes over the interpretation of EEA laws. However the whole EEA accord was thrown into doubt when the EC Court of Justice declared against the joint panel arrangements on the grounds that the panel would undermine its autonomy as the Community's supreme court. The EEA Joint Committee was therefore substituted at the last moment. This was cleared by the EC Court on the basis of an understanding that the committee's decisions would not be contrary to its own rulings.

Many of the economic arrangements outlined above are reminiscent of the kind of system which had existed in the European Community. However the EEA was based on a free trade area and not a customs union. The ex-EFTA states did not participate in the CAP. Nor were they involved in the EMS or committed to the EMU. They were also outside the Community budget (although they had to pay an 'entrance fee'), played only a limited role in the shaping of EC legislation and were excluded from participation in the CFSP (Department of Trade and Industry, 1992, pp. 29–30). This could have been regarded as an ideal arrangement. EFTA enjoyed the benefits of the larger market and retained some independence in areas such as monetary and foreign and security policy. Why, then, did the larger EFTA states quickly decide to apply for full membership of the European Union? Three reasons suggest themselves. First, while the larger market was attractive to the EFTA states, there was an economic and political cost in not fully participating in the process whereby internal market rules were set. The Norwegian prime minister made this point to the Norwegian parliament in December 1992:

In order to regain control of many of the forces that shape our daily lives, we must be able to make democratic decisions that truly enable us to meet our challenges. It is no longer possible ... to tell Norwegian voters that we can carry out all our tasks by means of decisions in Norway alone. If we cut ourselves off from the fora where important decisions are made, we are in reality restricting our own freedom of action ... Unless we ourselves decide otherwise, the EC may in a few years' time comprise all of Europe except for Norway, Iceland, certain countries in the Balkans and Russia.

A second reason is connected with neutrality. Austria, as we will observe in Chapter 10, had been precluded from economic union with Germany as part of the 1955 State Treaty. The ending of the Cold War lifted this inhibition. Thirdly it could be argued that neutrality was particularly significant in a polarized Europe, but participation in the CFSP was less of a challenge when the Cold War threat had largely evaporated. For countries such as Finland, the ending of the Cold War did not totally extinguish concerns about Russian intentions and the future direction of its political system. To Finland the EC was valuable because of the safe haven which it afforded.

The negotiations between the EFTA Four and the EC threw up a number of problems. Neutrality, which had always been seen as a stumbling block, certainly in the case of Sweden, Finland and Austria, proved not to be a problem – no doubt for the kind of reasons outlined above. The CFSP (and also cooperation on judicial and home affairs) were quite easily absorbed. In connection with the free movement of goods, one of the major concerns of the applicant countries was the need to maintain a high level of health, safety and environmental protection after accession. Closer inspection revealed that these fears were largely groundless, but for a limited range of cases acceding countries could maintain their own rules for four years. All the EFTA Four had specific rules regarding the purchase of holiday homes (secondary residences) by foreigners. They were allowed to retain these rules for five years. The Nordic alcohol monopolies were a matter of some concern. The Four agreed to modify their rules regarding import and wholesale monopolies. Given that the Court of Justice had not pronounced on retail monopolies, they were allowed to continue, provided that they did not discriminate against the products of other member states.

Road transit was a major issue for Austria, as regards the environmental impact. Whereas in the Community heavy goods vehicles normally enjoy unrestricted passage (provided certain rules are satisfied), the danger to Alpine passes and the narrow valleys leading to them had led the Community to conclude a bilateral agreement with Austria. This involved an 'ecopoint' system of transit licences. It was therefore agreed to continue with the plan for a target reduction of 60 per cent by 2003 in the pollution from heavy lorries in transit through Austria. To help achieve this, extra rail capacity and a new tunnel under the Brenner pass were identified as supportive measures.

Agriculture was bound to cause problems, since the national systems of the Four had to deal with difficult natural conditions, were important for environmental reasons and enjoyed price and support levels above those of the Union. The Four wanted transitional periods for prices and adaptations of the CAP which would take account of their particular problems. The Union, for its part, wanted to maintain a single market and insisted that the Four should adopt common prices immediately. This latter point was finally accepted, together with compensation payments to cover price reductions. These would be degressive but there would be a safeguard mechanism in case of market disruption. The mountain areas and less favoured areas, to be designated in the Four, would also be able to benefit from income support programmes designed to help farmers coping with difficult climates and terrain.

Fishing proved to be one of the most difficult problems, being, as we have already noted, of particular concern to Norway. Norway's initial position was quite firm: the Norwegian fisheries minister declared that Oslo 'had no fish to give away', a view not to the liking of the Spanish. Eventually a solution was found which involved the agreement of Norway to consolidate the fishing possibilities it had allocated to the Union in the context of the EEA agreement and the granting of certain additional fishing possibilities.

The acceding countries attached considerable importance to being able to continue their regional policies since, while generally prosperous, they do have areas of low income and high unemployment, together with problems stemming from low-density populations in remote northern regions. It was possible to envisage Burgenland in Austria as an Objective 1 region. It was also decided to create a new Objective 6, which would permit the designation of areas with very low population densities. In respect of the Community budget, the Four were expected in due course to be net contributors but, while accepting the *acquis* in full, they won a temporary budget rebate (disguised as a farm adjustment payment) which together with other sweeteners was worth 3.6 billion ECUs over four years. The necessary institutional adjustments were to be made (in the case of majority voting against some British objections) which included adding four more commissioners to the existing body of 17. This of course had the potentiality to cause problems since, as we shall point out in Chapter 10, it is widely argued that there are too many already.

In the event Norway, in a referendum, yet again rejected membership. This left an untidy situation, with Switzerland in EFTA (but looking for special arrangements), Norway in the EEA and the other three aspirants as full members.

CENTRAL AND EASTERN EUROPE

Until 1989, trading relationships between the Community and the CEECs were extremely limited. Sectoral trade agreements on textiles, steel and meat products had been made with some CEECs prior to the establishing of diplomatic relations. Romania was the only CMEA country with which the EC had a *general* trade agreement, concluded in 1980. A general agreement had also been concluded with Yugoslavia in 1970, but it was of course outside the CMEA (European Commission, 1993, p. 1; see also Fleming and Rollo, 1992). However the revolutionary events in Central and Eastern Europe changed all this. The two Germanies were reunited on 3 October 1990, the heads of state and government agreeing that this could be accomplished without a revision of the treaties.

Of extreme importance was the decision of the Group of Twenty-Four Countries (G24) to set on foot an aid package. This decision emerged from the Western Economic Summit held in Paris in 1989. It gave rise to Operation Phare. The Commission was given the task of coordinating this economic assistance. The Phare programme became operational in 1990 for Poland and Hungary and was subsequently extended to cover all the CEECs, including Slovenia but not the other states of the former Yugoslavia. The purpose of Phare was to support the process of economic restructuring and encourage the changes necessary to build a market-oriented economy and promote private enterprise. According to Brewin, a major aspect of the Phare programme is privatization. For example, it pays for the Polish Ministry of Privatization (Brewin, 1993, p. 78). The grant money made available under Phare has been accompanied by loan monies from various sources. The EIB has been authorized to extend its investment activity to Poland, Hungary, the Czech Republic, Slovakia, Romania and Bulgaria. The

Community has guaranteed these loans. The ECSC can also make loans to the CEECs for restructuring the steel and coal industries and has earmarked monies for this purpose.

Operation Phare also gave rise to the establishment of the European Bank for Reconstruction and Development (EBRD), which opened for business in London in April 1991. Its aim is 'in contributing to economic progress and reconstruction ... to foster the transition towards open market-oriented economies and to promote private and entrepreneurial initiatives in the Central and Eastern European countries committed to and applying the principles of multiparty democracy, pluralism and market economies'. The bank's capital, 10 billion ECUs, was initially to be provided by 42 shareholders: 40 countries, the European Community and the European Investment Bank (EIB). The Community, the member states and the EIB were to hold 51 per cent of the bank's capital, and the Community, represented by the commission, was to have one governor and one member on the board of directors. The EBRD is able to make or guarantee loans to enterprises in the private sector, and also for infrastructure improvements and to state-controlled enterprises being privatized or managed according to the principles of free competition. It is also able to invest in or finance investment in the capital of such enterprises. Up to 40 per cent of bank finance is for the public sector, the other 60 per cent of its funds being destined for the private sector.

A series of trade and cooperation agreements were concluded with most of the CEECs. Such an agreement was signed with the former Czechoslovakia, but not separately with the Czech and Slovak Republics. The agreement with the former Yugoslavia is no longer in operation but an agreement was signed with Slovenia in 1993. The agreements were subsequently replaced by association agreements referred to as Europe Agreements. These Europe Agreements (which are similar but not identical) were bilateral – between the Community and the country in question. They aimed to establish bilateral free trade in industrial products but were asymmetrical in that in each case the Community undertook to remove protection more quickly than the individual CEEC partner. Substantial protection was to remain, however, for a group of sensitive industrial products. This has attracted some criticism (Rollo and Smith, 1993) and had led to concessions on the part of the European Union.[4] Agricultural trade was mostly excluded from liberalization. The Community can impose voluntary export restraints (VERs) and has already done so in respect of some CEEC exports.

There are provisions for the right of establishment, freedom to supply services and free movement of labour. It would be a mistake, however, to assume that the latter provides for unrestricted movement of workers. Rather the agreements confirm existing agreements limiting the number of workers authorized to work in the European Union. In the second five years of the ten-year period, the Association Council can examine ways of increasing labour movement. There are also provisions relating to capital movements and currency convertibility in order to enable investment to take place and goods and so on to be paid for.

An important feature of the agreements is the insertion of competition rules and limits on state aids to industry. Financial cooperation is also covered and the Phare programme is incorporated in the agreements. There are political provisions, which open a so-called 'political dialogue'. The agreements seek to support the new political orders in the CEECs and to facilitate their integration into the community of democratic nations. The key question which they pose is that of ultimate membership of the European Union. The Europe Agreements 'only recognize that the final objective of the CEECs is to become EU members' (Baldwin, 1994, p. 125). However, as we have seen, the 1993 Copenhagen summit accepted that, if they desired full membership, they should have it. But there were qualifications. One related to the ability of the Community to absorb them – and that is where the real problem arises.

The burden on the Community budget of a Visegrad enlargement would be very considerable. This is partly because of the Four's agricultural structures (they are relatively dependent on agriculture). As a result, CAP spending would have to rise markedly. Additionally, because of their low incomes, combined with a total population of 64 million, structural spending would also escalate. If the Visegrad states enjoyed similar terms to those at present existing in the European Union, Baldwin argues that there would have to be a 60 per cent rise in Community budget contributions of the current (1994) members (Baldwin, 1994, p. xvii). Adding other CEECs would make matters worse. Reducing the generosity of current spending programmes would be a possible solution but would be violently opposed by the poorer current European Union states. Denying the Visegrad members access to CAP and structural spending would amount to second-class citizenship and would be offensive to them. Incidentally Baldwin identifies two other potential problems. First, the CEECs as full members could attempt to use their voting power to screw even more resources out of the European Union. Second, migratory flows, though not necessarily vast, could cause problems by being concentrated in particular areas.

The structural spending problem is of course partly due to the fact that the European Union was able to grant generous terms to its poorer states because, relatively, their populations are not overwhelming. Adding the Visegrad Four would significantly change the pattern of rich versus poorer states and *a fortiori* matters would be changed radically if all the CEECs joined. Baldwin has suggested a solution which also deals with a weakness of the present European Agreements which, being bilateral, do not adequately handle the need for liberalization in intra-CEEC trade. He suggests a staged process. The first stage would involve weaving the European Agreements into a single multilateral arrangement. At a later stage those who were in the vanguard of the reform movement could be admitted to an arrangement similar to the EEA discussed above. Eventually the process of economic development would mean that their budgetary impact would render them less of a problem as full members.

While the issue of membership has this far been largely viewed as economic, there is also a foreign policy and security aspect in respect of which progress also needs to be made. This is briefly discussed in Chapter 10.

NOTES

1. While the countries on the southern rim of the Mediterranean (specifically those involved in the Maghreb and Mashrek agreements) are not eligible for full membership, in October 1994 the commission did propose that they should be brought closer to the EC by being involved in arrangements similar to the EEA.
2. Visegrad is a small town on a bend of the Danube in northern Hungary. Here Hungary, Czechoslovakia and Poland held a summit meeting in 1991 at which they agreed a comprehensive cooperation statement which centred on European integration.
3. Bulgaria and Romania had also signed European Association agreements by 1994, and Slovenia was about to negotiate one.
4. These included a speeding up of tariff cuts, reducing the period for phasing out tariffs in sensitive sectors, increasing quotas for sensitive goods and increases in the scope for imports of agricultural products.

REFERENCES

Baldwin, R.E. (1994), *Towards an Integrated Europe* (London: Centre for Economic Policy Research).

Brewin, C. (1993), 'External Policy Developments', *Journal of Common Market Studies*, **31**.

Department of Trade and Industry (1992), *The European Economic Area* (London).

The Economist (1994), 'A touch of eastern promise', 26 March.

European Commission (1993), *European Community relations with the countries of central and Eastern Europe* (London).

Fleming, J. and J.M.C. Rollo (1992), *Trade Payments and Adjustments* (London: Royal Institute of International Affairs).

Laredo, T.L. (1992), 'The EEA Agreement: An Overall View', *Common Market Law Review*, **29**.

Pederson, T. (1991), 'EC–EFTA Relations: An Historical Outline', in H. Wallace (ed.), *The Wider Western Europe* (London: Pinter).

Pinder, J. (1991), *European Community: The Building of a Union* (Oxford: Oxford University Press).

Rollo, J. and A. Smith (1993), 'The political economy of Eastern Europe trade with the European Community: why so sensitive?', *Economic Policy*, **16**.

Weiss, F. (1989), 'EC–EFTA Relations: Towards a Treaty Creating a European Economic Space', in A. Barav and D.A. Wyatt (eds), *Yearbook of European Law* (Oxford: Clarendon Press).

10. Community dynamics and future problems

INTRODUCTION

The 50 years since the end of the Second World War have seen a transformation in the state of and relations between the nations of Western (and indeed Western and Eastern) Europe. Bitter hostility and division have been, and are still being, replaced by closer economic and political cooperation and integration and (notably in Western Europe) the economic devastation of the immediate postwar period has been superseded by an enviable level of economic prosperity. The original ECSC, confined to only two economic sectors and six member states, has been complemented by the overall economic integration associated with the EEC (now the EC) and it is now accompanied by a CFSP and by cooperation on judicial and home affairs. The European Union, as we now call this collective endeavour, has been successively extended to include first nine, then ten, 12 and now 15 states, with a host of aspirant East European and Mediterranean states impatiently waiting in the wings. The Union now looks forward to the possibility of yet a further deepening of economic integration by virtue of the transformation of the Common Market into an EMU. Additionally strong pressure continues to be exerted in favour of conferring greater decision-making powers and democratic legitimacy on the institutions of the Union. The prospect of defence being added to the CFSP was explicitly foreshadowed in the Maastricht Treaty. The peoples of the member states are, admittedly slowly, recognizing that they are citizens of the larger Union and thereby enjoy certain rights.

This is a remarkable transformation. In this final chapter we will endeavour to explain how this state of affairs has come about. What forces and processes have contributed to this closer union? These forces and processes will be described as European dynamics. At the end of the chapter we will recognize that problems still remain and the issues which still lie on the table will be identified.

THE DYNAMICS OF EUROPEAN INTEGRATION

Clearly a motivating factor was the devastation of two world wars, both of which involved Europe, the first being almost totally confined to Europe. In the first the military dead amounted, on minimum estimates, to some 8 500 000, while the civilian figure was of the order of 6 642 000. In the Second World War, but not just in the European theatre of operations, the military dead amounted to 15 600 000, with civilian dead being estimated at 35 899 000. To this must be added at least 5 100 000 Jews, gypsies and other groups who were exterminated. It should be added that some of these figures, notably those relating to civilians, have been said to be greatly under-reported. While 1945 and after, and the associated desire to turn over a new leaf and find a better way of conducting international relations, provides a realistic starting-point for the historian of European integration, we need to recognize that the European idea, in earlier times the concept of a Christian Europe and later of a European federal union, had a variety of advocates over the centuries. Nevertheless the really practical steps were post-1945 in origin. In the immediate postwar years numerous private organizations, dedicated to the federal ideal, sprang into existence and the climax of all this was the European Congress at The Hague in May 1948, organized by the International Committee of Movements for European Unity. Winston Churchill, President of Honour, opened the proceedings in the Netherlands parliament building. Eight hundred delegates from all over Western Europe attended. Significantly the Congress included a powerful German delegation, led by the future German chancellor, Konrad Adenauer. The result was the formation of the European Movement, with a National Council in each country. In due course it was to be principally responsible for the establishment of the Council of Europe, although this was a disappointment to the Europeans who looked forward to the development of European institutions which involved at least an element of supranational decision making and possibly a federal structure. Of course there were other bodies at work, such as the Action Committee for the United States of Europe, set up by Jean Monnet in 1955 as a purely private committee.

The goals of this broadly based European movement have continued to exert an influence on the course of European integration. Thus while, as we noted earlier, the word 'federal' did not appear in the European Parliament's Draft European Union Treaty of 1984, clearly it reflected such an aspiration and some of its aims were realized in the SEA and the Maastricht Treaty. Keen federalists have continued to rise to positions of major influence in national and European politics. Thus the UK opposition in 1994 to Jean-Luc Dehaene (the then Belgian prime minister) as a successor to Jacques Delors was partly grounded in his well-known sympathy for a federal Europe, although it has to be admitted that the main reason was the steamroller tactics of Germany and France.

The European movement has been a significant propelling force, but other factors have also been at work. We cannot ignore the 1963 Franco-German Treaty of Friendship and Cooperation. This was very much a product of two leading statesmen, President Charles De Gaulle and Chancellor Konrad Adenauer. De Gaulle was not a keen advocate of the Community method, and Franco-German relations have not always been smooth, but there is no doubting the fact that the reconciling effect of that Treaty on the two main actors, coming as it did after the bitterness engendered by two world wars, did help to underpin the development of closer relations in Western Europe.

This brings us to Germany which was, and continues to be, a major factor in the unification process. The first exercise in postwar economic integration, the ECSC, was precipitated by the need to decide how to react to the Germans. As we have seen, the answer to German economic expansion was that it could be contemplated provided it was locked into a European framework. More recently Germany has continued to be a formative factor, in that its enthusiasm for EMU was at least partly inspired by the expectation that such an earnest of good European intentions would evoke a matching acceptance by the rest of the Community of the unification of the two Germanies. The positive and leading role which Germany is now seen to play in the process of European unification was reflected in President Clinton's public declaration in 1984 of the overriding importance which he attached to US–German relations.

External forces also played a major role in the emergence and strengthening of the European Community. The first point to note is the encouragement which the USA has always given to the development of closer unity in Europe. Thus the Marshall Plan for aid to a devastated postwar Europe led to the convening of a conference and to the establishing of a Committee for European Economic Cooperation (CEEC). The attitude of the USA was that the CEEC would not just provide the USA with a list of needs. Rather the USA was of the view that aid giving should be accompanied by progress towards European unification and that aid giving should indeed be linked to such progress.

However an even more important external unifying influence proceeded from Eastern Europe, specifically from the USSR and its satellites. The Cold War provided a threat which impelled the countries of Western Europe to pool their efforts and at the same time, and for the most part, to look to the USA for defensive support. The threat which galvanized their collective responses was not just the prospect of Russian tanks advancing across the North European plain but also the possibility of internal political subversion: both France and Italy had large Communist parties. But the end of the Cold War did not mean that Eastern Europe ceased to provide a stimulus to the development of the European Community. Quite the contrary: it has released another set of influences which have served to further heighten its significance. First, the relaxation of East–West tension has meant that the 1955 State Treaty ban on economic union between Austria and Germany, which had previously been regarded as preventing full Austrian membership of the EC, could be set aside. Second, the newly independent and liberalizing economies of Eastern Europe (notably Poland, the Czech Republic, Slovakia and Hungary) now look to the European Union for aid, trade links, eventual full membership and, it is hoped, a security guarantee. The Community for its part recognizes the importance of responding positively, thus tying them into the democratic system. The decline of the Communist system has not of course led to a new political tranquillity. Some of the impulsion which has led EFTA, as well as East European states, to look to the EC has been the fear of political instability and ethnic tensions in parts of Eastern Europe, together with the possibility that, if the Yeltsin regime failed, Russia might lurch violently and dangerously to the extreme left or right.

These have been the broad influences which have helped to propel the European Community forward. In addition we have to take account of those factors, internal to the Community process, which have been conducive to success. First, we have to pay tribute to the intelligence, imagination and foresight of those who drafted the original Rome Treaty. This is rarely done. Such were the policy competences, decision-making powers and institutions which were written into the Treaty that most of the problems which could have arisen in the process of creating the Common Market were anticipated. It is true that certain specific powers were missing (such as an effective power to control mergers) and that the detailed methods of implementing certain policies were not specified in advance (for example, the CAP and CTP). However this did not constitute an insuperable problem. The architects of the treaty, wisely recognizing that differences existed, contented themselves with laying down the broad aims, or at least identifying key areas for action, and left the rest for determination later. In any case the treaty contained two forms of flexibility: Article 235 enabled extra powers to be taken to achieve already agreed objectives, while Article 236 enabled new objectives (with appropriate powers) to be identified. In short the Community was not saddled with a treaty which reflected the needs and aspirations of the 1950s: it could be adapted to meet future needs.

The institutional arrangements devised by the founding fathers were also imaginatively conceived. Three particular features of the decision-making structure stand out: the role and influential position enjoyed by the commission, the system of decision making within the Council of Ministers and the capacity of the Court of Justice on occasions crucially to move matters forward. The particular virtues of the first two are best appreciated by contrasting the Community system with that found in the now quite considerable range of integration exercises which exist in various parts of the globe. Not all integration exercises incorporate a permanent central executive body and, in the case of those that do, the body involved is usually quite small. Generally they seem quite weak when compared with the administrative resources but above all with the right of initiative and delegated enforcement powers enjoyed by the European Commission.

But the influential role played by the commission has not just been a product of these factors. It can be argued that the commission's authority has been reinforced by the fact that it holds the moral high ground. It is supposed to divorce itself from the service of particular national interests. Above all it, in particular, stands for a new and better means of progress in the reconciliation of diverse and conflicting national interests. By contrast, and perhaps trailing our coat a little, the Council of Ministers could be regarded as the villain of the piece, the place where national self-interests rather than the Community interest can be, and on occasions are, nakedly deployed. There is some evidence that the influence of this moral high ground is quite infectious. It was reported that at least one commissioner, put forward by Margaret Thatcher in the hope of stopping the rot, proceeded to disappoint her by going native. However too much should not be made of the contrast between the commission and the Council of Ministers. The infection which has been known to overtake individual commissioners is also capable of spreading to members of the national permanent delegations in Coreper. For example, Alan Clark observed in 1986, when attending a Council of Ministers meeting in Luxembourg, 'This morning I reported early to the Council Chamber and was soon closeted in the UKREP suite with officials. They were twitchy but curious. Totally Europhile' (Clark, 1993, p. 138).

The commission enjoys great potential influence within the system, but it is important to recognize that its effectiveness depends on the enterprise and skill of the commissioners and in particular the president of the commission. Under some presidents, as David Allen has reminded us (see Chapter 3), the Community has languished for a while. Here we have to acknowledge the reinvigoration which the Community has exhibited since 1985, under the energetic leadership of Jacques Delors. His achievements, in conjunction with individual commissioners such as Lord Cockfield, include the SEA and the completing of the single market, the Social Charter, the Delors I and II budget packages and the EMU programme. The achievements of the Delors Commission did not, however, just consist of pushing forward major programmes of action but were also characterized by greater ingenuity in ways of achieving policy goals. This point was emphasized in Chapter 4.

The second dynamic feature of Community arrangements is associated with the decision-making system of the Council of Ministers. We are of course referring to their capacity to take decisions by qualified majority vote. We can contrast this with integration exercises such as the Association of South East Asian Nations where unanimity is the invariable rule and the result is 'an endless process of consultations and negotiations. The outcome is that only a few common projects are implemented' (Jovanovic, 1992, p. 266).

The third body of particular importance in this context is the Court of Justice. It is important not just to see the court as a body on the sidelines which ensures that the major actors play by the rules. On a number of occasions the court has, through its judgements, removed logjams and moved matters decisively forwards. Two instances spring to mind. The first relates to airline deregulation where, prior to the SEA, no single market existed and competition was markedly absent. The problem was that the Council of Ministers was reluctant to introduce competition into scheduled airline operations and had not introduced an implementing regulation which would enable the commission itself to fully apply Article 85, including sanctions, to the airline sector. However, in 1986, a breakthrough occurred in the *Nouvelles Frontières* case (CMLR, 1986). This concerned a French budget travel company which had sold air tickets at lower prices than those sanctioned by the French authorities. The case was first heard by a French court which decided to refer the matter to the European Court of Justice for a preliminary ruling. The important feature of the court's verdict was the additional light it threw on the position which arises when an implementing regulation does not exist. This new light suggested that the commission's hands were not entirely tied: there was a way out. Thus the commission could at least investigate the various agreements entered into in the airline industry and might then decide to prohibit them, in which case *national courts* would have to take cognizance of the fact that the agreements in question were null and void. This would then open the door to lawsuits against airlines. Such cases would of course require that those bringing the suits had the required legal standing and that the commission had made the correct decision in the first place. Up to June 1986, the commission stayed its hand, hoping that the Council of Ministers would agree to a liberalizing package. When that failed to materialize the commission decided to commence proceedings against the airlines. These proceedings were obviously likely to provoke the ministers of transport into achieving an agreement, as it was always possible that the cases instigated by the commission would outlaw the restrictions in their entirety, whereas the Council of Ministers was willing to contemplate only a limited degree of competition. This move seems to have done the trick, since the ministers ultimately agreed to introduce the liberalizing package discussed in Chapter 4. The ministers having acquiesced to the introduction of competition, the commission then agreed to withdraw the cases.

Much the same kind of process arose in connection with the merger-controlling regulation of 1989. The commission had been unsuccessfully trying since 1965 to persuade the council to grant it such a power. The council was in part ultimately provoked into acceptance by the *Philip Morris* case (CMLR, 1988) in which the Court of Justice indicated that certain kinds of merger were capable of being attacked under Article 85, and this had the added advantage that there was no need to prove the existence of a dominant position. The commission took immediate advantage of the new situation, indicating that it would not hesitate to make full use of this new approach. The case also raised all kinds of procedural uncertainties and it became obvious that a regulation was necessary to restore some degree of legal certainty. Rather like *Nouvelles Frontières*, this case suggested to the council that it had to act if it was to retain control of the situation and in both cases the single market was as a consequence advanced and the commission emerged as the winner.

We turn now from the properties of the institutions to the characteristics of the processes which the Community has employed in order to deepen and widen the integration of the economic and political systems of the member states. A key characteristic has been the *top-down* nature of the process. To a large extent, European integration has been elitist in origin: political, business and professional elites have judged it to be a good idea and the citizenry have been disposed to accept their judgement. European unity cannot be said to have been delivered because the mass of the people positively demanded it. This top-down process has been successful because, certainly until recently, it has been characterized by what may be called the 'incremental approach'. The conferment of powers on the Community institutions, at the expense of the member states, has been incremental – using the word in the mathematical sense of a relatively small change. In other words, individual changes, transfers of sovereignty and so on have not been so dramatic that they could not be sold back home, by heads of state or ministers, to their parliaments and electorates. This was certainly the case until recently. However, as we indicated in Chapter 7, there is some evidence that at Maastricht the elite got more than a little ahead of their citizens: ditching the Deutsche Mark is, after all, more than just another incremental change.

A good example of the cumulative consequences of incrementalism is provided by the European Parliament. It started out with relatively little power. It was in no sense a legislature. It had to be content with being consulted. Its only significant power was to censure the commission, but it had no say over reselection. But by a series of small steps it has grown in significance. First it acquired a power over some kinds of budget spending which, incidentally, will over the next few years become proportionately more important. It also acquired a power formally to adopt or reject the budget as a whole. Following a report of the Court of Auditors it was also empowered to grant a formal discharge of previous budget spending. In the 1986 SEA, the new directly elected parliament moved forward to the cooperation procedure and acquired positive assent powers over trade agreements and new members. At Maastricht it was granted a negative assent power and now played a key role in the appointment of the commission. Each step was relatively small and in itself not greatly controversial (even Margaret

Thatcher and John Major agreed to some of it) but the cumulative effect was significant and there may be more to come.

Allied to all this has been the 'ratchet principle'. A ratchet is of course a toothed wheel which can move round in one direction, with a catch mechanism preventing the wheel ever moving backwards. In short the movement is all one-way. This has been the case in the relationship between member states and the Community institutions. The former have handed powers over to the latter – but not the reverse. The proposal to renationalize the CAP would have been an example of the latter, but it never happened. However if, following an enlargement from Eastern Europe, the cost of the CAP became excessive it might yet happen. The Community has also extended its policy competence with a process which can best be described as exploiting treaty generalities. The classic case is environmental policy. As we noted in Chapter 4, the word 'environment' did not appear anywhere in the Treaty, but that did not stop the Community of the 1970s from introducing directives which went well beyond the needs of the single market. The secret was to view them as measures which led to 'an accelerated raising of standing of living', while the prevention of noxious gases blowing across frontiers could no doubt be said to facilitate 'closer relations between the member states': in short, the generalities of Article 2 came to the rescue.

The Community has also embraced what may be described as the 'foot-in-the-door' principle. Here is an abstract example. One way of extending the Community's competence is first to get the policy area on the Community agenda, that is, at least to have it formally declared to be an area of Community concern and collective endeavour. Next time round it may be possible to invite member states to contemplate the possibility that progress might be facilitated if the area could actually be brought within the legislative process; to avoid too much provocation this might be broached as subjecting it to unanimous voting. At yet a later stage it might then be possible to invite the member states, in the interest of greater effectiveness, to agree to shift, perhaps selectively, to qualified majority voting. Aspects of social and environmental policy are areas where a progressive change of status has been evident.

The process of integration was also facilitated by the spillover process, which was discussed in Chapter 1. There seems little doubt, in the light of EC experience, that economic integration both generates forces and provides rationales which lead to greater integration, both economic and political. It is also important to recognize that economic integration does not proceed purely through the legislative process, as with directives designed to harmonize product standards or financial regulation. It also operates through the agency of market forces. Thus, once the cross-frontier trade in goods has been liberalized, some degree of fiscal harmonization is ultimately likely to follow, even if no specific tax rate-harmonizing directive has been agreed. For example, in the case of VAT, the destination principle may eliminate one form of distortion (that is, imported goods are taxed at the same rate as home-produced goods) but this does not prevent cross-frontier shopping as consumers take advantage of lower VAT rates abroad. This is likely to generate pressures, notably from high-rate country retailers in border regions, for some compensating adjustment of tax rates.

The Community has also benefited from two-tier integration. When first enunciated this was felt to strike at the very heart of what the word 'community' really meant. In practice it is a means by which the Community can make progress without being held back to the lowest common denominator. It is not unreasonable to expect that the laggards will ultimately come into line – all the more so if the previously controversial move proves advantageous. The process worked in respect of UK membership of the ERM and has now been formally assumed since under Maastricht EMU does not require 100 per cent membership. In a more diverse Community, embracing East European economies, two (even three) tier arrangements seem highly likely (see below).

Another factor which has facilitated the integration process has been the ineffectiveness of those member states which were least enthusiastic about it. Here the UK was well to the fore. Lord Cockfield has argued (Cockfield, 1994, pp. 131–45) that Margaret Thatcher was less than fully conversant with the basic treaty texts and does not seem to have been aware of the underlying dynamics and implications of the EC. To be effective those who seek to resist change must be as well briefed, indeed better briefed, than their opponents. There is also the point that it is difficult to say no to everything. Some concessions, conscious or unconscious, have to be made, and were indeed made.

This description of Community dynamics would be greatly deficient if it did not draw attention to one other aspect of the way in which Community policies have unfolded. At first glance it might be concluded that, given the commission enjoys a right of initiative and is required to act with independence, the policies which emerge are essentially a product of an objective assessment of the needs of the

Community, untrammelled by sectional interests. However such a view would fall well short of the truth. In fact what emerges is the product of trade-offs in which member states grant concessions in return for concessions. Sometimes such trading relates to a particular issue, but it may be that a concession on one issue is granted in return for a concession received on another. The emergence of the CAP was a classic instance of this process at work. Indeed the Community made progress through a series of minor crises. For quite long periods the original Six failed to resolve their problems. The solution to them was left to marathon sessions of the Council of Ministers, during which package deals were evolved. It has to be added that threats and blackmail played their part. The evolution of the CAP owed a good deal to veiled threats from the French that they would withdraw if *appropriate* progress was not made. The history of the Community is littered with examples of strong-arm tactics. The Spanish demand for a transfer of resources as a condition for its agreement to EMU is a case in point. In 1994, we witnessed a naked example of linkage. This arose in connection with Italy's failure properly to implement milk quotas, a case which is referred to later. Italy faced the prospect of a massive fine and judged that in any appeal before the Court of Justice the balance of probabilities was that it would lose. In order to head off an outright legal confrontation but secure a reduced out-of-court settlement, it implied that, if forced into court, it would not find itself able to ratify the 1992 Community budget agreement. Spain was also involved.

PROBLEMS STILL ON THE TABLE

Lord Cockfield has observed, 'The Community always goes forward; never backward ... At times progress may be slow to the point where it appears almost to have stopped: but in due time progress will be resumed' (Cockfield, 1994, p. 64). If this process is to continue, what are the problems that will have to be addressed?

One concerns the general shape of the Union: must all the member states move forward in parallel at all costs or will it be necessary to accept the emergence of a two-tier or even a three-tier structure? Some concern has already been registered about the untidiness of the Maastricht settlement, notably in respect of EMU and the Social Charter. We have expressed the view that the dangers of the variable speed approach can be exaggerated. In any case the untidiness of Maastricht may be a temporary phenomenon. It is difficult to imagine that on the monetary front the UK would want to be permanently consigned to a semi-detached membership role, since this could have adverse consequences on the inward flow of foreign investment from Japan and the USA and could undermine the position of the City of London. As for social matters, a change of political control in the UK would bring it back into the fold.

Recent policy pronouncements in France and Germany have indicated that there is some political support for the idea of approaching further integration on a two- or three-tier (or two- or three-concentric circle) basis. Some of this may be a bargaining tactic. In the three-circle plan the inner circle would consist of those countries who were enthusiastic and strong enough to forge ahead with further integration. This would include Germany and France and presumably the Benelux countries. The membership of the other two circles tends to vary from account to account. It seems likely that the next circle would take in current Union members who are less enthusiastic or lack the economic strength to forge ahead. The outer circle would include current outsiders such as the CEECs. More will be said on their position below.

The single market remains a problem. The date 1992 should not fool us into assuming that it is now a reality. When the commission reported in December 1993, it noted that, while 95 per cent of the 1985 Cockfield White Paper measures had been enacted, the position was much less favourable when the question of transposition into national law was considered. Transposition varied between member states from 94 per cent to 75 per cent (House of Lords, 1994, p. 14). When the commission further commented in May 1994, it drew attention to the fact that countries were dragging their feet, particularly in respect of financial services and public procurement (*Financial Times*, 1994, p. 1), a point which had also been made by Sir Michael Butler on the basis of evidence accumulated by the UK's European Committee on British Invisibles (House of Lords, 1994, p. 15). Fiscal harmonization is a notable area where considerable progress still has to be made. Then of course there is the equally important point that member states must not just transpose legislation but, once it is on the statute book, must also implement it. In one sense the single market will never be a *fait accompli*: companies (via cartels) and governments (such as the French government in 1994 in respect of state aid to Air France) will continue to act in ways which distort competition or need justification.

Another problem is EMU. It seems unlikely that in the long run a group of countries trading so intensively together will not move towards a single currency. However all the signs are that the requirements of convergence (which Germany is bound to insist on) are such that full EMU will not occur in 1996 and that the earliest feasible date is 1999. This is the view of the president of the EMI, who has also suggested that the final stage may be approached in two phases. Exchange rates could be fixed irrevocably and then there might be a substantial interim period before the single currency made its appearance. The possibility that EMU will be approached on a variable speed basis seems highly likely, particularly if the Community embraces the economies of Eastern Europe. While Maastricht appears to provide for an automatic transition in 1999, it is difficult to see how it can occur without an act of will on the part of those who propose to participate. Incidentally, while business favours a single currency, it is evident that the public is not enthusiastic, as seen, for example, in Germany. One feature of the EMU programme which has been neglected is the absolute emphasis which is laid on price stability. In a stimulating article, Mark Blaug has expressed astonishment at the degree to which governments, bankers and the public have been, in his words, persuaded to accept the dogma 'that inflation is the root of all economic evil and that price stability is the key to growth and full employment' (Blaug, 1993, p. 399). His conclusion is that the costs of unemployment vastly exceed the costs of inflation. He also anticipates that political sensitivities on the subject of unemployment versus inflation may change. Whether the ESCB will in any case achieve price stability is open to doubt. The kind of correlation between central bank independence and price stability discussed in Chapter 7 could be misleading. It could be that countries which fear inflation will insist on bank independence and therefore it is this fear, rather than the bank's constitutional position, which explains price stability. The ESCB is not likely to enjoy the same popular anti-inflation support that has underpinned the Bundesbank.

It can be argued that the fiscal design of the EMU plan needs to be re-examined. We noted in Chapter 7 that the asymmetry of the debt provisions was likely in certain circumstances to build a deflationary bias into the Maastricht system. But this is not the only cause for concern. Under EMU the scope for monetary action at national level is largely eliminated. This has led some economists to emphasize the need for some compensatory scope on the fiscal front if and when member states are faced with asymmetric shocks. A reform of the community budget, increasing its size and building into it a capacity to generate automatic and stabilizing inter-country fiscal flows needs to be considered.

Unemployment is a major problem in the Community and its extremely high level has been attracting more attention at Community level. This was apparent at the Edinburgh summit in December 1992, when the heads of state and government adopted a Declaration on Promoting Economic Recovery in Europe. At the Copenhagen summit in June 1993, apart from extending the subsidized EIB credit line for trans-European networks agreed at Edinburgh, Jacques Delors was commissioned to produce a White Paper on the Eurosclerosis problem, Eurosclerosis on this occasion being defined to cover problems of low growth, lack of competitiveness and high unemployment. The resulting White Paper, *Growth Competitiveness and Employment* (European Commission, 1993) was received at the Brussels summit in December 1993. It was not formally approved by the council but was described as constituting 'a reference point for future work'.

The White Paper pointed out that the European economy's potential rate of growth had shrunk from around 4.5 per cent to just over 2 per cent a year. Its competitive position had worsened relative to the USA and Japan. But unemployment was the key problem; indeed the commission opened by saying that the one and only reason for the White Paper was unemployment. In the Community as a whole it was 12 per cent, as compared with 6 per cent in the USA and 3 per cent in Japan. Unemployment had risen steadily, cycle by cycle. The long-term unemployment situation was particularly serious: about 45 per cent of the unemployed were long-term unemployed, as compared with about 5 per cent in the USA. The House of Lords, in its report on the White Paper, noted that, since the population of working age was expected to grow by 0.5 per cent per annum, a growth rate of 2.5 per cent was needed merely to hold the line and only a rate of growth of 3.5 per cent would make any significant inroads into the problem in the medium term.

The White Paper recognized that the role of the Community in dealing with these kinds of problem was limited. *A good deal would fall to the member states.* The factors which inhibited employment and so on varied from state to state. States would have to review the ideas contained in the White Paper and appropriately address their approaches to such matters as education, access to vocational training, labour laws, employment and redundancy practices, their provisions for geographical mobility, their social security benefit systems and the ways in which such systems heaped non-wage costs on employers.

Nevertheless there were some opportunities for a Community contribution. The first was the completion and effective implementation of the single market. The second was the introduction and financial support of trans-European networks which, while they would not immediately have a major impact on unemployment, would make a valuable contribution to increased cohesiveness, efficiency and competitiveness. The third was the development of information highways – systems for the transmission of data throughout the Community which would make it possible to combine transmission of information, sound, text and images in a single high-performance system. The fourth was the need to strengthen R&TD activity.

With respect to the second opportunity, an indicative list of 26 projects in the field of transport, together with lists of possible gas and electricity networks, were set out in the White Paper. Commissioner Christopherson was charged with the task of selecting a priority list, while the information aspect was remitted to Commissioner Bangemann. Some differences did arise in connection with the financing of the trans-European networks, the commission having proposed to fill the financing gap by itself issuing Union Bonds. However the idea was shelved. At the Corfu summit in June 1994, 11 transport links were approved and it was agreed that supportive measures would be taken if these priority actions ran into financial difficulties.

During 1984, the German economics minister Gunter Rexrodt gave strong backing to the desirability of deregulation as a means of increasing competitiveness and employment. In this he was strongly supported by the British but received a hostile response from Jacques Delors. At the Corfu summit it was agreed that a task force should be established to carry out a cost–benefit analysis, not only of European Union but also of national legislation which created obstacles to job creation and greater competitiveness.

The macroeconomic framework within which the Eurosclerosis problem would be tackled was not discussed in detail in the White Paper, it being assumed that its key characteristics were already determined by the ongoing EMU programme. The task of setting the framework was the responsibility of the European Council (following Article 103 of the Rome Treaty as prescribed at Maastricht). The plan agreed in December 1993, and later formally adopted by the Council of Economics and Finance Ministers, declared that the purpose of the policy framework was indeed to reinforce the competitiveness of the European economy. To this end it stressed the importance of low inflation, sound public finances and so on; in short, it emphasized the continuing requirement to satisfy the convergence criteria. This latter point was criticized by the House of Lords, which argued that the process of cyclical recovery could be inhibited by an undue short-term emphasis on the need for adherence to strict public deficit criteria (House of Lords, 1994, pp. 28–9).

Agriculture has always been high on the Community problem list and is unlikely to disappear in the coming years. The jury is still out, in the sense that the McSharry reforms are still in process. The Community Budget Financial Perspective to 1999 indicates that expenditure on the CAP will continue to grow in real terms, but as a proportion of budget spending it will fall. On the positive side there is the prospect that the CAP will be less offensive to outside food producers and that it will be more environmentally friendly.

Some commentators have also identified economic and social cohesion as an area of possible future concern– regional imbalances may increase. However the evidence, at least to date, is not discouraging. Button and Pentecost, taking the period 1975 to 1988/9, have shown that there was convergence in terms of the growth rate of regional GDP. However they do report that unemployment rates have diverged, 'although during the 1980s there is some sign of convergence to a higher level of unemployment as the EC economies faced economic recession' (Button and Pentecost, 1993, p. 9). Evidence has also been provided by Barro and Sala-I-Martin to the effect that the EC experienced convergent growth of GDP per capita over the period 1950–85 (Barro and Sala-I-Martin, 1991). Armstrong has pointed out that this study was largely confined to the more prosperous regions and excluded certain EC states. He has conducted the analysis on a broader basis, bringing the results up to 1990, and concluded that the findings lend support to the catch-up view of regional GDP per capita growth among EC regions (Armstrong, 1995).

A major problem for the future is bound to be further enlargement. The Union decision-making system already has to cope with the increase in its number following the adhesion of Austria, Finland and Sweden. The number will of course grow still further if the Mediterranean aspirants and the CEECs achieve their ultimate goal. However a Central and East European enlargement poses not just a numbers problem but also an economic and financial one. Quite simply, as indicated in more detail in Chapter 9, the direct budgetary cost would be quite substantial. Added to this is the possibility that the CEECs might use their voting power to screw extra resources out of the richer members. Further problems could arise from uncontrolled migratory flows from the east. A solution on the lines of winding up current agricultural and structural spending would be violently opposed by the poorer states of the present Union. Admitting the CEECs, but excluding them from the benefits of such funding, would be an unacceptable slap in the face. One rather guarded solution consists of recognizing that full unqualified membership is a long way off: it will depend on economic development reducing the size of the agricultural sector and raising income levels. In the meantime a relationship involving an intermediate but progressive status is called for which keeps the long-term goal in sight and fosters the movement towards it. Such a plan has, as we saw in Chapter 9, been proposed by Richard Baldwin (Baldwin, 1994).

The decision-making system of the Union, including the role to be played by the European Parliament in the light of the Delors democratic deficit argument, is bound to be closely scrutinized in the 1996 review.[1] Inevitably those with federal aspirations will return to the attack. Such an attack would no doubt include proposals for greater use of majority voting on economic and social issues in the Council of Ministers, a power of initiative and a conventional colegislative role for the parliament, together with the bringing of the CFSP into the majority voting system (Gardner, 1994, p. 12). However a federalist versus anti-federalist-dominated agenda would be very stultifying and would do little to advance the Union's cause. Federalist-inspired proposals would probably automatically provoke the veto of the UK, and possibly others. It would be much more productive if the debate was conducted on different lines, such as how to make the Union system more effective and efficient in the context of an expanded and probably expanding membership. To such a debate the UK could not avoid contributing constructively, since it has been one of the keenest advocates of enlargement.

This issue needs to be set against the background that the Community of Twelve at Maastricht could by virtue of EFTA and other enlargements end up as a Community of between 20 and 30. Much depends on how the Union reacts to the problems identified by Baldwin (see Chapter 9), but whatever approach is adopted in relation to that problem, a substantially enlarged Community as compared with Maastricht is on the cards. This raises all kinds of issues, such as the effectiveness of the Council of Ministers if every national delegation must have its initial say before the hard bargaining can begin. A *tour de table* of ten minutes per minister among 30 adds up to five hours of preliminaries! This worries some, but others do not see it as a problem since they envisage that groups of countries will select one state to be their spokesperson (Ersboll, 1994, p. 415). It has also been pointed out that more members means more seats in the European Parliament and that this could undermine efficiency in a significantly enlarged parliament. Views differ as to how proper Parliamentary accountability (i.e. tackling the so-called democratic deficit problem) can best be achieved. While some see it in terms of beefing up the powers of the European Parliament, others identify a way which gives national parliaments a more influential role (Neunreither, 1994). The size of the commission has already spiralled up from 17 to 20, thanks to the EFTA enlargement, and threatens to get even larger, although it is widely argued that the appropriate figure would be ten. A larger number of states and greater diversity seem to point to the need for more streamlined voting processes in the council and for a vigorous approach to the concept of subsidiarity. An awkward issue which is likely to come up is the disproportion between the council votes and national populations. Following the completion of the EFTA negotiations it was pointed out that Luxembourg had one vote for every 186 000, whereas Germany had one for every 8 million people (*The Economist*, 1994, p. 37).

A major problem area concerns the CFSP and its development into a common defence policy and a common defence. Here a number of issues arise. The first is the problem of the cohesiveness of the CFSP in the virtual absence of majority voting. Its predecessor, EPC, had its high points, such as keeping EC states together in the Conference on Security and Cooperation in Europe, issuing the 1980 Venice Declaration on Palestinian self-determination and in preparing the way for sanctions against Iraq, South Africa and Argentina, but it has also had its failures, and its achievements in securing common votes on UN General Assembly resolutions have been modest. Between 1975 and 1990 (excluding uncontested resolutions) the percentage of successes ranged from a high of 65 to a low of 31 (Buchan, 1991). The cohesiveness of the CFSP will be tested by greater numbers and greater diversity. A number of new members who previously valued their neutrality seem to have had no difficulty in accommodating themselves to the prospect of a CFSP. Will they find it so easy to come into line when major real-world issues have to be faced?

The question of the appropriate arrangements in relation to defence were, as we noted in Chapter 5, a matter of dispute prior to Maastricht. However Maastricht achieved a resolution of this problem: the nine-member WEU would implement decisions and actions of the Union which had defence implications, but the policy of the Union had to respect NATO obligations (see, on all this, Anderson, 1994). The Maastricht Treaty Declaration on Western European Union in effect opened WEU up to all Union members. The 1992 WEU Petersburg Declaration followed this up by deciding that WEU membership should be more closely aligned with that of the Union, and in November of the same year Greece became a full member and Denmark and Ireland became observers. Trevor Taylor has pointed out that this aspect of the Maastricht Treaty could lead to near-automatic expansion of NATO membership:

> Given the stated desire of the Central European States (Poland, the Czech Republic and Hungary) to join NATO, it is predictable that if and when they achieve EC membership they will ask also to be WEU members. Yet it would be potentially very awkward to have Europeans covered by the WEU but not the NATO guarantee, since this could mean (for instance) that WEU states could get involved to their east in a crisis in which the United States had no formal voice. The obvious solution would be to expand NATO along with the WEU, but this would require ratification by North American legislatures. (Taylor, 1994, p. 3)

The possibility of NATO membership for CEECs has been approached cautiously for fear of provoking right-wing reactions in Russia. The policy has consisted of inviting former Warsaw Pact countries to join Partnership for Peace arrangements which allow for participation in NATO activities but fall short of full membership and do not involve an assurance of a NATO response in the event of an attack on such a cooperating member.

Taylor has pointed out that, if the CFSP is to be credible, three further developments are called for. In the first place the Maastricht Treaty is 'long on objectives and short on methods' (Taylor, 1994, p. 7). A strategy document is needed which identifies the key and pressing problems and *indicates how they might be tackled*. Second, the Union has been dangerously weakened by defence cuts and this process needs to be brought to an end. Third, the Union members need to cooperate effectively on equipment (Taylor, 1994, pp. 7–15). This latter element involves preserving an appropriate industrial base but also achieving greater competition and cost-effectiveness in spending and contract letting. Rome Treaty Article 223, which allows members to shield defence industries from normal competition rules, almost certainly needs to be looked at.

Attention will also have to be given to the tasks assigned to the various bodies in Europe which have security and defence roles to play. For example, what kind of relationship should exist between NATO's Rapid Reaction Force and an expanded Franco-German brigade? Douglas Hurd (1994, p. 427) has also pointed out that a weakness of the old EPC machinery was that it did not provide for any forward-looking analysis and planning. He has observed that, if the CFSP is to be successful, it will need, not a massive bureaucracy, but a dedicated back-up and one which is separate from the commission. He argues that the strengthened CFSP section of the council secretariat will be important in this context. Whether this proves sufficient, only the future will tell.

One of the perennial problems faced by the Community has been the failure of member states to implement Community law. We have already seen that it was felt necessary in the Maastricht Treaty to tighten up the Article 169/171 procedure, thus enabling fines to be imposed on governments who refused to conform to Court of Justice rulings. In 1994, a quite spectacular episode occurred in connection with the failure of certain member states to implement the requirements of Community law in respect of milk quotas which had been agreed in 1984 (see above). As a result, they had produced excess milk, whereas farmers in law-abiding states had been forced to slaughter dairy cows. The states in question were Italy and Spain. The original fines imposed by the commission were £2 billion and £1.4 billion, respectively. Apparently both countries refused to pay the fines, arguing that their original quotas had been too low. The commission then agreed to a retrospective increase in their quotas, which had the incidental effect of reducing the size of overproduction and therefore the fines. This was opposed by the UK, which launched a Court of Justice case alleging that in granting the retrospective quota increases the commission had exceeded its powers. In the end the UK agreed to drop its case when Italy and Spain finally agreed to pay reduced fines of, respectively, £1.52 billion and £1 billion.

Fraud is another embarrassing problem that the Community has yet to tackle. In November 1994, the president of the Court of Auditors drew attention to a list of transgressions in connection with the use of

Community budget monies. This continuing saga of misappropriation undermines the credibility of the European endeavour. There is a suspicion that some member states have been mainly concerned with extracting money out of the Community budget and have been little concerned about what happened to that money thereafter.

The reader cannot fail to have noticed that as the Community has developed, its decision-making processes have become increasingly complex, indeed obscure. For example, single issues such as the protection of the environment can be subject to a diversity of different arrangements. If the Community wishes to command the respect and interest of the public, it should give some serious consideration to simplifying and streamlining its procedures so that they are capable of being understood by ordinary mortals.

It is the view of the author that, although all of these problems demand solutions, the highest priority ought to be given to that posed by the CEECs and particularly the Visegrad Four. When the history of the postwar period is written, the really key events will be the fall of the Berlin Wall, the collapse of the Communist system and the diminished threat posed by Russia. The Community for its part will in significant measure be judged by its response to this issue. There will be immediate costs but also long-term benefits. Action, not rhetoric, is called for.

NOTES

1. There is a real need to heighten the public's perception of the important role which the parliament can play. In 1979 the turn-out for the European Parliamentary elections was 63 per cent, but it had fallen to 56 per cent in 1994 and in the UK in 1994 it was a miserable 36 per cent.

REFERENCES

Anderson, S. (1994), 'Maastricht: Negotiating a Security Agreement without an Enemy', in A.J. Williams (ed.), *Reorganizing Eastern Europe* (Aldershot: Dartmouth).

Armstrong, H.A. (1995), 'Convergence Among European Community Regions 1950–1990', *Papers in Regional Science*, forthcoming.

Baldwin, R.E. (1994), *Towards An Integrated Europe* (London: Centre for Economic Policy Research).

Barro, R.J. and X. Sala-I-Martin, 'Convergence across States and Regions', *Brookings Papers*, vol. 1.

Blaug, M. (1993), 'Public Enemy No. 1: Unemployment not Inflation', *Economic Notes, Monte dei Paschi di Siena*, **22**, (3).

Buchan, D. (1991), 'A long march towards Euroarmy', *Financial Times*, 18 October.

Button, K. and E. Pentecost (1993), *Testing for Convergence of the EC Regional Economies, Economics Research Paper No. 93/5* (Department of Economics, Loughborough University of Technology, Loughborough).

Clark, A. (1993), *Diaries* (London: Phoenix).

CMLR (1986), Ministère Public *v.* Lucas Asjes and Others (Nouvelles Frontières), *Common Market Law Reports* [1986], 173.

CMLR (1988), British American Tobacco Company Limited and R.J. Reynolds Industries Inc. *v.* E.C. Commission (Philip Morris), *Common Market Law Reports* [1988], 24.

Cockfield, Lord A. (1994), *The European Union: Creating the Single Market* (London: Wiley Chancery Law).

The Economist (1994), 'Indigestion Strikes Europe', 12 March.

Ersboll, N. (1994), 'The European Union: the immediate priorities', *International Affairs*, **70**, (3).

European Commission (1993), *Growth, Competitiveness and Employment, Bulletin of the European Communities Supplement 6/93* (Luxembourg).

Financial Times (1994), 'Brussels to name single-market laggards', 23 May.

Gardner, N. (1994), 'Just when you thought Maastricht was over...', *Fabian Review*, **106**, (4).

House of Lords Select Committee on the European Communities (1994), *Growth, Competitiveness and Employment in the European Community*, 7th Report, Session 1993–4.

Hurd, D. (1994), 'Developing the Common Foreign and Security Policy', *International Affairs*, **70**, (3).

Jovanovic, M.N. (1992), *International Economic Integration* (London: Routledge).

Neunreither, K. (1994), 'The Democratic Deficit of the European Union: Towards Closer Cooperation between the European Parliament and the National Parliaments', *Government and Opposition*, **29**, (3).

Taylor, T. (1994), 'West European security and defence cooperation: Maastricht and beyond', *International Affairs*, **70**, (1).

Index